# UNFINISHED BUSINESS

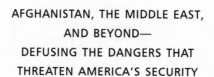

AFGHANISTAN, THE MIDDLE EAST,
AND BEYOND—
DEFUSING THE DANGERS THAT
THREATEN AMERICA'S SECURITY

# UNFINISHED BUSINESS

AFGHANISTAN, THE MIDDLE EAST,
AND BEYOND—
DEFUSING THE DANGERS THAT
THREATEN AMERICA'S SECURITY

# HARLAN ULLMAN

WITH A FOREWORD BY
Senator John S. McCain

**CITADEL PRESS**
Kensington Publishing Corp.
www.kensingtonbooks.com

CITADEL PRESS BOOKS are published by

Kensington Publishing Corp.
850 Third Avenue
New York, NY 10022

All Kensington titles, imprints, and distributed lines are available at special quantity discounts for bulk purchases for sales promotions, premiums, fund-raising, educational, or institutional use. Special book excerpts or customized printings can also be created to fit specific needs. For details, write or phone the office of the Kensington special sales manager: Kensington Publishing Corp., 850 Third Avenue, New York, NY 10022, attn: Special Sales Department, phone 1-800-221-2647.

Citadel Press and the Citadel Logo are trademarks of Kensington Publishing Corp.

First printing: June 2002

10  9  8  7  6  5  4  3  2  1

Printed in the United States of America

Library of Congress Control Number: 2002102878

ISBN: 0-8065-2431-6

If the United States does not lead, there will be no leadership. . . . If we fail to live up to our responsibilities, if we shirk the role which only we can assume, if we retreat from our obligations to the world into indifference, we will, one day, pay the highest price once again for our neglect and shortsightedness.

—George H. W. Bush, forty-first President of the United States
from *A World Transformed*

It takes time to ruin a world, but time is all it takes.

—Fontenelle

# Contents

# Foreword

The title of this book, *Unfinished Business*, is exactly right. The horrific events of September 11th, and the extremism that caused them, killed more than three thousand innocent people. This callous attack was a final warning. Until the causes and consequences of this assault, as well as other crucial pieces of business left over from the Gulf and Cold Wars, are redressed, the United States and its friends are in serious danger—danger that may be the gravest since World War II.

In *Unfinished Business*, Harlan Ullman clearly articulates the reasons why this situation is so serious. Before September 11th, the United States had the false luxury of believing it was safe and secure from direct attacks on its cities and citizens at home. We acted on that basis and therefore deferred or ignored confronting too much unfinished business. However, we now know that Osama bin Laden is not only a menace out to kill Americans and inflict as much devastation as he can, but that he is using the "openness" of democratic societies as an instrument for death and destruction. What to do?

On the one hand, we must recognize that our freedom and openness make us vulnerable to damage and disruption especially from extremists and terrorists willing to die in the process. But if we overreact to these threats, we risk doing far greater harm to our democratic way of life. The dilemma posed by this danger demands intelligent, thoughtful, and creative action. The first steps, including the campaign in Afghanistan to remove the al Qaeda network and Taliban rule, have proven successful. But there are greater challenges—Iraq, Iran, the Israeli-Palestinian conflict, the India-Pakistan nuclear and conventional standoff, and the extremism of bin Laden's perversion of Islam—that will fully test the resolve of America.

We need to make sweeping reforms. In the area of national security, I thoroughly agree with and support the conclusions that Harlan Ullman offers. First, people are the best line of defense. Until we fix the "people deficit," no long-term solution will work. Second, we need to restructure the national security posture of the United States and revise the fifty-five-year-old National Security Act to bring it in line with the present and future rather than the past. We need to ensure that "enforcement of the law" and a list of newer national security tasks are assigned to the proper agencies and offices and then give them the authority, responsibility, and resources to carry out their missions. This restructuring must also include Congress as a full and cooperative partner with the executive.

Furthermore, the American people must insist that their appointed and elected officials change their habits. In the past decade, politics have become highly "campaign-centric." Fueled by money and dominated by attempts to play to the media, politicians are behaving more like celebrities and movie stars than leaders and statesmen. Politics have become distorted, governance has suffered, and one-liners and five-second sound bites have begun to pass for debate and argument. This must change and government officials must begin to draw on the renewed sense of patriotism and non-partisanship in finishing this business and keeping America and her friends safe and secure.

All of this means that "reform" is vital. For reform to work, it must begin with values, leadership, and people. For 2003, we plan to spend more than $400 billion on national security and defense. However, before this money is spent, we must ask ourselves whether the nation will be safer and more secure as a result of these expenditures. If we cannot positively answer yes, we must decide on the correct priorities to achieve that end.

Since September 11th, no American will shrink from sacrifice or duty if called on to provide for the common defense. Our task is to direct this support and commitment. The proposals set forth in *Unfinished Business* are an excellent beginning if we are to prevail in the coming struggle against forces of true darkness and evil.

Senator John S. McCain

# Author's Note

In light of the horrendous attacks of September 11th, 2001, against Manhattan's World Trade Center and the Pentagon in Washington, D.C., Walter Zacharius, founder and CEO of Kensington Publishing Corp., had the idea of reexamining President George Herbert Walker Bush's decision not to march to Baghdad during the Gulf War in 1991 to eliminate Saddam Hussein. The inference was that such an investigation might reveal certain cause-and-effect relationships. My own interest was less concerned with Saddam's involvement in September 11th and more focused on less visible "legacies" and pieces of unfinished business that would bring such terror to the United States and, by extension, turmoil to much of the world as well. The combination and collaboration of these perspectives became the basis for this book.

The stakes in this new era may, surprisingly, turn out to be greater than during the Cold War. Ironically, unlike the Cold War, when tens of thousands of nuclear weapons were at the ready but never used in anger, mass-destruction weapons have already been unleashed, in the case of the United States possibly by home-grown terrorists. Internationally, as the United States and Great Britain, supported by a broad-based coalition, took the fight against terrorism and terrorists into Afghanistan, other trouble spots, "book ends" for the region, raise the specter of an outbreak of war in the shadow of these frightening weapons.

India and Pakistan, the latter vital for waging any military campaign in Afghanistan, came close to the brink of war after a suicide bomber struck the Indian Parliament. India blamed Pakistan. In the Middle East, the Arab-Israeli-Palestinian conflict raged.

India, Pakistan, and probably Israel have nuclear weapons. Use of other mass-destruction weapons—chemical and biological agents—is no longer a hypothetical question. Anthrax-laden letters mailed in the United States killed five Americans and terrorized the nation. The danger is clear and present. These old conflicts could explode. Saddam still lives. And no one knows what the surviving al Qaeda members may be capable of doing.

Despite the very real dangers, there is also opportunity. But opportunity will not be risk-free. Whether the legacy of September 11th is lasting or not, the United States has been warned. We may not have another chance to resolve much of this unfinished business before a greater catastrophe unfolds.

Throughout this crisis, the media focused on President George W. Bush and his performance as chief executive and commander in chief. The first eight months of his presidency were marked with stumbles and missteps. These followed the most contested presidential election in the nation's recent history. Then, after September 11th, the media reported a transformation in the presidency and the president. Clearly, that the son might have to deal with the unfinished business of his father has been a continuing story. However, this book seeks to avoid a rush to judgment regarding short-term assessments of what might or might not prove to be a brilliant presidency or an exciting news story.

A brief word on methods, sources, and references may be useful to the reader. This book is not meant to be a comprehensive history. Selectivity is the rule. The intent is to use the various pieces of unfinished business as organizing themes around which relevant fact and record are assembled. However, not every event is used. Much of the material, especially quotations and points of view of important participants, has been taken from the historical record and from the many autobiographies that have been written. The major sources are listed in the reference section.

Emerson wrote, "In analyzing history, do not be too profound, for often the causes are quite superficial." The causes are often long in forming. That is the book's subtext.

HARLAN ULLMAN

Washington, D.C.
March 15, 2002

# UNFINISHED BUSINESS

## BUSINESS

---★---

AFGHANISTAN, THE MIDDLE EAST,
AND BEYOND—
DEFUSING THE DANGERS THAT
THREATEN AMERICA'S SECURITY

---★---

# Introduction

---

# Unfinished Business

The Cold War between the United States and the Soviet Union rested on a remarkable and unprecedented historical paradox. For most of that war, each antagonist possessed more than enough nuclear weaponry to annihilate the other. Crises from blockades in Berlin to missiles in Cuba caressed the nuclear trigger. But that trigger was never pulled. War was successfully avoided and not a single American or Russian was obliterated under a nuclear cloud. In 1991, the Cold War ended peacefully. The Soviet Union disintegrated. Eastern Europe was free. But the danger from these and other weapons of mass destruction has not been eradicated.

On September 11th, 2001, nineteen terrorists armed only with box-cutters and loyal to a cause not to a country, hijacked four commercial airliners flying over the east coast of the United States. Three were turned into deadly weapons of mass destruction and deliberately crashed into the twin towers of New York City's World Trade Center and into the Pentagon in the nation's capital. It is likely that the fourth, apparently brought down by heroic passengers, targeted either the White House or the Capitol. Over three thousand innocent victims from many nations were killed.

Americans were profoundly shocked by the enormity of this outrage, brought home to millions by the searing image of the horrendous collapse of the twin towers captured live on television. These unprecedented events shattered America's sense of invulnerability to major attack. Not during the Cold War with the danger of societal immolation or since the British burned the White House in the War of 1812 had the continental United States been so frontally assaulted. The physical as well as psychological damage left the nation reeling.

September 11th was immediately likened to an earlier day of infamy, December 7th, 1941, the date of Japan's surprise attack on Pearl Harbor. At least one major disconnect is clear. December 7th held sufficient justification for the United States to declare a war that lasted for three and a half years. The combined menace of Nazi Germany and fascist Japan was defeated unconditionally. The United States and its allies won the war. More importantly, the United States and its allies won the peace. Nazi Germany and fascist Japan became exemplary democracies.

Will September 11th have the enduring force of December 7th? Less than a year before, the country was embroiled in another crisis. Election day, November 2000, came and went. It took another six weeks to determine who won. Yet, the experience of one of the most contested elections in the nation's history is largely forgotten. How much long-term effect September 11th will have on the collective American psyche remains to be seen.

As the United States responded to these tragic yet tectonic attacks, Osama bin Laden, a wealthy exiled Saudi and the founder and chief underwriter of the al Qaeda terrorist network, was quickly identified as the chief suspect. The question of complicity or indeed instigation on the part of Saddam Hussein's Iraq also surfaced. To some, there was little doubt of Saddam's involvement, although convincing evidence of it was and still is lacking.

To others, the destruction of the twin towers and a portion of the Pentagon provided the tempting opportunity to clean up one piece of unfinished business left over from the Gulf War of 1991. While Kuwait was liberated and much of the Iraqi military crushed, Saddam was not removed from power. With a penchant for acquiring both so-called weapons of mass destruction and the territory of immediate neighbors, a nuclear-armed Iraq is a hazard to peace and stability. In these views, the time had come to rectify that mistake once and for all by eliminating Saddam and his despotic rule. Given the lopsided victory in 1991 and the sudden collapse of the Taliban and enemy forces in Afghanistan a decade later, advocates of retribution believe that smashing Saddam again would not prove difficult in the face of overwhelming U.S. military force.

As this book will show, other pieces of perhaps more substantial unfinished business lingered in the war's wake. Many of these pieces were either in their infancy or simply awaiting a catalyst to turn them into grounds for global turmoil and terror. None of them—from bin Laden to the anthrax-infected mail attacks launched against Americans that quickly followed—sprang to life full-grown as Athena from Zeus's brow. Much of this unfinished business transcends presidents, prime ministers, and time, threatening not only the United States but many other nations as well.

What are these pieces of unfinished business that must be resolved? First, the "openness" of the United States and other democracies creates vulnerabilities that can be exploited by those wishing to do evil. This is the paradox of a free society in which ready access to its public and "critical infrastructure" is virtually impossible to restrict. Extremists will attempt to use this openness against us. And, to the degree that the nation overreacts and restricts freedom and democracy on the grounds of self-defense, terror will have succeeded.

Second, critical infrastructure includes the sectors on which the nation's livelihood depends: transportation, power and energy generation and distribution, public utilities, banking and financial services, telecommunications and electronics, emergency and health services, and food production and distribution industries. These can all be attacked or disrupted by either individuals or organized groups. The assaults on computers and computer networks are irrefutable proof that these vulnerabilities are real and tempting targets.

Third, the U.S. government is simply not well organized to provide for its security. One part of this limitation is due to the nature of the political process that makes a rational approach to providing for the common defense more difficult. Time is often the enemy.

New administrations increasingly take longer and longer to staff. By the time an administration is in place, a year or more may have elapsed. Biennial Congressional elections loom. Political capital, already in short supply, is lost along with the opportunity to make the most of the first months or year in office.

To evaluate national security, Congress convened the bipartisan United States Commission on National Security Strategy/21st Century (composed of distinguished American citizens and co-chaired by former senators Gary Hart and Warren Rudman). The prestigious panel reported its finding in February 2001. The commission described the current national security structure as "dysfunctional" and badly in need of overhaul. This assessment is true of the Congress and the presidency, the two chief branches of government responsible for protecting the nation.

Part of this dysfunction, reinforced by the American political system of "checks and balances," has made genuine reform of key national security agencies from the CIA to the FBI to the Defense Department exceedingly difficult. And, while reform must accommodate the emergence of law enforcement and counterterrorism as more urgent national security matters, this will not be easy. Dealing with Saddam, bin Laden, al Qaeda, the Taliban in Afghanistan, and what may come next in what George W. Bush calls a "new" type of war almost certainly will require new tools and substantial structural changes. All of this is part of the nation's unfinished business. And, with the President's call to arms to oppose a new "axis of evil" consisting of Iraq, Iran and North Korea, the traditional organization of government will be further tested.

Success will also require a greater ability on the part of the president and his key advisors to think through more thoroughly the consequences of actions they are contemplating. As we will see, from Jimmy Carter's approval of the ill-fated Desert One rescue operation to Ronald Reagan's decision to arm the mujahadeen in the fight against the Soviet Union in Afghanistan to George W. Bush's ordering of Operation Enduring Freedom to capture or kill the members of al Qaeda and eliminate Taliban rule in Afghanistan, the understanding of both intended and unintended consequences of chosen actions is critical to assuring success.

Fourth, like it or not, the Arab-Israeli and Palestinian disputes provide sadly fertile grounds for breeding extremism. U.S. security is now directly linked to security in these faraway regions. Oceanic protection cannot keep violence from these disputes away from American shores. And the potential use of weapons of mass destruction remains a daunting possibility.

Any resolution must appreciate that regimes in the Arab world and elsewhere are autocratic and often antidemocratic. As long as substantial numbers of people are estranged or antagonized by political rule and tightly controlled distribution of power, animosity will follow. In these circumstances, others like bin Laden who come from middle- and upper-middle-class families will become alienated and therefore prospects for seduction by radical causes seeking to overthrow the regimes in charge. And, the breeding grounds for such extremists have already extended beyond the Gulf to parts of Africa, South Asia, Asia, and Latin America.

Finally, in fashioning any long-term and lasting solutions, the roles of Russia and China will be crucial. So, too, are India and Pakistan critical to creating a measure of peace and stability in this troubled region. Beginning in 1991, Bush the elder was unable to fashion a new world order to his liking. The circumstances were not right. The effects of the disintegration of the Soviet Union and the animosity to China's repression of students in Tiananmen Square in 1989 still had to run their courses.

A decade after Desert Storm, there is historical irony in the fact that the son, now the nation's forty-third president, must deal with specific legacies, some of which are attributable to the father, the nation's forty-first president. In 2002 and beyond, President George W. Bush will need to craft a new set of relationships among the great powers. Whether he will have the opportunity and skill to do so remains to be seen. The challenge is that the circumstances of today are far more complicated than those in 1991. Global turmoil and terror are no longer isolated from America's shores.

Prior presidents, too, have passed on their legacies. Clearly, some of them—such as the Arab-Israeli conflict and the China-Taiwan dispute—have proved to be beyond the capacity of any individual to resolve, even one as accomplished in foreign affairs as Bush the elder. In other ways, facets of these legacies and unfinished business have become more intractable and difficult to handle. During the Cold War, the United States had the advantage of leveraging much of its power off the fulcrum provided by the rival Soviet Union. That fulcrum is long since gone. The Clinton administration could claim the benefits of being the "world's sole remaining superpower." To others, the term had little meaning and less political utility.

The two Bush presidents are linked in other ways beyond the ties of blood. Whether bin Laden will prove to be the bête noire to the younger Bush that Saddam was to his father remains an open question. But the son may have to deal with both adversaries. And, if the extremism bin Laden represents moves to a higher level of violence, the danger could be far greater than that posed by Iraq. As with his father, Bush's performance will be judged in the next presidential election. Despite the extraordinary popularity of the president in 1991, Bush senior lost in 1992 to Bill Clinton, an opponent completely without foreign policy, military, or wartime experience.

In waging the "war on terrorism and those that harbor terrorists," George W. Bush is relying on many of the same chief lieutenants who served his father. Dick Cheney was secretary of defense in 1990 and is vice-president now. General Colin Powell was then chairman of the Joint Chiefs of Staff, America's top military officer. Today, he is secretary of state. Andrew Card, then White House Deputy Chief of Staff, has moved up to the top spot. Condoleezza Rice was on the staff of the National Security Council (NSC) for the president's father. She is now the president's adviser for national security. Other lieutenants, including Deputy Secretary of Defense Paul Wolfowitz and State Department policy planning head Richard Haass, were in senior positions ten years ago.

The president has promised to win this war on terrorism, vowing to bring justice to the perpetrators and the perpetrators to justice. But, unless and until this unfinished business is addressed, other, possibly more dangerous and capable versions of the current "evil ones" will emerge. A sinister reminder is the evolution of radical movements in the late nineteenth and early twentieth centuries. The culmination was Hitler's Germany and the Bolshevik Revolution that created the Soviet Union. Of course, it is possible that bin Laden is more akin to Pancho Villa than to Lenin. The September 11th attacks could turn out to be isolated incidents, as was Villa's sortie into New Mexico in 1916. On the other hand, the current Bush administration warns of a long, hard struggle against terrorism.

Reinforcing the warnings about the future of things to come, the National Security Strategy Commission also concluded that "within twenty-five years, there will be a potentially catastrophic terrorist attack against the United States," almost certainly with weapons of mass destruction. The commission's forecast was prescient. It took only seven months to materialize.

Less than three weeks after the September 11th attacks, the nation received a second wake-up call. Anthrax-laden letters were mailed through the U.S. Post Office to various American media and government offices, including the U.S. Congress. Five Americans died and eighteen others were infected but recovered. In some ways, citizens were as alarmed by the use of something as commonplace as mail for delivery of a biological attack as by the fear of an attack itself. While the identity of these bioterrorists is unknown (and possibly not linked to bin Laden or Saddam), the harsh reality is that any country is vulnerable to this form of terrorism. Indeed, for centuries, nature has visited on mankind the horseman of the Apocalypse called Pestilence. The prudent question is not whether but when the next round of manmade disease will occur.

After the war in Afghanistan is over and terrorism is on the run, the president will have to deal with what comes next. With a midterm election looming in November 2002, an unpredictable economy, and a truculent Congress (not dissimilar to the one his father faced in 1990), Bush may justifiably claim victory and go on to other business. After all, this has been very much the American practice. Indeed, the administration of President Bill Clinton eschewed decisive foreign policy action in favor of what sensibly seemed a less risky but politically acceptable alternative.

After the bombings of U.S. embassies in Africa in 1998 and the attack on the destroyer USS *Cole* in Yemen in 2000, the Clinton administration chose to regard bin Laden's actions as a criminal matter not requiring a call to arms or a wartime footing. Retaliation with a handful of cruise missiles was deemed appropriate. Landing Special Forces to capture or kill him and his associates would have been more decisive but was seen as too risky. The use of larger numbers of ground forces would have risked incurring casualties.

The same constraints and considerations applied to other crises. The disintegration of Yugoslavia was a tragic example of unfinished business left over from the first Bush administration. For Clinton's entire presidency, the former Yugoslavia was a geopolitical and humanitarian nightmare. Finally, in the midst of the president's impeachment and trial in Congress, the administration realized it had no alternative to using force to prevent Serbia from completing a campaign of "ethnic cleansing," that is, murder, against the Muslim Kosovars.

Operation Allied Force began on March 24th, 1999, and lasted seventy-eight days. It succeeded in forcing Serbian President Slobodan Milosevic to withdraw his forces from Kosovo and stop the massive violence. But the original expectation of the Clinton team, led principally by Secretary of State Madeline Albright, National Security Adviser Samuel (Sandy) Berger, and United Nations (UN) Ambassador Richard Holbrooke, was that Milosevic would quickly capitulate after only a few bombs fell. In deciding on this course of action, not one of the principals expected an eleven-week war that would come close to dissolving the political integrity of the North Atlantic Treaty Organization (NATO). Making predictions, especially about the future, observed movie mogul Sam Goldwyn, "ain't easy." However, a common and chronic flaw spanning every administration has been to give short shrift to thinking through longer-term consequences.

The president and his advisers must recognize that this may be the nation's last opportunity to deal directly with this unfinished business. No one is predicting a nuclear catastrophe through a terrorist attack or in a war in the Middle East or South Asia. However, the danger cannot be dismissed. That crescent of crisis (a term coined by Carter National Security Adviser Zbigniew Brzezinski), from the Arab-Israeli-Palestinian conflict to the west, Iraq and Iran in the center, and Afghanistan and India and Pakistan to the east, is a ticking time bomb. Something must be done to defuse it.

In the future, the nation will not wish to look back in anger for failing to take the necessary steps, no matter how politically difficult they now seem. Given the degree of its potential vulnerabilities, ease of access to its population and critical infrastructure, reservoir of potential enemies wishing the nation ill, and the persistent presence of biological and nuclear weapons and agents of mass destruction, the United States is the largest and most likely future target for these types of attacks. The crucial question is clear: Will America ever be safe again?

# ★ 1 ★

# From the Jaws of Victory

## Every War Has Unfinished Business

The major wars of the last century share at least one common feature. Whether in August 1914 when World War I began or the day after Pearl Harbor when the United States entered World War II, no political leader had the foggiest idea of how those wars would end and what the shape of the postwar world would resemble. World War I was declared by President Wilson to be the "war to end all wars." Instead it became the incubator for fascism and communism. Twenty years later the world would be at war again with even greater devastation and loss of life.

In 1941 neither Roosevelt nor Churchill envisaged a future in which the enemy powers would be occupied, defanged, and democratized. Nor could anyone foresee a "Cold War" that would continue for nearly five decades after the axis powers were defeated. Similarly, many of the technological triumphs from the war—from nuclear weapons to the jet engine to penicillin and wonder drugs—and their consequences could not have been predicted.

The unfinished business from one war has always had profound effects on the future and has laid the ground for the next conflict. Perhaps the end of the Cold War has finally halted this deadly progression of the twentieth century—but perhaps it has not.

The Gulf War to liberate Kuwait was no world war. Nor was it comparable to the Korean and Vietnamese wars. The air war lasted thirty-eight days. The actual ground campaign lasted only one hundred hours. The sixth largest army in the world was routed at the cost of 148 dead Americans, a quarter of whom were felled by "friendly fire." Of the other statistics, one in particular characterized the magnitude of that rout. In conducting the now famous "left hook" to trap Saddam's forces in Kuwait, the U.S. Army's VII Corps destroyed more of the enemy's "things"—from tanks to personnel carriers to artillery pieces—in four days than did the same army in Europe against Hitler's forces from 1944 to 1945.

Critics of the war—who demanded to know in retrospect why Desert Storm was not more decisive in ending Saddam's regime and why so many forces loyal to Saddam were permitted to survive—have stirred debate and controversy. But that criticism avoids the larger pieces of unfinished business on which America's future safety will depend.

The first critical question is what unfinished business has been left over from Desert Shield, Desert Storm, and the related events. The second is whether the consequences of this unfinished business will be comparable in scope and magnitude to what happened in the years following 1918 and 1945. And, if the answer to the second question is yes, what can be done to limit the future risks and dangers?

## The Context

At exactly 8:01 A.M., February 28th, 1991, Gulf time, hostilities between the U.S.-led coalition of some thirty-five states and Iraq officially ceased. Kuwait, invaded and occupied by the forces of Iraq on August 1st, 1990, had been liberated and its legitimate government, a monarchy headed by the al Sabah royal family, would be shortly restored. Much of Iraq's once-vaunted military power had been reduced to a rabble, and a portion of its arsenal of mass-destruction weapons had been destroyed. United Nations' weapons inspectors would soon be posted inside Iraq to finish the task of eliminating both the remaining mass-destruction weapons and the means for their production.

At the time, George Herbert Walker Bush had been America's forty-first president for two years. The assessment of the administration was that Saddam Hussein could not remain in power. This view was shared by each of the coalition partners. Saddam's ignominious military defeat created the expectation in Washington, Riyadh, Damascus, Cairo, London, Paris, and Moscow that Iraq's supreme leader would be overthrown by a vengeful military, much in the manner that Saddam had seized power more than a decade earlier. In fact, Secretary of Defense Dick Cheney bet a *New York Times* reporter dinner that Saddam would be gone in six months.

But Saddam did not cooperate (and Cheney lost his bet). If anything, paradoxically, the dramatic defeat in Kuwait enabled the despot to tighten his control on power, unlike the leaders confronting him. Saddam not only outlasted George Bush; John Major, then British prime minister, was turned out of office. Mikhail Gorbachev was an earlier political casualty. Jordan's King Hussein and Syrian President Assad died and were succeeded by their respective sons.

Of the leaders who remained in power, almost all were in the region. Fahd is still the Saudi king, although his health is tenuous. The Sabahs continue to rule Kuwait. Hosni Mubarak remains Egypt's president.

Saddam's longevity regrettably sets the context for the war against Osama bin Laden and those who support his type of terrorism. In 1991, bin Laden had already cut his teeth in the nearly ten-year-long Afghan war against the Soviet Union. Along with the less visible forces that were building, the effect would be to metastasize yesterday's unfinished business into much of today's turmoil and terror. But, at the time, the future consequences were taking form.

Substantial U.S. military presence in Saudi Arabia would last. It would have a dark side. Saudi culture and values would suffer. Political problems would emerge, bin Laden the most visible. Yet, without American presence, there might not have been a kingdom.

Against this broader context, we can better understand the question of whether eliminating Saddam in 1991 was wise or even possible and could have influenced the events of September 11th and we can put the inherent difficulties in dealing with these pieces of unfinished business in a proper perspective.

## The Bush Experience

When George H. W. Bush took the oath of office on January 20th, 1989, he was the president most qualified in foreign policy since General Dwight Eisenhower was sworn in thirty-six years earlier. A graduate of Phillips Andover Academy and Yale University, Bush had served with distinction in World War II as a Navy fighter pilot, the second youngest in the fleet. Shot down after strafing a Japanese-held island, he bailed out and was rescued by an American submarine. Following his father's footsteps, he was elected to Congress. After losing a bid for the Senate, he served in high office during the Nixon administration as ambassador to the United Nations and to China and as Director of Central Intelligence. He was Ronald Reagan's vice-president for eight years before winning the presidency.

During the Reagan years, Bush was witness to and participant in an array of foreign policy triumphs, tragedies, and disasters. Some events would be indelibly etched in his memory; others would return to test his tenure. The triumphs principally related to Europe, the Soviet Union, and ending the Cold War; to China; and perhaps most importantly, to creating the image of a vibrant and powerful America. The tragedies and disasters arose from Reagan's attempts to defeat communism in Latin America, to bring peace to the Middle East, and to contain Iran's influence in the region during the eight-year-long war with Iraq.

The latter issues, of course, never went away. And two major military incidents occurred during the Reagan watch that would magnify earlier American failures, beginning with the Vietnam experience. Significant changes in the law would arise regarding the organization of the Department of Defense. These, too, would become important in waging war and keeping peace.

Reagan strongly supported those in opposition to communism.

In Afghanistan, the mujahadeen were armed to greater purpose by the CIA with Stinger missiles and other weapons. Ultimately, the Soviets would be driven out. However, other conditions were created in Afghanistan that would return to test American policy and successive presidents. Bin Laden and many of his al Qaeda followers honed their skills and resentments in battle with the Soviets.

In Latin America, the Contras were fighting against the left-wing parties aiming to control Salvador and Nicaragua. There, the administration was waging a not-so-secret war but without the full involvement or knowledge of Congress. The Director of Central Intelligence, William Casey, a veteran of World War II's famous OSS (Office of Strategic Services), was largely in charge. Casey was an independent operator who neither sought nor needed much help from Congress in carrying out his president's wishes. When the story of the CIA's mining of Nicaraguan waters broke, there was a firestorm on Capitol Hill. Casey survived nonetheless.

It was the Iran-Contra scandal, however, that nearly destroyed the administration. Reagan's support of the Contras and his likening of them to America's revolutionary leaders intensified the already supercharged partisan debate over his policy toward Latin America. However, genuine constitutional issues over the responsibility of the president for the conduct of foreign policy and the role of Congress for oversight and funding were at stake. Democrats in Congress, through legislation offered by Representative Edward Boland (D.-Mass.), placed restrictions on U.S. aid to the Contras. Funding was cut off in three separate amendments bearing Boland's name.

The Reagan administration believed that its constitutional responsibilities for foreign policy superseded those of Congress. The White House acted to circumvent the admittedly ambiguous language in the Boland amendments to do what was needed to defeat Nicaragua's Sandanistas. That meant keeping the Contras alive with money and weapons. But a collision was in the making with another aspect of the Reagan policy, in this case as it concerned Iran.

In June 1985, Reagan's third national security adviser, Robert (Bud) McFarlane, attempted to create a strategic opening to Iran. In a draft National Security Decision Directive (NSDD) titled "U.S.

Policy Toward Iran," McFarlane proposed a dialogue with Iran. To demonstrate American intent, a transfer of U.S. arms was part of the package. McFarlane, a veteran of NSC service when Henry Kissinger held the job, envisaged the Nixon administration's opening to China as the strategic model for dealing with Iran. Secretary of State George Shultz and Secretary of Defense Caspar Weinberger strongly objected, to the point of condemning the idea. After all, Iran was a terrorist state. And Reagan had pledged never to deal with terrorists. Despite these warnings and contradictory policy aims, the White House proceeded with the overture.

Ultimately, according to Colin Powell's book, 4508 Tow antitank missiles and repair parts for anti-air Hawk missiles were transferred from the Defense Department to the CIA for subsequent shipment to Iran. By then, McFarlane had resigned as national security adviser and was replaced by his deputy, Vice-Admiral John Poindexter. Marine Lieutenant Colonel Oliver North, serving on the NSC staff and acting (as it turned out) on his own, recycled some of the proceeds from the sale of the missiles to Iran, brokered through Israel, to the Contras. All of this was purposely concealed from Congress, the public, and much of the administration.

Keeping a secret in Washington is difficult. On November 1, 1986, *Al Shiraa*, a magazine in Beirut, broke the story. Washington was reported to be secretly selling arms to Ayatollah Khomeini's regime. In light of Reagan's pledge never to deal with terrorists, his use of illegal funds to support the Contras, and the perjured testimony offered by key White House officials to Congress were explosive revelations. The administration was trapped and nearly destroyed.

The subsequent investigating commission, chaired by Senator John Tower (and including Brent Scowcroft as one of the commissioners), portrayed Reagan as "detached, confused and uninformed." A major housecleaning of Reagan's key advisers also ensued. Chief of Staff Donald Regan and Admiral John Poindexter were fired. Frank Carlucci, a seasoned professional and Reagan's first deputy defense secretary, was brought in as the new national security adviser and Colin Powell became his deputy. Throughout, Vice-President Bush claimed he "was out of the loop," playing no role in this policy disaster. Had Reagan not been so personally popular with members of both parties of Congress, impeachment would have been a distinct possibility. His televised public apology went a long way toward defusing the overheated situation.

In the summer of 1983, the United States intervened in Lebanon in an attempt to facilitate the withdrawal of all foreign troops in the country. The Lebanese Army and Syrian-backed Shiite units were fighting each other in the Shouf mountains. Syrian forces were in the north of Lebanon. Israel had occupied southern Lebanon in 1982 in an effort to rout out the Palestinian Liberation Organization (PLO) and its threat to Israel. In the early days of that occupation, the massacre of Lebanese refugees at the camps at Shattila and Sabra occurred. Many placed responsibility for the atrocity on Ariel Sharon, now Israel's prime minister.

To many Arabs and Muslims, Israel's occupation of Lebanon was the provocation needed to legitimize such terrorist organizations as Hezbollah and Hamas. Bin Laden and his colleagues may not have been sparked by this legacy, but surely many Arabs and Muslims were. Hence, the weight of the past is relevant to the problems and challenges of this decade. Peace in the Middle East was elusive then. It has become dramatically more so.

The Reagan administration landed U.S. Marines to take up positions near the Beirut airport, directly between the two major warring armies—the Lebanese and Shiites. This turned out to be less than an ideal plan. To simplify logistics and support, a large building was turned into the Marine headquarters and barracks. On October 23rd, an explosive-laden truck crashed through the gate and was detonated by the driver. The suicide attack killed 241 Americans and destroyed the Marine barracks. The bombing was a tragedy and a foreign policy nightmare. Critics were emboldened by this disaster to condemn the competence of both the administration and the military. After Beirut, the movement for military reform would become irresistible. French forces were bombed as well.

The Beirut bombing was also the first real instance of a calamitous "kamikaze-like" attack against American forces since World War II. It would not be the last. The Reagan administration soon withdrew the Marines stationed in Lebanon and took a step back from the peace process. But suicide bombers were not new. Over a hundred years before, on March 1, 1881, after eight separate attempts, a suicide bomber from the Russian terrorist group *Narodnaya Volya* (people's will) assassinated Tsar Alexander II, killing himself in the blast.

Two days after Beirut exploded, the administration intervened in the Caribbean island of Grenada. The Marxist-leaning leader, Maurice Bishop, had been assassinated. In the chaos, the administration publicly worried that American students enrolled in a local medical school were at risk. However, there was an unstated reason for intervention: to prevent a left-leaning government from taking power.

The military intervention did not go smoothly. Marred by poor communications, little interservice cooperation, and micromanagement from Washington, U.S. forces appeared uncoordinated and clumsy. Despite the light opposition, it took nearly a week to subdue the resistance, take the island, and rescue the students. Fortunately for the administration, the media largely overlooked the conclusion of the force commander, Vice-Admiral Joseph J. Metcalf, that the students were never in danger. Major General Norman Schwarzkopf, then commanding the 24th Infantry Division, was sent to Metcalf's staff at short notice to provide someone experienced in ground combat.

Both Beirut and Grenada became the poster children for critics alleging U.S. military ineptness and incompetence. After Beirut and Grenada, the conditions were ripe for military reform. George Bush would see the fruits of that reform—the Goldwater-Nichols Act, named for Senator Barry Goldwater and Representative Bill Nichols—when he became president. That act, passed into law in 1986, strengthened the role of the chairman of the Joint Chiefs of Staff (JCS) as the principal military adviser to the president, downplayed the role of the Joint Chiefs, and made operational "jointness"—that is, the better integration of the Army, Navy, Air Force, and Marines in actual deployment and use—a requirement. Later, when the chairmanship was filled with an officer of Colin Powell's ability, the authority of the office of the chairman would be strengthened even further.

The Reagan administration also dealt with terrorism and homeland defense. U.S. servicemen were killed and injured when a disco was bombed in Berlin in 1987. Libya and its leader, Colonel Muamar Quadaffi, were held responsible. A punitive strike, called Eldorado Canyon, was ordered. Air Force and Navy jets attacked Tripoli. One of Quadaffi's children was killed. The Reagan administration claimed a victory and relaxed its anti-Quadaffi rhetoric. In 1988 Pan American Flight 103 was downed by terrorists, almost certainly in retaliation for the egregious downing of a commercial Iranian Air Bus over the Persian Gulf by the American warship USS *Vincennes*. But terrorism remained outside the continental United States.

In March 1983, Reagan announced his plan for a strategic defense initiative, called SDI. His aim was to defend America from Soviet missile attack. Strategic defense would make nuclear missiles "impotent and obsolete." The debate was and remains fierce. As George W. Bush seeks to implement a miniature version of strategic defense, controversy will continue.

## The New Captain of the Ship of State

Bush won his party's nomination for president and easily defeated former Massachusetts governor Michael Dukakis in the 1988 election. He entered office without major crises or controversies at hand. In June 1989 the Chinese bloodily repressed the student "democracy" protest in Beijing's Tiananmen Square. U.S.–Sino relations collapsed despite the president's stint as ambassador to China.

In November two events, one small and the other seminal, captured the president's attention. A coup in the Philippines threatened the regime of President Corazon Aquino. With prompt American action and a show-of-force fly-over of Manila by U.S fighter aircraft, the danger quickly receded. But several weeks before, on November 10th, the Berlin Wall had cracked open. Bush was witnessing what would become the end of the Soviet Union.

At year's end, Bush was confronted with a crisis in Panama and

growing danger to Americans stationed there. Panama and its dictator, Manuel Noreiga, had long been an irritant to the United States.
Noreiga and his regime were corrupt and involved in the drug trade.
In 1988 the Justice Department indicted Noreiga for drug trafficking
and racketeering.

In October 1989, an attempted coup against Noreiga failed. He
stepped up his anti-American activities. Americans stationed in Panama largely to protect the canal were put at some risk. On Saturday,
December 16th, a Panamanian Defense Force (PDF) roadblock
stopped four U.S. officers in civilian clothing. When the soldiers
attempted to pull the Americans from the car, the driver sped off.
Shots were fired. Marine Lieutenant Robert Paz was hit and soon
died. The situation deteriorated. Navy Lieutenant Adam Curtis and
his wife, Bonnie, who witnessed the shooting, were detained by the
PDF. Taken to a police station for questioning, Curtis was assaulted
and threatened with death. His wife was harassed and physically
abused by PDF soldiers.

The next day, Sunday the 17th, the Bush administration national
security team met in the White House and made a decision for
strong action. Colin Powell, then two months into his four-year
chairmanship of the Joint Chiefs of Staff, cited the reasons: "Noreiga's contempt for democracy, his drug trafficking and indictment,
the death of the American marine, the threat to our treaty rights to
the canal. . . . And, unspoken, there was George Bush's personal
antipathy to Noreiga, a third-rate dictator thumbing his nose at the
United States. I shared this distaste." This would not be the last case
in which Bush's personal feelings would loom large.

Originally code-named "Blue Spoon" and planned by Army
General Maxwell Thurman, the U.S. commander in Panama, the
operation was renamed "Just Cause" and 25,000 American servicemen went into action ultimately to capture Manuel Noreiga.
Although they had difficulty finding him, Noreiga was finally hunted
down and arrested. Twenty-three U.S. servicemen were killed in the
process. Noreiga is serving life imprisonment in a U.S. jail.

Ten months later, in late July 1990, Saddam stepped up his rhe-
torical attacks on Kuwait. Iraq had long regarded the tiny kingdom

and its vast quantities of oil as its thirteenth province. Iraq and Kuwait had quarreled over oil production and prices. Iraq had accused Kuwait of illegally producing and pumping more oil than authorized by OPEC—the Organization of Oil Petroleum Exporting Countries—thereby keeping the price down and limiting Iraq's oil revenues. Iraq claimed some $2.5 billion had been lost due to Kuwait's antics. Another dispute focused on the boundaries of the rich Ramallah oil fields and Iraqi access to the Gulf. Saddam had eyed two Kuwaiti-held islands—Bubiyan and Warba—that blocked Iraqi access to the Gulf. As Powell noted, Saddam regarded the Kuwaitis not as Arab brothers but as "greedy lapdogs" of the West.

Controversy between Iraq and Kuwait was not new. Nearly thirty years earlier, in 1961, Iraq, under a different regime, threatened Kuwait. The United Kingdom, then still possessing an "east of Suez" presence, landed an undersize battalion of Royal Marine Commandos in Kuwait. Even though these marines had virtually no ammunition or staying power, the display worked. The Iraqis were deterred and no attack took place.

The U.S. ambassador to Iraq, April Glaspie, was about to depart Baghdad on home leave. Her instructions from Washington, however, were to discourage Saddam from using force and to call for a peaceful resolution. At the time, the general American assessment of Iraqi intent was one of bluster and not a full-scale military attack. Glaspie informed Saddam directly that peaceful resolution was imperative. However, she added that the U.S. government had "no opinion" on fault and did "not take a stand on territorial disputes" between regional states.

The American expectation was that the parties in the region should resolve the dispute. On the diplomatic front, President Hosni Mubarak of Egypt and King Fahd of Saudi Arabia mediated the dispute between Iraq and Kuwait. Saddam had given his word to both leaders that he would take no action until their effort had run its course. Despite assurances to the contrary, Saddam massed his forces on the Kuwait border, all under the watchful eyes of American spaced-based satellites and reconnaissance systems. By the time it became clear to Washington that Iraq was almost certainly preparing a full-fledged invasion of Kuwait, it was too late for either preventive options or active diplomacy.

## America at War—Almost

At 8:20 P.M. on Wednesday, August 1, President Bush was in the White House Medical Office receiving heat for a sore shoulder aggravated by "hitting too many golf balls" when his national security adviser, Lieutenant General Brent Scowcroft, and senior NSC staffer Richard Haass burst in with the news that Saddam's army was on the move. As a footnote, General Scowcroft currently serves as the chairman of the president's Foreign Intelligence Advisory Board and Haass is director of the State Department's policy planning office.

Perhaps in a curious twist of fate, earlier that morning Secretary of Defense Dick Cheney and chairman of the JCS Colin Powell had briefed the president on a proposed new strategy for the post–Cold War period. Part of the strategy was a "Base Force" that no longer needed the current 2.1 million personnel on active duty; 1.6 million were enough. The Base Force also envisaged Korea and the Gulf as the two most likely regions for future conflict.

After the invasion, Washington had few immediate options. The U.S. presence in the Gulf was principally naval. With Saudi permission, American land-based fighter and support aircraft could quickly be deployed. The excellent bases that had been built in the Saudi Kingdom were perfect for accommodating large numbers of aircraft. General Norman Schwarzkopf, now commander in chief of Central Forces Command and the general responsible for that region estimated that five tactical fighter squadrons and a carrier battle group could be on station in a week.

Lieutenant and later General Chuck Horner, who would command the air war, was prepared to deploy four hundred F-15 and F-16 fighter aircraft in eleven days once the order was given. Because the Saudi Air Force also flew U.S. F-15s and F-16s, a reservoir of common repair parts and aviation fuel was on hand. Additional carrier battle groups and supporting Marine Amphibious forces could be dispatched to the Gulf. But longer transit times meant that it would take several weeks before a powerful sea-based force could be on station.

Bush was scheduled to deliver an important speech the next day at Aspen, Colorado, and then to meet with Britain's Prime Minister Margaret Thatcher. The two heads of state would be able to confer on responses to Iraq's invasion of Kuwait. Bush admitted in his memoirs, co-authored with Brent Scowcroft, that the suddenness of the attack left him no time to assess the implications or indeed to gather more than bits of information as to what was happening in Kuwait. Hence, Bush had drawn no conclusions about possible future courses of action. Nor had he ruled any out.

Thatcher's reaction was no different than in 1982 after Argentina seized Britain's Falkland Islands at the tip of South America. Britain went to war, sending a substantial force ten thousand miles to recapture territory that was practically, but not symbolically, of little value. (Interestingly, British intransigence registered heavily on the Soviets, who took Thatcher more seriously thereafter.) Thatcher assumed a tough stance, demanding Saddam's withdrawal, peacefully or with the force of arms. She was quoted as telling the president, "Don't go wobbly on me, George." Bush would not. However, fashioning the policy and coalition that finally would evict Saddam from Kuwait would take time, patience, skill, and a bit of luck.

The invasion also entailed a certain embarrassment. For much of the eight years of war between Iran and Iraq, the United States had "tilted" toward Iraq. Saddam was close to being a quasi-U.S. ally. Bush, of course, as Reagan's vice-president, was "fully in the loop" regarding Iraq.

The Reagan administration, mindful of Iran's seizure of the American embassy in 1979 and stung by the Iran Contra disaster, had an ambivalent Gulf policy. Hence, the tilt to aid Iraq in that war was an understandable step. The two nations exchanged intelligence, and American military observers were permitted to visit the Iraqi front.

In 1987, two Exocet missiles, inadvertently fired from a French-built Iraqi Entendarde aircraft, hit and nearly sank the frigate USS

*Stark* on patrol in the Gulf. Iraq apologized, cooperated in the investigation, and offered compensation for the damage. Despite the unsavory nature of the regime, Iraq was of temporary use to the United States in counterbalancing the more hostile Iran. When Bush entered office in 1989, his major strategy review, National Strategy Review (NSR)-10, concluded that no change was needed in U.S. policies in the Gulf toward Iraq.

On a personal note, during the war I was a frequent television commentator. On August 6th, I appeared on *Larry King Live*. Pat Buchanan, the moderator, was pessimistic about would happen next in Kuwait, fearing American inaction. My reaction was different. "It will be over in six months. Saddam will be out of Kuwait." Buchanan was disbelieving.

The record of the Bush administration in the handling of the war and its aftermath has been well documented by the principal participants as well as by historians and reporters. In retrospect, as in the early days of the two world wars, nascent issues were present that would become the unfinished business left over from reversing Saddam's aggression. But, as the administration began drafting plans for forcing Iraq to withdraw from Kuwait, the historical antecedents were as distant to Bush as they had been to prior presidents and predecessors on the eve of war.

The first of these had to do with the "openness" of democratic societies and their inherent vulnerabilities. In 1990, the United States was protected by its geographic separation from sources of conflict. The Cold War had not ended. Political leverage as a counterbalance to the Soviets remained. U.S. vulnerabilities were largely economic. Despite many warnings and a Cold War that could have become white hot with nuclear exchange, terrorism and violence from afar had not reached American shores. The vulnerability of the infrastructure was largely theoretical. Yes, security in airports had increased since the 1970s to prevent aircraft hijackings, but otherwise few outward signs reflected any heightened security. It would be five years before Timothy McVeigh destroyed the Murrah Building in Oklahoma City; bin Laden's network was three years from launching its first and unsuccessful attack against New York's twin towers.

The principal economic consequence of Iraq's occupation of Kuwait rested in access to and potential control over most of the world's proven oil reserves in the Gulf. In 1973 and 1974, after the October Arab-Israeli War, OPEC imposed an "oil embargo." Americans alive then will recall the enormous lines of cars at gasoline stations and the subsequent "energy crisis." Cheap and accessible gasoline is viewed almost as a basic American right. A quarter of a century later, when premium gasoline cost $2 a gallon, the public was outraged. Iraq, in charge of the region's oil reserves, would have an embargo weapon at the ready and an economic dagger pointed at the West. That was not a tolerable condition.

Later during the Gulf conflict, when pushed by reporters to answer what U.S. vital interests were involved in this fight, Secretary of State James Baker had a simple reply: "Jobs, jobs, jobs." His point, an unstated reference to oil, was obvious. For geopolitical as well as economic reasons, an aggressive and unpredictable Saddam could not be allowed to sit astride the oil crucial to the West.

Domestically, the economy was sputtering. Bush's most famous campaign promise and one he later came to regret was his repeated "Read my lips. No new taxes." Bush's budget had stalled in the Democratically controlled Congress. And that promise would be tested.

With Saddam in Kuwait and the prospect of war real, Congress and the White House had no agreement on the most pressing issues, including the budget—a vital need at a time of emergency. But who would give in—the Republicans or the Democrats? On both sides of the aisle, Congress was not well disposed to war. Reinstalling a despotic leadership to power in a faraway sheikdom from the grasp of even such a villain as Saddam Hussein was not seen as a vital role for the United States. Most members of Congress favored sanctions as an alternative to war. Bush blinked first on the budget. He would not do so on the war. As it turned out, the budget and not the war would be more important in the November 1992 elections.

Bush clearly understood that public support was essential.

Hence, one of his first aims was to convince the public of the need to reverse the invasion, whether or not force ultimately was used. Quickly, sanctions were imposed. The United Nations became a vehicle for internationalizing the scope of those sanctions. Fortunately, the fear of terrorist attacks by Iraq or parties favorable to Iraq against the United States was measured. A massive homeland defense campaign did not seem necessary to counter the threat that Iraq was likely to pose.

The Arab-Israeli conflict loomed. Bush did not have warm feelings for Israeli Prime Minister Yitzhak Shamir. The sentiment flowed both ways. Indeed, U.S.–Israeli relations would be stretched to the limit by subsequent events. On October 8th, a riot on Jerusalem's Temple Mount led to Israeli security forces' killing twenty-one Palestinians. The Arab world was outraged at a delicate time in building the anti-Iraq coalition. During Desert Storm, Saddam launched Scud missile attacks on Tel Aviv. The understandable Israeli passion to retaliate had to be cooled—a test for any American administration.

The so-called moderate Arab states—Egypt, Saudi Arabia, and the United Arab Emirates (UAE)—had misgivings about the staying power of the United States. The memory of Vietnam lingered. The failed attempt to rescue the fifty-two Americans taken hostage by Iran in 1979 during the seizure of the U.S. embassy was a national embarrassment (as well as one of the reasons for the defeat of President Jimmy Carter in 1980 to the Reagan-Bush ticket). And, of course, the Beirut bombing and U.S. withdrawal reinforced regional concerns about American staying power.

Thus, while Iraqi forces were menacing the Saudi border from positions in Kuwait, King Fahd was ambivalent on the United States. Clearly, Saudi Arabia needed protection and some form of defense against the vastly stronger Iraq. However, the Saudis were not prepared to grant the United States instant access and basing, or even to permit the stationing of foreign troops on Saudi soil without strong assurances that the United States would honor this commitment.

Jordan was a separate and difficult case. King Hussein and President Bush enjoyed a good relationship. Jordan, however, was dependent on Iraq for oil and for protection. Hence, the king would be forced to side with Iraq despite his friendship for America and George Bush.

In Europe and in NATO, reactions to the Iraqi invasion were mixed. Britain was the strongest advocate for taking decisive action. However, other members of the alliance were reluctant to react. France did substantial business in Iraq. Iraqi debts were large. France had no wish to jeopardize them. And, if force were required, the alliance would have to accept redeployment of American troops from Europe to the Gulf at a time when Moscow was in the midst of profound change. NATO states would also have to authorize access and overflight rights—something that was not done during the U.S. resupply missions to Israel in the October 1973 war or in Eldorado Canyon strikes against Libya.

Mikhail Gorbachev was ending Soviet occupation of Eastern Europe and imposing *perestroika* (reform) and *glasnost* (openness) at home. The effect would inadvertently trigger the disintegration of the Soviet Union. Clearly, the U.S.–Soviet relationship was in great flux. Russia was Iraq's principal supplier of weapons and was owed several billions of dollars in past-due payments. Hence, in August 1990 no one could predict where or how the Soviet leadership would come out over whether to support reversing Iraq's invasion.

Even then, Afghanistan was an emerging worry. The Soviets had just beaten a retreat from the nearly decade-long war there. About sixteen thousand Russians had been killed as a scantily armed but determined Afghan resistance deftly bloodied the Red Army. The United States had helped the army of mujahadeen through two administrations—Carter and Reagan. The Stinger missile had become famous as one of the deciding military factors for defeating the Soviets by reducing their advantage in air power. When the Soviets left, so did the Americans. Afghanistan would have to fend for itself, a policy that would end in tears.

Finally, this was to be the first war fought under the Goldwater-Nichols reorganization. Powell as chairman was the principal military adviser. Working with Secretary of Defense Cheney, Powell and his staff, along with CentCom (Schwarzkopf), formulated the plans and issued the orders. The rest of the Joint Chiefs were largely out of the loop operationally.

If there was any question over who was in charge, Air Force Chief of Staff Michael Dugan learned the hard way. Returning from a trip to Israel in late August, Dugan had made indiscreet comments to the press disparaging the probable American reaction to U.S. casualties. The conversations appeared in the Sunday *Washington Post*. Cheney was furious. Dugan was dismissed virtually on the spot.

The war against Iraq would bear a striking resemblance to the U.S. plans for fighting the Soviet Union. The national security structure was well organized and prepared for that task. The forces were designed to counter the Soviets. Instead of charging to the Fulda Gap on the German plain to defeat the Soviet Army, American forces would maneuver in Kuwait. The desert, because it lacked obstructions such as forests and cities, would prove the ideal battleground for the vastly superior American technology, weather permitting.

Heavy armored and mechanized ground forces would destroy Iraqi ground forces, themselves modeled on those of the Soviet Union. Air forces would seize control of the skies and wage a strategic bombing campaign against Iraq's important military targets—air defenses, logistics, command and control, supply and support, communications lines, and military–industrial targets including suspected chemical, biological, and nuclear sites. At the same time, air forces would begin striking Iraqi forces in Kuwait, preparing the battlefield for eventual ground attack.

Since Iraq possessed no real navy, American warships would have uncontested command of the sea and air. Naval forces would support the air campaign and prepare for an amphibious assault, should one be required. The main danger, outside of some form of Iraqi kamikaze attack, was from mines; two U.S. warships would be hit and damaged by these underwater explosives. Still, the Navy was exceedingly lucky. Most of the ships in the Gulf steamed, unknowingly, in mined waters. Fortunately, Iraq had inserted the exploders backward in most of the devices, rendering them useless.

The president and his secretary of state would conduct the diplomacy vital to put in place an international coalition to legitimize any action against Iraq. Intelligence would support battlefield preparations and deal with preventing terrorism. In other words, the organization for a possible war in the Gulf flowed from the preparations for fighting the Soviet Union.

The ultimate plan would be complex and require careful coordination both abroad and at home. On August 1, the president had insufficient information to formulate any plan that would last even a week. Since Saddam's intentions were unknowable—he could withdraw from Kuwait whenever it suited him—it was impossible to guess the degree to which force, as opposed to diplomacy, would be the ultimate arbiter. Bush understood that there were several choices. However, he also understood that each depended on fashioning some form of supporting coalition.

Sanctions were the first available tool. The administration had already suspended certain commodity credits to Iraq. It would soon impound Kuwaiti and Iraqi assets in the United States. But sanctions took time to work, and history offered few examples in which sanctions had forced one country to relinquish territorial gains. True, South Africa's apartheid regime partially succumbed to sanctions, but those sanctions had been in place for years. In facing Iraq, while Congress had broad political support for sanctions and far less for war, the administration understood the limitations of any economic strategy to deny Iraq access to the world at large.

Second, diplomacy could impose strong pressure on Iraq. Regional leaders in the Arab and Muslim worlds had some influence on Saddam. Whether any pressure would be effective remained to be seen. Bringing other states, particularly the Soviet Union, to bear was an intelligent approach. However, given the ambivalence of Congress and many Americans toward the use of force, diplomatic options had to be pursued to exhaustion.

This reality gave the advantage to Saddam. While diplomacy was inducing him to leave Kuwait, Iraq could agree to accept certain terms and perhaps even start a partial withdrawal. Iraq could also stall once negotiations were underway. The start-and-stop option, if Iraq were to exercise it, would almost certainly remove any opportunity to use force. Then, the holy month of Ramadan and the hot season of 1991 would delay the military option even further.

Third, if military forces were to be deployed, two basic options presented themselves. The first was to mount a defense to protect Saudi Arabia from any form of Iraqi attack. Strategists considered an American force of about a quarter of a million soldiers, airmen, sailors, and marines enough for the mission of keeping Saudi Arabia and the peninsula secure. However, the long-term consequences of maintaining such a large foreign presence in Saudi Arabia would present major complications for both the Saudis and the United States. The United States then had about three hundred thousand service personnel deployed around the world. The logistics of another sustained deployment would be significant and would affect the size and type of presence elsewhere. More significant would be the impact of large numbers of foreigners (infidels to some) on Saudi culture, religion, and society, and therefore on the authority of the ruling regime.

The second option was to deploy an offensive force powerful enough to drive Saddam out of Kuwait and, in the process, eliminate as much of Iraq's military power as possible. The size of that force was estimated at about twice the size of the defensive package or about half a million Americans. However, in August 1990, Iraq's army enjoyed a certain reputation based on eight years of fighting Iran. Battling that army could prove expensive. American casualties were a crucial political consideration. And America had not fully emerged from the dark shadow of Vietnam. Its fighting capacity had not been proven and the memories of Desert One, Beirut, and Grenada lingered.

## Shield before Storm

Just as Roosevelt had no immediate plan for winning World War II immediately after Pearl Harbor and Lyndon Johnson had no strategic blueprint regarding Vietnam after the Tonkin Gulf incident in August 1964, Bush too needed time to assimilate sufficient information before proceeding. On Sunday August 5th, Bush flew back to the White House from Camp David in the Maryland mountains west of Washington. Climbing down from his helicopter on the South Lawn, Bush purposely walked over to a crowd of waiting reporters. In answer to the questions swirling around him about Iraq's invasion of Kuwait, Bush revealed the general direction of his thinking: "I am not going to discuss what we're doing in terms of moving forces. . . . But I view it [the invasion] very seriously. . . . This will not stand, this aggression against Kuwait."

For much of the fall, the administration crafted the means for dislodging Saddam. The best case was that a combination of diplomacy and sanctions would take its toll. Saddam would recognize that his long-term interests were best served by peaceful settlement and withdrawal. This approach held two obvious risks. First, sanctions required time. Results could be measured in months and even years. The longer Iraq remained in Kuwait, the greater the odds against negotiation of a peaceful exit. Saddam also would have more time to dig in and to prepare his defenses, including laying tens of thousands of mines—a daunting prospect.

Second, to work, any action—whether sanctions or force—required international cooperation and support, if not full-scale approval. Sanctions were only as good as their enforcement. Even a single leak could provide Iraq the means for selling oil.

But the Bush administration had to consider the worst case. Suppose Saddam refused to budge. Suppose Iraq was determined to stay in Kuwait. And, if Iraq remained, what would it take to keep adjoining states, particularly Saudi Arabia, secure? Only military force could provide answers to these questions.

Military force, of course, entailed great risk. More international cooperation would be needed to authorize force, including UN resolutions. Access to the Gulf was difficult. A number of nations would have to consent to the use of their bases and facilities for deploying forces. The United States would need military forces from other nations for political as well as operational reasons. A broad coalition would help persuade Congress and the American public to support the use of American forces. In particular, how could senators vote against using force if Egypt, Syria, and Poland, for example, committed troops to evicting Saddam? A broad coalition might persuade Saddam to withdraw short of war.

Meanwhile, the administration had to contend with outside interventions and wild cards. The Soviet Union was anxious to play a role. Gorbachev had already shocked the world by taking down the Berlin Wall. Now, would he attempt even bolder diplomatic initiatives in the Gulf, in part to build his credibility at home? The UN was essential for legitimizing international action. However, the United States was outnumbered ideologically there. Ensuring that the UN member states could be persuaded to cooperate or at least not to thwart American responses would prove a testing exercise.

The administration embarked on a plan that would keep its options open. An international coalition was joining together to sustain sanctions and support a military campaign. Under the name Desert Shield, defensive forces surged into the peninsula. Beyond the immediate defense of Saudi Arabia, the administration was considering what force it would take to evict Saddam if it came to that. An "air-only" campaign was politically attractive. Such a campaign would minimize American casualties. However, there were grave doubts among Bush's military advisers that bombing alone would force Iraq to leave Kuwait.

On September 24th, Cheney and Powell requested an audience with Bush. Powell believed it was important to brief the commander in chief on the two feasible military options. The first was the offensive plan. The second was the defensive option, which protected Saudi Arabia but relied on sanctions to compel Iraqi withdrawal. Powell told the president that the decision to choose the offensive option could not be delayed past October. Otherwise, sufficient forces would not be in place for an attack early in the new year, well before Ramadan and hot weather could impede any military operations. Bush understood. If an offensive were to be mounted in January, his approval to deploy the remaining forces must come by late October. The choices were starkly clear.

October 30th was the day of decision. Congress had adjourned two days before. That morning Bush met with a special bipartisan eighteen-member congressional team headed by Majority Leader

George Mitchell and House Speaker Tom Foley. Foley handed the president a letter carrying an "expression of concern" about the role of Congress in the event of war in the Gulf. Signed by eighty-one members, the letter noted recent reports that the United States had shifted "from a defensive to an offensive posture and that war may be imminent."

Congress was clearly worried about war and about its constitutional responsibilities, especially with an election only a week away. The letter went on to state: "The consequences would be catastrophic—resulting in the massive loss of lives including 10,000–50,000 Americans. This can only be described as war. Under the U.S. Constitution, only the Congress can declare war."

If that was not sufficient warning, the signatories informed Bush that "we are emphatically opposed to any offensive military operations" without giving sanctions a chance to work and without a declaration of war. This congresssional statement is a reminder of how tense the situation was for the Bush administration and how fragile the coalition and support actually were. In retrospect, that Bush successfully navigated these dangerous political waters was a remarkable tribute to his skills and perseverance. As Bush later expressed it, if he failed or stumbled, he expected Congress to bring impeachment proceedings against him.

At 4:00 p.m. that day, the national security team, less Vice-President Dan Quayle, who was out of town, met in the White House. Bush opened the meeting. The fundamental question had been posed in August: Does the United States limit its activities to defending Saudi Arabia and depending on sanctions to drive Saddam out? Or does the nation take steps to drive him out with force? As Powell put it, "defend or eject?"

The president was clear in his aim: "Either way [defend or eject], I want everyone to know that my commitment to seeing Saddam leave Kuwait unconditionally remains firm." Eventually the discussion worked its way around to the offensive campaign. Powell describes his briefing in his autobiography, and quotes Scowcroft asking: "What size force are we talking about?" Powell records that his reply—"nearly double" the 250,000 needed for the defensive option—evoked some heavy breathing.

After further discussion, Bush gave the order. The DOD was to move its forces into the region. If sanctions did not work and Iraq was still in Kuwait in three months' time, the United States would have the forces in place to take the offensive. In mid-January, if Saddam had not backed down, the United States and its allies would go to war.

My vantage point throughout all of this was as continuing television commentator and a friend of many of the participants, including Colin Powell. Tuesday November 6th was election day. I was scheduled for a private lunch with the chairman in the Pentagon. Around noon, Nancy Hughes, Powell's secretary, escorted me into the chairman's office, Room 2E-872. Over a cheeseburger, talk meandered around the crisis in the Gulf. Powell usually preferred to listen, so he began quizzing me. His first question was, "What should I be worried about most?" "Three things," I responded. "Saddam could mine Suez and close it. That happened in 1967 during the Six Days War. It would add a week or two to swinging forces in from Europe, as well scare the Egyptians and everyone else about what could follow as the next escalation. Second, he could begin to withdraw or promise to withdraw from Kuwait. That's the biggest problem in my mind. Finally, he could use biological or chemical weapons. The biological ones are the scariest because of the psychological impact. I doubt he'll use chemicals and besides, we can defend against those." Powell nodded in agreement.

The October 30th meeting had been reported in the press. Powell described, in careful terms, the general flow of the discussion that day including his presentation of the offensive option. "What's going to happen?" I asked. "Beats me," or words to that effect, was Powell's response. Powell's confidence and calm were impressive. It was crystal clear that the president and the secretary of defense had been given the best military advice. This was not going to be another Vietnam. If war occurred, Powell was deadly serious and determined, as he later put it, "to cut it [Saddam's army] off and kill it." The operational unveiling of the doctrine of decisive force was just two and a half months away. No one on either side of the Saddam line in Kuwait could have guessed just how decisive and overwhelming that force would prove, not even Powell.

With Congress out of session, the administration focused its efforts on strengthening the coalition and urging the United Nations to pass the necessary resolutions authorizing the use of force. On November 29th, the Security Council passed Resolution 678 by a twelve-to-two vote. Cuba and Yemen voted no. China abstained.

The resolution authorized the use of "all necessary means" to remove Iraq from Kuwait. While the Americans compromised on that euphemism, preferring the term "military force," Resolution 678 was a remarkable document and an extraordinary diplomatic feat. The coalition was building. Egypt and Syria had agreed to send 50,000 troops. However, the resolution was unambiguous. The license was good only for freeing Kuwait. It did not authorize occupying Iraq and removing Saddam's government. The UN and international support were explicitly clear in how far and where the coalition could proceed.

## Shield Becomes Storm

As 1990 ended, American and allied forces were continuing to pour into Saudi Arabia and the Gulf. Despite the UN resolution and the magnitude of the coalition forming against Iraq, Saddam was unyielding. Barring a diplomatic breakthrough or a clever withdrawal, force was almost certainly going to be necessary. Congress convened on January 3rd and immediately scheduled hearings to discuss whether "jaw" (i.e., sanctions) or "war" was the better course of action after the UN deadline for withdrawal by January 15th expired. The hearings produced divided counsel. Public opinion supported the president and his handling of the crisis.

On January 12th, 1991, both houses of Congress voted on a joint resolution authorizing the use of force pursuant to UN resolutions. In 1941, Congress had voted unanimously to declare war on Japan (it took a unilateral declaration of war by Hitler to bring the United States into the European conflict two days later). The Gulf of Tonkin

Resolution in August 1964, giving Lyndon Johnson virtually a blank check to wage war in Vietnam, had been opposed by only two senators casting negative votes.

The vote to authorize force against Saddam passed by the smallest margin in American history ever to send the nation to war. The House passed the Solarz-Michel resolution 250–183. The Senate's Warner-Lieberman version passed 52–47. With the close vote over, after January 15th, the nation could find itself at war.

On Monday January 14th, my twice-monthly broadcast for NHK, Japan's largest television station, was to go out. Unlike American television, the Japanese prefer longer programs for discussion of serious issues. As the moderator, I often found that a challenge. In October 1989, I hosted an all-day special marking the fortieth anniversary of the formation of the People's Republic of China. Less than four months after Tiananmen Square, China was a pariah. Encouraging broader discussion was difficult. The program, which was billed as "live" from Beijing and Tokyo, had little life in it.

Guests that January day were Admiral William Crowe, chairman of the JCS under Reagan and Bush; General Alexander Haig, Reagan's secretary of state and former NATO commander in Europe; Representative Lee Hamilton, thoughtful chairman of the House Foreign Relations Committee; and Senator John Warner, a former secretary of the navy and strong supporter of national defense. Crowe had just testified to Congress against war, arguing that sanctions should be given more time.

That panel represented the general views across the United States. With the UN deadline about to expire, the crucial question was, what would happen next. John Warner suggested that there would be neither "peace nor war," a politically astute comment suggesting that Saddam might come to his senses and withdraw before force was used. Crowe believed that war was now inevitable and was worried about the extent of U.S. casualties. Privately, he agreed with Powell's concern about an Iraqi withdrawal. But it was Haig who proved most prescient. Haig was characteristically blunt. There would and should be war. Aggression could not be allowed to stand, especially by a "two-bit punk." And, if it took American forces more than two or three days to finish the job, we ought to be ashamed of ourselves. Haig was right. When the ground offensive began five weeks later, it would last exactly one hundred hours. Saddam's army would be beaten to a pulp and forced to flee for its collective life.

## After the Storm

U.S. F-117 Stealth fighters and Tomahawk cruise missiles were the first of the coalition forces to strike deep into Iraq. The history of the war is well known and need not be repeated. After thirty-eight days of the intensive air war, at 4:00 A.M. Riyadh time on February 24th, U.S. Marines, supported by an Army brigade and followed by a panoply of Saudi, Egyptian, Kuwaiti, and Syrian forces, crossed into Kuwait. Far to the west, XVIII Airborne Corps began its push into Iraq with its left flank covered by the 82nd Airborne Division and a French light armored division. The 101st Air Assault Division and the 24th Infantry (Mechanized) Division (ID) of XVIII Corps streamed north toward the Euphrates River valley. Between the Marines and XVIII Corps, VII Corps, with the 1st British Armored Division, stood by to launch the left hook encircling Kuwait and cutting off all escape routes.

The attack was virtually flawless. Two Marine divisions, under the command of Lieutenant General Walter Boomer, quickly slashed through the Saddam Line and were racing toward Kuwait City. Lieutenant General Gary Luck's XVIII Corps was faring as well. Over three thousand Iraqis were captured the first day at the cost of one American wounded. Major General Barry McCaffrey's 24th ID drove sixty miles into Iraq. The Iraqis had been stunned by the aerial bombardment, led by Lieutenant General Charles A. Horner, the overall air war commander, and Vice Admiral Stanley Arthur, who commanded the naval forces operating offshore.

Attack hour for VII Corps was advanced by fifteen hours. Lieutenant General Frederick Franks had the task of cutting off the Iraqi army and killing it with his M-1 tanks and attack helicopters. At every point, Iraqi resistance was crushed. Iraqi prisoners kept pouring in as coalition forces pushed into Kuwait and Iraq. From a tactical perspective, the attack worked too well.

Boomer's Marines moved so quickly into Kuwait that the Republican Guard divisions in reserve were unable to respond promptly. By the time they were prepared to move south, Franks's VII Corps had been racing north and was turning east to close the "door" before the reserve Iraqi divisions could engage. While the coalition was inflicting heavy losses, literally destroying everything in its path, the trap was sprung too quickly. The Republican Guard divisions held in reserve would not be committed. The bulk of the Iraqi army in Kuwait that had not been destroyed began a headlong retreat north. They were literally fish in a barrel for Horner's air forces to shoot.

By February 27th, the war aims were met. Saddam's army had been eviscerated. Kuwait was about to be liberated. Little more could be achieved, beyond killing more Iraqis and the continued ravaging of their forces. Iraq's army was trapped heading north on what the press called a "highway of death." Unwilling to kill Iraqis for the sake of killing and very conscious of public opinion, particularly in the Arab world, Bush was prepared to call a halt.

In preparation for the endgame, earlier, Powell had circulated excerpts of *Every War Must End*, written by Fred C. Ikle. Ikle had served in senior defense and state positions in earlier Republican administrations. His book argued that in war, "fighting often continues long past the point where 'rational' calculation would indicate that the war should be ended." Hostilities were suspended on February 28th with thousands of Iraqi forces trapped on the highway of death.

The aftermath of the very successful military campaign provoked major controversy. The key criticisms were the alleged failure to destroy more or all of Saddam's Republican Guard, to march to Baghdad if necessary to remove Saddam and the Baathist regime and allowing Saddam to continue to fly his helicopters. Without question, the killing of Iraqi forces could have been continued for another day or two.

In the administration's analysis, the continuing the attack would have been counterproductive. Saddam kept more than half his divisions deployed in Iraq. Their purpose was to protect the regime. Hence, even if all of Iraq's forces in Kuwait had been killed or captured, Saddam would still have had substantial forces at his disposal. Given Iraq's population of some 22 million, as opposed to Kuwait's 1.9 million, further destruction would have not changed that balance.

To Americans, would risking the lives of U.S. service personnel to kill more Iraqis have been justified? The Iraqi army had been smashed. Its ability to attack south in a coherent manner would take years to rebuild. So, on balance, the Bush decision to terminate hostilities probably held less significance than its critics have implied.

The more significant criticism attacked the failure of the Bush administration to end Saddam's regime, if necessary by seizing Iraq. The line of argument was well put in *The General's War* by retired Marine Lieutenant General Bernard (Mick) Trainor and *New York Times* reporter Michael Gordon (to whom Cheney had lost the dinner bet over Saddam's longevity). Trainor had also been the *Times*'s military correspondent.

Trainor and Gordon argued that the United States could easily have continued to Baghdad, destroying whatever Iraqi army units got in the way. The Saudis, they said, gave tacit and private support to removing Saddam. The United States could have relied on the Kurds in the north and the Shiites in the south to oppose Saddam. The army, mostly Sunni, was not loyal to Saddam and, in their view, would have surrendered. Trainor believed that senior Saudis, including Prince Bandar, their ambassador to the United States, agreed with this scenario. Furthermore, the Saudis dismissed the prospect of Syrian or Iranian intervention as unlikely.

The authors cited the absence of guidance given to Schwarzkopf, as he met with Iraqi generals at Safwa to dictate a ceasefire and virtual surrender, as indicative of the failure to have a broader strategic plan. Trainor attributed the lack of a more aggressive strategy to Bush and his key advisers, Scowcroft and Baker. In Trainor's critique, they were unprepared to take further risks and content to rest on the overwhelming victory won in Kuwait. Furthermore, the assumption that Saddam could not stay was taken as a given.

The other side of the argument is more persuasive. In forging the armed coalition, the officer placed in overall command was Saudi Lieutenant General Prince Khalid bin Sultan. Schwarzkopf was in command of all U.S. forces and technically Khalid's deputy. The distinction signified a crucial constraint. Western forces were serving in Saudi Arabia with the consent of King Fahd. Despite what might have been said behind closed doors or off the record, there was scant possibility that the Saudis, or for that matter any of the other Arab states including Egypt and Syria, would have sanctioned a full-fledged invasion of Iraq.

Operational realities also precluded going much beyond Baghdad. VII Corps had covered more territory faster than any other major military operation in history, including General George S. Patton's historic run north to relieve Bastogne during the Battle of the Bulge. While General Franks was confident that his forces could have gotten to Baghdad, destroying any resistance in its path, an occupation of the entire country would have required logistics, particularly fuel, that were unlikely to be available. Similarly, XVIII Corps and the French division in Iraq could have marched north to seize Baghdad if required. However, occupying the entire country would have been logistically difficult to sustain.

Franks also recalled a troubling incident. When VII Corps finally moved south from Iraq to King Khalid Airfield before returning home in May, his corps was provided fresh lettuce. The lettuce was contaminated. Overnight, part of his corps contracted diarrhea and intestinal malaises. A significant number of Franks's troops reported to sickbay, rendered ineffective by the complaint. Fortunately, the war was over. However, the effects, whether from natural or man-made germs, were serious.

From a geopolitical perspective, a partitioned or divided Iraq would favor Iran and Syria. Instability in Iraq could have spilled over to Turkey as well. Furthermore, Saddam's replacement might not have been any more compliant. The circumstances were worlds away from 1945 and unconditional surrender. Occupying Iraq, defanging it, and imposing a Jeffersonian democracy were out of the question. Despite "what might have been," the reality was different. Whether there will be action to change the leadership is now up to the current president Bush.

Finally, UN Resolution 678 simply did not authorize such action against Iraq. The resolution called only for liberating Kuwait. In going beyond it, the coalition would have risked collapse. Soviet support would have disappeared. If the Saudis hesitated and restricted basing rights, the United States would have been physically incapable of mounting an effective invasion. The logistics and fuel that Franks and Luck would have required would have had no port of entry for transshipment.

Regarding the decision to allow Saddam to fly helicopters, Iraq used those aircraft to attack the Kurds. In retrospect, the decision was an error. However, Saddam also had ground forces that were capable of conducting those operations. So, in any event, the Kurds were vulnerable.

Critics will continue to criticize. After a decade, the danger has shifted. The issue is whether Saddam and his attempts to acquire deadly weapons can be contained or neutralized only by another war and the use of force. That is a fair question, and one of the unfinished pieces of business the younger Bush must face.

## Small Expectations

With the war over, the victory parade completed, and the forces brought home, the administration had the opportunity to put in place a "new world order." The end of the Soviet Union provided much of the impetus. In some ways, Bush believed that the Gulf War presaged a new world in which the United States would not necessarily need to use force so actively to protect its interests. The emasculation of Saddam and the end of the Soviet threat appeared to be profoundly positive steps toward enhancing peace and stability.

But, as well as the administration had planned and thought its way through mobilizing and then leading the coalition that vanquished Saddam, for whatever reasons, it did not apply the same rigor to considering the postwar environment. Evicting Saddam from Kuwait seemed enough. Reckoning with him in the future was rendered unnecessary by the expectation that Saddam could not last. The status quo ante was good enough. Kuwait was "liberated" and Saddam was no longer an immediate threat to his neighbors.

As a result, no one in the White House had any appetite to shape this new world order. The system had worked well. True, Bush had problems with Congress. But all presidents did. American forces had shattered the image of the Vietnam syndrome and, along with it, any lingering concerns of military ineptness. Fundamental change or reform seemed unnecessary. The old saw of "don't fix what's not broken" applied. Lessons that would be learned from the war would be sufficient guidelines for making any improvements.

The Arab-Israeli dispute was not on the boil. Israeli restraint in the face of Iraqi Scud attacks and the success of coalition Arab forces in the war tended to calm the dispute, not intensify it. And Yassir Arafat, who supported Saddam, was discredited by the enormity of the victory. In fact, the Arab-Israeli conflict waned. In 1993, Israel and the Palestinian Liberation Organization signed the Oslo Accords and a real peace finally seemed close at hand. Turmoil and terror were waning. The dismantlement of Saddam's ambitions had a mollifying effect on the region, at least for a few years.

Bush always intended to return the al Sabah regime to power. He strongly believed it was up to the people of Kuwait, not an outside force, to determine their leaders. And it was clear that the Saudis would have resisted any attempt at forced democratization in Kuwait. The fact that the Kuwaiti people had absolutely no say in determining their future had little impact on Bush's decision. In retrospect, perhaps the largest omission by the Bush team was not seeking broader democratization in the Arab states. The fundamental issue of whether an Islamic state could be "modern" while retaining its culture and values had been deferred. A decade later, bin Laden would force the most profound reexamination of this question.

At that point, the forces of globalization that were drawing the world closer were still forming. The term then was "interdependence," implying economic integration. The erosion of all forms of boundaries between states and cultures was beginning to eliminate borders. Relevant journal articles and books in 1991 reflected this view. But the full power of globalization was not yet recognized. The world of 1991 had not yet been "McDonaldized." It would take another few years for the impact of globalization to be fully felt.

For these reasons, Bush saw no reason to change either basic policy or the national security structure. The Base Force was approved. The force would be a third smaller. That seemed enough of a reduction for the time being. Theater nuclear weapons were reduced. However, after the success of Desert Storm and the end of the Soviet Union, the Bush administration showed little interest in making further major change or imposing reform since none seemed necessary.

As it would turn out, one of the controversies of the war was Goldwater-Nichols and the power given to the chairman. Powell, having presided over one of the most spectacular one-sided military victories in history, was to be criticized for usurping too much power. Perhaps the American condition was such that too much of a good thing could not be tolerated by some.

After Desert Storm, the administration faced two further foreign policy crises. The first was growing chaos in post-Tito Yugoslavia. The second was famine and starvation in Somalia. As Secretary of State Baker described the first, the United States had "no dog in that hunt," referring to Yugoslavia and its partition.

Bush was also advised by two of the nation's best Yugoslav experts. Baker's replacement as secretary, Lawrence Eagleberger, had served as ambassador to Yugoslavia during his distinguished career in the Foreign Service. National Security Adviser Scowcroft had written his Ph.D. dissertation on Yugoslavia. Both advised caution. Both recommended against deploying U.S. forces or even taking sides among the parties.

Somalia was a humanitarian tragedy. Televised images of Somalis starving to death filled nightly news reports. The UN had embarked on a relief effort supported by modest American military transport and personnel assets. However, foodstuffs were not getting through. Local warlords stole food from warehouses and hijacked relief trucks. The suffering could be alleviated only with greater American support.

In December 1992, Bush ordered U.S. Marines and Navy Seals

to Somalia. Called Operation Provide Hope, the effort was designed
to ensure that food got to the people who needed it. The intent was
to exit Somalia by January 20 and not leave the brand new Clinton
administration with a foreign policy headache. But the crisis was due
less to a natural famine and more to the battle among warlords. The
United States would not be out by inauguration day.

It remains extraordinary that a president with an unprecedented
level of approval in 1991 could be defeated in 1992. Several factors
were at work. The economy was struggling. Bush and his pollsters
misread the political impact of the downturn. They believed that the
war would continue Bush's popularity through the election. Ross
Perot, a mercurial billionaire, abandoned the Republican Party to
run as an independent. Perot siphoned off votes that otherwise
would have gone to Bush.

Bush also did not take Bill Clinton very seriously. It is fair to
wonder on Bush's behalf how a "draft-dodging, dope-smoking liberal" could defeat a successful incumbent. One reason was that Clinton was a conservative Democrat, occupying precisely the political
spot toward which most of the country was leaning. Clinton also
knew that "it was the economy, stupid." The attacks on his character
and experience were simply not registering with the voters.

Bush had also been taking medication for an irregular heartbeat
caused by a thyroid condition called Graves' disease. At one point,
five separate drugs had been prescribed to arrest the condition. Bush
himself recognized a "slowing down of the mental process." He was
passive and often detached—in stark contrast to the way he normally
acted. The campaign reflected these characteristics and foundered.

Diagnosed with this condition in 1991, it is possible that the
medication had contributed to his reluctance to take on a broader
agenda then. Bush never considered himself a visionary. However,
after Desert Storm, U.S. power and influence, with the Soviet Union
disintegrating, were preeminent, perhaps as much as in 1945. Bush
was not able or did not choose to exploit these opportunities. That
these conditions would return as unfinished business was an unintended legacy. Because of the economy, Clinton's shrewdness in

exploiting it, and the Perot diversion, Bush lost. Clinton became president with a plurality of 43 percent of the votes.

## Sayonara Saddam

Suppose, however, that Saddam had been overthrown or replaced. How might that have affected future events in general and the ultimate disposition of Osama bin Laden? Clearly, how Saddam would have been deposed or replaced and the nature of the successor regime would determine the answer. Two possibilities provide the best routes for speculation.

The most positive probable outcome was a regime that put U.S.– Iraqi relations on a footing similar to that of the 1980s, when Iraq was neither friend nor foe. In this case, the regime would have remained autocratic but capable of governing. It also would have allowed UN inspectors greater access to verify that the programs for production of weapons of mass destruction had been stopped.

The most negative probable outcome would have been a partitioned Iraq. The parallels are the former Yugoslavia with its warring factions and indeed Afghanistan after the Soviets left and before the Taliban took over in 1996. The danger was instability. Rather than Iraq's posing a direct threat to its neighbors, the threat would be reversed. It would be Iraq's neighbors—particularly Iran and possibly Syria—that would prove dangerous should chunks of Iraq be carved up.

In both cases, the effects on the pieces of unfinished business are clear. In the first case, the effects would have been minor. The vulnerability of open societies to outside forces would have been unchanged. Other factors would have contributed to exacerbating the Arab-Israeli conflict, particularly after the optimism of the Oslo Accords in 1993 faded. Arab regimes would have remained autocratic. And the Soviet Union would still have collapsed.

The one exception was the strain long-term American presence would pose on Saudi Arabia. The huge differences in societies and cultures would produce great tensions. Osama bin Laden railed at this presence. To him it was destructive to Islam. But to balanced

observers, American presence would exacerbate some of the para-
doxes of Saudi society, tensions that the Saudis would have preferred
to keep less visible. General Horner, himself well versed in Saudi culture and Islam, had hoped that after the war, a large American presence in the kingdom could be avoided. Some of the consequences of
this larger presence are discussed in Chapter 7.

The pessimistic case would probably have contributed to turning
the pieces of unfinished business into more dangerous quantities
and probably more quickly. The Arab-Israeli situation would have
deteriorated faster. Arab regimes would have become more and not
less autocratic as a means of protecting their ruling leaders. And perhaps extremists would have found a home in Iraq much as bin
Laden did in Afghanistan. While parallels to the former Yugoslavia
are inexact, a partitioned and unstable Iraq, post-Saddam, would
present a very serious security challenge. Without the proximity or
equivalence of NATO states whose security was linked, bringing stability to an unstable Iraq would have proven exceedingly difficult.

The fact is that Saddam has not gone. He simply could not be
removed from office. That was a bridge too far for the Bush administration and the international community to travel. As a result, more
than a decade later, the sins and virtues of the father have been
thrust on the son. After the 1992 election, the legacies of the Bush
administration regarding Somalia and the former Yugoslavia would
plague Bill Clinton.

As these pieces of unfinished business metastasized, the consequences for turmoil and terror grew more profound. It was not that
the last decade of the twentieth century would be the most turmoil-
and terror-filled in history. Clearly, it was not. But, for the United
States, a dangerous agenda was getting worse, and there were competing temptations.

In the United States, the call for "engagement" and intimate U.S.
involvement abroad was countered by caution against overextension
and the case for less U.S. military presence. Idealism was in conflict
with pragmatism, traditional points of contention in American attitudes toward foreign policy since the republic took form. And
abroad, bin Laden and terrorists like him, long tempted to take the
attack to the United States, had means as well as motive.

# ★ 2 ★

## Deadly Legacies—Turmoil and Terror

### What a Start

On January 20th, 2001, George W. Bush was sworn in as the forty-third president of the United States. His domestic priorities were education and the economy. He promised a new brand of "compassionate conservatism" and vowed to change the "tone" of government in Washington. He would, however, have to deal with unexpected turmoil and terror that were neither clear nor present dangers when he took office.

His inauguration followed an extraordinary presidential election that took weeks to decide. Bush's opponent, Bill Clinton's vice-president, Al Gore, won about half a million more popular votes. The Constitution mandates that the Electoral College, not the popular vote, determine the president. The Founding Fathers were unwilling to cede to the public the right to elect the nation's chief political leader directly.

The election hinged on Florida. Bush appeared to have won the Florida popular vote and therefore the election. In the winner-take-all system, he was entitled to Florida's entire twenty-seven electoral votes, giving him the winning majority. In close elections, Florida law provides for a recount. The Gore team, citing voting irregularities and claiming fraud, went to court to ensure a recount. Bush mounted a strong legal defense to maintain his narrow victory. And, as the drama unfolded, it did so under the eyes of Florida's governor, Jeb Bush, younger brother of the candidate, and Florida's Republican Secretary of State, Katherine Harris, who was legally responsible for certifying the winner of the election.

The dispute made its way through the Florida state court system and was "fast-tracked" to the U.S. Supreme Court. An anxious nation watched the battle intently. In a five-to-four decision, the Supreme Court voted in favor of staying the recount. Bush was declared the winner and president. To Republican partisans, the court's decision vindicated the electoral system, the election, and the constitutional process. It also put an end to four more years of a "Clinton-like" regime. To Democratic partisans, the election was stolen. The Court's decision was taken not for good legal reasons but because the Court seated one more Republican than Democrat.

Despite the fiercely fought legal battle, once the election had been decided, the public readily accepted the results. The transfer of power was smooth. The nation's highest elective office requires only three credentials. The president has to be native born, must be thirty-five years of age or older, and must win a majority of votes in the Electoral College. No other requirements for experience and competence are required by the Constitution. And, once the Supreme Court resolved the Florida election dispute, Bush filled all three criteria. However, the electoral crisis and delay in determining the winner were warning shots about the potential fragilities of the political system.

The system survived. Americans went about their business. The crisis receded. There is the obvious question of whether one of the more contested election in American history will have any lasting impact. But there is another, less visible worry: whether anyone wishing America harm took careful note. We know that four commercial airliners were turned into deadly weapons of mass destruction. Are there vulnerabilities at the heart of the political process that someday might be turned against the nation? Continuity of government, that is, who succeeds if or when the president is disabled or dies, has taken on new significance. It is not just a matter of sending the vice-president to an "undisclosed secure location." Suppose a number of congressmen are disabled or elections disrupted and disqualified. Who succeeds to office and how does the legislature function short of a mandated quorum? And what about the continuity of the courts and judicial system? These questions were not relevant to the Founding Fathers. They are today.

Of the last five presidents, four had made their political marks as governors. Like the three other governors before him—Carter of Georgia, Reagan of California, and Clinton of Arkansas—Governor Bush took office with little national experience, particularly in foreign policy and defense. Only the senior Bush had serious credentials in these areas.

Bush had no apologies and acted as if he had won a broad popular mandate. However, the six-week delay in resolving the electoral dispute gave no favors to the Bush administration. The eleven weeks from Election Day to inauguration were short enough a transition period to put a team in place. Clearing nominees had become a time-consuming and politically explosive process. Cutting the transition time in half was ludicrous. If and when the structure of the national security system is revised, that is one lesson that cannot be ignored.

The national security team that Bush would assemble was highly accomplished and experienced. Bush was not. A graduate, like his father, of Andover and Yale, he received an M.B.A. from the Harvard Business School. He served briefly in the Air National Guard as a fighter pilot and went into the oil and then baseball businesses. He ran unsuccessfully for Congress in Texas and was twice elected its governor. To critics, given his lineage, Bush was anointed as the party's presidential candidate. He did not earn it. And, in the primaries, Senator John McCain gave him a scare after winning in New Hampshire.

McCain, the son and grandson of admirals, was a navy pilot shot down over North Vietnam in 1967. He displayed uncommon valor as a prisoner, his captivity made harsher because his father was the admiral in command of the Pacific forces fighting in Vietnam. Many Republicans and more independents believed the best man had not won the nomination. Bush's inexperience was a major concern. However, relatively unnoticed was the reality that the younger Bush did benefit from observing his father's twelve years in the White House.

The Bush team was, in many ways, a re-run of Bush I. Dick Cheney was, of course, vice-president. Colin Powell served as secretary of state. Condoleezza Rice became the national security adviser. Andrew Card was made Chief of Staff. And, at defense, Donald H. Rumsfeld was the choice. With the exception of Rumsfeld, each of the president's key national security advisers had served Bush's father. Rumsfeld was a pedigreed Republican. Thrice elected to the House of Representatives, he joined the Nixon White House as counselor to the president. Nixon later sent Rumsfeld to NATO as U.S. ambassador. Dick Cheney was a Rumsfeld protégé.

With Nixon's resignation over the Watergate scandal, Vice-President Gerald Ford became chief executive. Among his first decisions was to make Rumsfeld, a colleague and close friend in the House, chief of staff. In 1975, Rumsfeld moved over to become secretary of defense, replacing Nixon appointee James R. Schlesinger. In this shift, Cheney replaced Rumsfeld as chief of staff. When Ford lost to Jimmy Carter in 1976, Rumsfeld left government for the private sector.

Rumsfeld went into the pharmaceutical business, where he chaired G. D. Searle at the time it was bringing the artificial sweetener "Nutra Sweet" to the market. From Searle, he went on to head other firms in the technology and telecommunications fields. From 1983 to 1984, the Reagan administration recalled him to serve as special envoy to the Middle East. He contemplated a run for the presidency in 1988. During the Clinton administration, he chaired two national commissions—one on assessing the ballistic missile threat to the United States, the other on space. He will also have the distinction of serving as both the youngest and the oldest secretary of defense in history.

Fortunately, despite the truncated transition, for much of his first year in office, Bush faced no real crises. The unfinished business and legacies from earlier administrations had not reached the danger point. All of that was to change on September 11th. However, that day of infamy was not an isolated event perpetrated by chance.

## Legacies of Turmoil and Terror

As all wars leave unfinished business, good and bad legacies are left from one administration to its successors. In dealing with these legacies, there is normally a huge resistance to change. In part, this comes from the Constitution and the purposeful balance of power between the branches of government. To a large degree, with the exception of crises, ships of state rarely embark on swift and dramatic course changes. And, in the heat of campaigns, promises for change, whether Bush's "read my lips, no new taxes" or Clinton's condemnation of the "butchers of Beijing," are often lost in the actual practice of policy.

Part of the reason for this resistance to change is that many policies are enduring and simply do not require major change every four or eight years. Dealing with the Soviet Union or its Russian successor, China, NATO, and other foreign policy staples has been required since the end of World War II and the Cold War. And part of the reason is that while administrations come and go, the same turnover does not affect Congress and most of the rest of the federal government. Virtually 90 percent of incumbents in Congress are reelected. Civil service and other government employees are not normally dismissed with a change at the White House.

In campaigning, Carter promised he would never lie. Reagan promised a smaller government, a stronger defense, and lower taxes. Bush offered a "kinder, gentler" America and the pledge of no new taxes. Clinton fixated on the economy. All except Bush senior arguably had "vision," whether Carter's concept for peace in the Middle East or Reagan's Strategic Defense Initiative to render nuclear weapons "impotent and obsolete." Bush made light of the "vision thing," preferring to substitute pragmatism and judgment for governing. In practice, all of these presidents had to make significant policy changes from campaign platforms and promises.

Carter could rightly claim recognition of China and the Camp David Egyptian-Israeli peace accords as great achievements. His strong stand in Europe over nuclear weapons strengthened NATO. And, while he was criticized for his handling of defense, his administration created the Rapid Joint Deployment Task Force for a Persian Gulf scenario against the Soviet Union. The force was described by its first commander and later Marine Corps Commandant General P. X. Kelley as not rapid, joint, or deployable. However, it evolved into Central Command and showed its value in the Kuwaiti war. Paul Wolfowitz, then a relatively junior official at defense and today Bush's deputy secretary, was a key architect of the new strategy.

The defining year for the Carter administration was 1979. Early in the year, the Shah fell in Iran. The dreaded Ayatollah Khomeini returned from exile in France. Iranian "students" stormed the U.S. embassy in Tehran, taking fifty-two Americans hostage. The attempt to free the American hostages would end in tragedy and wreck Carter's tenure.

In the summer, Carter savored the diplomatic triumph of Camp David and the Middle East peace accords. Then, in December, the Soviets stormed into Afghanistan, catching Carter off guard and making the administration look duped. Carter would also be blamed for "gutting" the CIA's covert and clandestine services. His director of central intelligence was his Naval Academy classmate Admiral Stansfield Turner. Turner was ordered by Carter to "clean up" the CIA and its "rogue elephant" image after a series of hearings and investigations, principally the Senate panel headed by Idaho Senator Frank Church, uncovered serious CIA wrongdoings and misdeeds in 1975. The economy, with soaring inflation and interest rates, would make Carter's reelection impossible. But Desert One was the last nail in Carter's political coffin.

The raid to rescue the fifty-two Americans taken hostage when the U.S. embassy was seized in Tehran was launched on April 24th, 1980. It was called Desert One. Eight Navy RH-53 helicopters, flown by Marine crews from Navy ships in the Persian Gulf, and six C-130

Hercules transports, along with a complement of commandos, darted into Iran. Fierce sandstorms impeded the ingress. Three helos were knocked out of action by a combination of mechanical failure and weather. Six helicopters were needed to complete the mission. Faced with this report, Carter ordered the mission aborted, with the hostages still in Tehran.

The failure quickly disintegrated into a tragedy. During refueling for the return flight at a remote location inside Iran, one of the surviving helos accidentally struck a C-130 on the ground. Eight Americans died in the explosion and fire. The rescue attempt turned into a debacle. Along with Grenada and Beirut, Desert One made military reform inevitable. It also reinforced the image of a weak president and a military that could not shoot straight.

Reagan would lighten the mood of the country. Under his presidency, an unprecedented economic boom would begin. The Soviet Union would begin to dissolve. Yet the presidency was almost lost due to huge gaffes and errors of judgment in relatively distant regions in Latin America and the Middle East over seemingly minor matters.

Reagan's brushes with foreign policy disasters were outlined earlier. On balance, Reagan was Reagan. A great communicator, as president he was largely "hands off," with a management style charitably described by the Tower Commission as "aloof." Yet, despite the foreign policy crises and disasters that nearly crippled his tenure, Reagan's personality won out. And, as the Soviet Union unraveled, many assigned the credit to him and his constancy of purpose in ending the "evil empire." He also had eliminated the so-called intermediate range nuclear weapons in Europe in a sweeping arms control agreement with the Soviets (called the Intermediate Nuclear Forces or INF treaty) and embarked on further negotiations to discard all such weapons. At a summit in Reykjavik, Iceland, Reagan went so far as to propose to Gorbachev that both superpowers do away with all strategic nuclear weapons.

Bush had Desert Storm. During his watch, the Berlin Wall came down. Yet the economy was in trouble. Despite his huge popularity, Bush would not win reelection. And, to illustrate the potential fragility of any presidency in time of crisis, had Bush stumbled in Kuwait, he risked impeachment.

Clinton was the first of a new breed of old-time politicians. He understood where the public stood. Political polling was his life's blood. And Clinton reacted to it. The old poker adage of knowing precisely when to hold and when to fold aptly described the operating philosophy of this gifted politician.

A "New Democrat," he considered himself to be "conservative" on economic and foreign policy issues and "liberal" on social issues, particularly race and gender. He was also entirely pragmatic. He favored the Gulf War and, while originally opposed to the death penalty, accepted it as politically necessary because most Americans favored it. When he was a governor, he appalled his liberal supporters by permitting the execution of mentally retarded murderer Rickey Ray Rector, in 1992. The forthcoming election had everything to do with the decision.

He also had serious character flaws. His dalliance with a young White House intern was inexcusable. Nonetheless, the "comeback kid," as he was called in the press, survived the affair after impeachment by the House winning acquittal by the Senate. His gifts were so plentiful that if the Constitution allowed a third term, he probably would have won against G. W. Bush.

While each of these four presidencies was unique in style, substance, and personality, they had several characteristics in common. Administrations since Eisenhower's have been criticized for an absence of "long-range" planning. This really means that administrations were simply not good at either considering or forecasting the probable consequences of their policy actions and key decisions beyond the short term. Johnson and the Tonkin Gulf Resolution in 1964 is a tragic example of policy myopia. In addition, each of these administrations worked with a government organized for national security much as it had been in 1947 when the National Security Act was passed.

Of course, new agencies—from the supersecret National Security Agency (NSA), which does the nation's electronic eavesdropping, to the Drug Enforcement Agency, to help "win the war on drugs"—

have been created. However, fundamental questions pertaining to the divisions of authority and responsibility among and between the agencies and departments remain unresolved. With law enforcement becoming a more crucial national security imperative and extremists such as bin Laden becoming greater dangers, resolution of these questions is essential to keeping America safe.

Similarly, as we will see, Congress and the White House have chronically been incapable of apportioning responsibility and authority for national security in ways that make sense. A look at the budget process and charges of "pork" (if it is Congress's fault) or "waste, fraud, and abuse" (if it is the executive's problem) is instructive. The failure of the White House and Congress to reach agreement on an economic stimulus package in December 2001—something that could very much have affected the nation's security—is more rule than exception.

As global turmoil and terror increasingly affect the United States, new tools will be needed. Definition of authority and responsibility for taking action and making decisions has been, thus far, missing. And people, the most crucial ingredient to the success or failure of any endeavor, have paradoxically also become a neglected resource in this interaction between branches over ensuring that the nation is kept safe and secure.

## The Clinton Legacy of Unfinished Business

Clinton came into office with the war cry "it's the economy, stupid" and a "laser-like focus" on domestic politics. From Clinton's perspective, there was keen intellectual interest in and curiosity about foreign policy. But elections were not won over foreign policy, only lost. Carter's ill-fated Desert One was still a source of concern among Democrats.

As the Democratic convention settled into New York City in July 1992, Clinton was out jogging early one morning in Central Park. He literally ran into his friend and Yale Law School classmate Jerry Hultin. Hultin was at the convention and had first sponsored Clinton's introduction to key politicians in his home state of Ohio.

Hultin jokingly asked, "What are you going to do to save the world, Bill?" His intent was to provide to the candidate a list of good ideas he had put together on foreign policy. He recalls Clinton's lack of responsiveness. Hultin pictured the thought balloon over Clinton's head—it's the economy, stupid! Clinton's focus was at home. He would appoint Hultin Under Secretary of the Navy, but even from inside the administration, Hultin was unable to persuade the president to focus on big foreign policy ideas.

Clinton, as memorialized by his sometime political alter ego and Svengali Dick Morris, believed in political "triangulation." Stake out a position. See what the opposition does. Then usurp the strengths of both to triangulate a third position. All the while, marginalize political risks.

This philosophy, which would prove politically effective, conflicted with Clinton's intellect. Clinton had the brainpower to see and to understand complicated aspects of any political issue. He had the capacity to conceive of solutions that were bold or sweeping enough to work. Yet, in his disastrous attempt at reforming health care in 1993, when he appointed First Lady Hillary Clinton to lead the effort, he learned an important lesson. Bold, sweeping, and rational solutions, no matter how brilliant in theory, did not assure political success.

Foreign policy would be secondary to domestic politics and would be shaped in light of domestic considerations. Seeking the politically acceptable path, soon to be known as "politically correct," particularly in foreign policy, was a virtue in itself. Risk overseas was calculated in terms of domestic politics and priorities.

On paper, Clinton's national security team seemed strong. Vice-President Al Gore had more than two decades in Congress. In the Senate he was well versed on arms control and interactions with the Soviet Union. Warren Christopher was secretary of state. A lawyer, Christopher had served as deputy secretary of state under Carter. Dour and unassuming, Christopher was seen as intelligent and competent. When it came to strategy, he was no Kissinger or Brzezinski. However, he had few enemies and knew his way around Washington.

Clinton chose as his first secretary of defense Les Aspin. Aspin was chairman of the House Armed Services Committee. A true defense intellectual, Aspin had studied at Oxford (at his own expense) and earned a Ph.D. in political science from MIT. Representing Wisconsin for twenty years, Aspin had matured from an irritating defense critic to one of the few Democrats to support George Bush and the Kuwaiti war. He was rumpled and disheveled in appearance, and his management and organizational styles shared the same traits. Despite intellect and experience, Aspin would not survive in the job.

The national security adviser's position went to Anthony Lake. Lake began his professional life as a young Foreign Service officer in Vietnam. Identified as a "comer," he went to work for Kissinger in the Nixon White House. After the United States invaded Cambodia in 1970, Lake resigned in protest. He had served under Carter and turned to teaching.

For the CIA, Clinton selected R. James Woolsey. Woolsey, like Clinton, was a Rhodes scholar. A lawyer, he had served on the staff of the Senate Armed Services Committee. He was under secretary of the Navy for Carter. In the Reagan adminstration he was appointed an ambassador for arms control and negotiated successfully with the Soviets. A conservative Democrat, Woolsey had high grades for his intelligence, experience, and enthusiasm for public office.

What happened? A preview of how the Clinton administration would fare came with the press conference introducing Lake, Woolsey, and several other members of the national security team. Press Secretary Dee Dee Myers did not know Woolsey. She tried to identify him by calling out "Admiral Woolsey," the name on the press release. Woolsey was startled. As former Navy under secretary, he understood how serious the faux pas was; as a former Army captain, he was probably impressed with the promotion; as a future CIA director, he must have worried how the administration came by its information.

The first several years of the Clinton administration turned out to be a shambles. Health care reform stumbled. And, in the Department of Defense, the most efficient and probably best managed of the executive departments, all was not well either. Aspin came aboard with the intent of performing a "bottom-up" review of the department. His approach was to start with basic military missions and tasks and then build a complete force structure and budget program. Three impediments stood in his way.

First, in the campaign, Clinton promised to integrate homosexuals into the military. As president, it was his first directive. It was a disaster. The military strongly disagreed on many grounds, including privacy and culture. Congress was even more strongly opposed to the policy. And Aspin, anxious to protect his president, was caught in the crossfire. From his first moments in office, Aspin's days were numbered because of this issue and his handling of it.

Second, Aspin moved aggressively to man his department with "the best and the brightest" from the policy world. In essence, he was creating a mini–State Department inside the Pentagon. This might not have bothered Secretary of State Warren Christopher, but it certainly made no friends in Foggy Bottom or the White House, where people thought Aspin was exceeding his authority.

Last, Colin Powell was still chairman of the Joint Chiefs. His term would not end until September 30th. No chairman has had greater prestige or clout. And Powell was unwilling to see his forces and "his army" subjected to a review by an administration that was openly hostile to the military and a secretary of defense who had long been his adversary on Capitol Hill. A friendly truce prevailed. Powell was loyal and carried out Aspin's directives. But after the homosexual fiasco, which was finally resolved by the "don't ask, don't tell" policy, the administration did not wish further dissension from the Pentagon. Hence, unsurprisingly, Powell's Base Force became the foundation for Aspin's "bottom-up force."

During the summer of 1993, Aspin convened several private dinners in the Pentagon with outsiders to critique his review. Just after 6:00 P.M. on July 26th, I arrived at the River Entrance for one of these dinners. Lacking a building pass, I told the guard I was to see the secretary of defense. He skeptically pointed me to a phone. There was no answer from Aspin's office. He had adjourned to his large private dining room.

On the way in, I had noticed Powell's limousine parked outside. I dialed his office, which was scarcely fifty feet away. Before I could explain my dilemma to his secretary, Nancy Hughes, the chairman was on the line. "I'll be right out," he said. The gate guard was startled when the large figure of the chairman (or chairperson, as he called himself) materialized. "He's OK. Let him in." Powell asked about my destination. I told him. He replied, "Let me know what happens."

The briefing was unexceptional. Powell's not-so-invisible hand was unmistakably present. Aspin had decided on a "capabilities"-based strategy very similar to the Base Force. Two major regional contingencies—wars to the layman—formed the basis for the force structure. The wars likely to be fought were defending Korea and the Persian Gulf. And planning had to include the possibility that both wars might be fought more or less simultaneously. The size of the force was slightly reduced from the Base Force 1.6 million to an active duty force of about 1.45 million. Otherwise, there was little difference from the plans of the Bush administration.

My biggest contribution was locking myself in the secretary's private bathroom and making enough noise to attract attention and get freed. A letter sent the next day to Aspin listed follow-on ideas. None were taken. And, as I compare that letter with one written to the current secretary, the themes remain remarkably unchanged—the need for innovation, dramatic steps to alleviate the gross inefficiencies of the process, and above all a strategy for using the forces in action.

Aspin would soon resign. His stand on the homosexual issue had put him in dangerous political waters. Aspin was not a good manager. His forte was as a legislator. His brilliance was better suited to other endeavors. Sadly, Aspin died in 1995, a relatively young fifty-six. Woolsey would leave after less than two years. Lake resigned after the first term, as did Christopher.

In the summer of 1993, the Clinton administration had changed the mission of U.S. forces in Somalia from humanitarian feeding and resupply to nation building. Part of nation building required pacifying local warlords peaceably or, if necessary, with force. Mohammed

Farah Aideed was one warlord who seemed to understand only force.

After forces under his control attacked and killed twenty-four Pakistani soldiers assigned to the United Nations, Admiral Jonathan Howe, Bush's former deputy national security adviser, had been asked by the Clinton team to become the UN High Representative to Somalia. After the Pakistanis were killed, Howe issued a $25,000 reward for Aideed's apprehension. Finally, U.S. forces were assigned the job. Based on local intelligence reports, on October 3, 1993, the Army's Delta forces, supported by U.S. Rangers to secure the operating area, were sent in to seize Aideed and his key lieutenants. It was a trap. The information was bait.

An intense firefight erupted. Eighteen American soldiers were killed and seventy-seven others wounded. The body of one dead American was dragged by a mob through the streets of Mogadishu, Somalia's capital. Virtually every television station in the world broadcast videos of the spectacle. In 2002, a movie based on the book *Black Hawk Down* was released and was highly popular. The film was a graphic presentation of the violence and carnage of the daylong battle between the U.S. Army and Somali irregular forces.

That the vastly outnumbered U.S. soldiers acquitted themselves well in the fight, killing hundreds of the attackers, made no difference. America had been humiliated by the incident. Reinforcements were dispatched to Somalia but Clinton set a withdrawal date of March 31, 1994, for all U.S. forces. As with the Beirut bombing in 1983, the administration looked weak, inept, and beaten.

The pattern of a seeming lack of foresight was to continue. In January 1994, Clinton went to a meeting of NATO heads of state in Brussels. There, he proclaimed the Partnership for Peace or PFP program. The PFP was designed as a halfway house for aspiring NATO members. With the dissolution of the Warsaw Pact and the democratization of Eastern Europe, many of the former Soviet satellites were clamoring for membership in NATO. PFP was the stepping-stone.

But the stumbling block was clear. As Poland, Hungary, the Czech Republic, and the Baltic States lined up to join the alliance, what was to happen to Russia? NATO moving east would be of little comfort to Moscow. If not handled with care, Russia could react negatively and even precipitously. Unfortunately, the administration assumed that problem away. The close personal relationship between Clinton and Russian president Boris Yeltsin would, it was hoped, permit a smooth settlement of the differences.

Three states have so far moved from the PFP into NATO. In two regards it has proven successful. NATO has expanded. And the military-to-military contacts between the alliance and the PFP members have helped the former East European states in their transition to full democracy. But the Clinton administration failed to resolve the dilemma over Russia and NATO. Clinton's preference to move only so far and to defer tough choices was clear. It is now the responsibility of the Bush administration to deal with Russia and NATO expansion.

The administration was badly chastened by Somalia. That did not mean the policy of engagement would be abandoned; it would merely be refined to minimize the risks. In 1994, Haiti loomed large. Haitian refugees were streaming into Florida to escape violence on the island. Haiti, of course, was close to American shores. The crisis presented a two-fold problem: coping with the coup that was causing the humanitarian disaster and stemming the tide of illegal Haitian refugees landing in Florida. Ultimately, domestic politics forced action. The United States intervened militarily.

A negotiating team comprised of former President Jimmy Carter, General Colin Powell (who retired in 1993), and Senator Sam Nunn was dispatched by the administration to secure a peaceful transfer of power and an end to the violence. The team negotiated with General Raoul Cedras, who led the military junta. The aim was to restore Jean-Bertrand Aristide and the legitimate government to power. The official version reveals that just prior to the landing of American forces, a peaceful settlement was reached. Cedras stepped down with the intervention of Emile Joanssaint, Haiti's president. The unofficial story is more exciting.

Carter, Powell, and Nunn, in this version, knew only in general terms when H-Hour—that is, the time U.S. forces were to land—

was scheduled. As the talks dragged on, Major General Jerry Bates, the delegation's escort officer representing the Joint Chiefs of Staff, grew more agitated. Finally Powell sensed the problem. Clinton had also warned him that Carter might be prone to delaying the negotiations to obtain a settlement. Observers posted outside the XVIII Airborne Headquarters in North Carolina on troop movements updated the Haitians. A Haitian officer burst into the meeting with the news that "the 82nd Airborne had just taken off." At the last minute and only with the strongest persuasive language from the U.S. side was the settlement was reached. But, had this not happened, three very important Americans could have become hostages.

Clinton also had Yugoslavia on his hands. There was a series of mini-crises as Serbs, Bosnians, Croats, and Muslims engaged in mutual genocide. Debate swirled in NATO and Washington over what to do. Europeans, mindful of Sarajevo in 1914, were afraid of instability spilling over the borders of the former Yugoslavia. Generally, these states favored intervention, but they were reluctant to intervene without the United States. Operational if not symbolic reasons mandated participation of U.S. forces.

The United States was divided. Strong humanitarian reasons called for intervention. Yet which parties were the aggressors and which were the victims was not clear. Every ethnic group fell into both categories. Clinton was reluctant to become engaged by risking American troops on the ground. In part, his own lack of military experience and the anti-military image of the White House contributed to inaction. However, no simple or easy solutions presented themselves. Yugoslavia was a political mess.

By 1995, the crisis was boiling over. "Ethnic cleansing," the unfortunate euphemism for the obscene killing, was spreading. The Balkans were the powder keg for World War I. NATO was intermittently bombing the warring factions in an attempt to disengage them. Peacekeeping forces were required. If NATO were to engage, U.S. forces would have to accompany them.

The administration agonized and then agreed to deploy a small peacekeeping force. Secretary of Defense William J. Perry, Aspin's successor, and chairman of the Joint Chiefs Army General John M.

Shalikashvili, Powell's replacement, testified to Congress on the mission. Both assured Congress that the task could be completed in a year. That was to prove impossible. U.S. peacekeepers remain in the former Yugoslavia. There is no probable date for withdrawal.

In 1996, crisis threatened the Taiwan Straits. China, attempting to intimidate Taiwan on the eve of its first democratic elections, embarked on a series of military maneuvers including missile firings. The rhetoric grew hot. The United States responded to China's military maneuvers by sailing two aircraft carrier battle groups into the South China Sea. The battle groups remained hundreds of miles away from the Taiwan Straits but close enough to be able to close in a crisis.

The elections were held; the maneuvers by the Chinese ended. The Clinton administration declared a victory and spun the presence of the carriers as a key consideration in convincing the Chinese not to escalate the crisis further. However, to the Chinese, in many ways, the show of force was a show of weakness. A more convincing and less visible signal, such as sending a nuclear submarine to the Taiwan Straits, would surely have made a more powerful impression.

There were, of course, other foreign policy challenges. In Rwanda and Zaire, the United States intervened with belated attempts to end the genocide and provide aid in the humanitarian disasters unfolding. The former Yugoslavia continued to boil. And enforcement of the no-fly zones over Iraq kept U.S. and British warplanes busy.

Clinton clearly recognized that foreign policy could not get a president elected. But it certainly could help lose an election. He also understood that new forms of danger such as the juncture of the proliferation of mass-destruction weapons and the ability of terrorists to seize and use these frightful instruments had to be addressed. All of these worries were carefully and competently documented in public statements and documents including the presidentially issued annual National Security Strategy document.

Terrorism was becoming a staple of the administration's daily agenda. On February 26, 1993, five weeks after Clinton took office, Ramzi Yousef, a bin Laden disciple, bombed the World Trade Center. The bomb fizzled. Five were killed. In November 1995, a powerful explosion destroyed a U.S.–leased building in Riyadh. Six more Americans died. Then, on June 25, 1996, nineteen U.S. military personnel were killed when a truck bomb leveled the Khobar Towers dormitory at the King Abdul Aziz Air Base in Saudi Arabia. At about the same time, the Aum Shinrikyo cult used Sarin gas to kill twelve passengers in a Tokyo subway.

The accumulation of these events was to fixate the administration on terrorism and, later, the stunning threats posed to the nation's "critical infrastructure." A national commission was convened and issued its report in 1997. The report was a catalogue of vulnerabilities and weaknesses that exposed the nation to grave danger.

The administration understood that action was imperative. However, typically, that action was bureaucratic, not operational. There was a firestorm of activity to rewrite wiring diagrams and form new committees and intergovernmental steering groups. The National Security Council was reorganized to reflect the rising priorities of countering terrorism, halting proliferation of weapons of mass destruction, and protecting critical infrastructure. The great success in preparing for the much reported and worrisome "Y2K bug," when computers not programmed to read the year 2000 would presumably fail with great consequence, should have paved the way for real action. It did not. Government leaders did not change budgets, reprogram dollars, or realign priorities. Homeland security had become an important declaratory program, but it was only rhetoric without the resources to turn it into a viable program.

To no one's surprise, the House of Representatives had gone Republican in 1994. That the Senate came under Republican control was unexpected. In many ways, this reversal was due to public backlash against the Clinton administration and a referendum on its performance. Clinton learned the lesson. Triangulation was widely employed. Clinton was reelected in 1996, easily defeating Senator Majority Leader Robert Dole. However for Clinton, the second term and 1998 and 1999 in particular, would be the most testing years of his presidency.

In the summer of 1998, U.S. embassies in two African states were bombed. Over two hundred people, mostly Africans, were killed. Twelve were Americans. The perpetrator was identified as Osama bin Laden. Bin Laden, known to the intelligence community, was beginning to come into the public view.

The administration chose to regard these attacks against the embassies as serious crimes and not reasons for declaring war. This decision had several advantages. Law enforcement seemed the appropriate instrument rather than the possibly massive use of military power to catch or punish the murderers. As a criminal, bin Laden would have less propaganda leverage than if he were accorded a more visible status. And the administration would spend fewer valuable foreign policy "chips" using law enforcement to bring the perpetrators to justice. Military action would require foreign support, if only for bases, and would raise the risk of casualties, both American and civilian.

Still, the attacks could not go unpunished. The political symbolism of a failure to retaliate would suggest weakness and indifference under attack. More and not less violence could arise. Something had to be done. The question was what and how much.

There had been a perpetual quandary in the Clinton adminstration over using force. The military rightfully asked the purposes of such use of force and then the "what ifs," should problems arise as in Desert One and Somalia. Colin Powell was the most forceful and credible of the Joint Chiefs of Staff. But his successors, first John Shalikashvili and then Henry H. Shelton, shared these views.

In 1997, "Shali" as he was affectionately known, retired. The first non–U.S. born chairman (Georgia, USSR, was his birthplace), Shalikashvili, the press releases noted, had learned his English from watching John Wayne movies. Perry had stepped down as secretary. William S. Cohen, a former Republican senator from Maine, replaced him. Cohen's choice for a new chairman was Air Force General Joseph Ralston, serving as the vice-chairman.

Political correctness and the political backlash against allegations of the president's womanizing conspired to derail Ralston's appointment. At the time, an Air Force lieutenant, Kelly Flinn, had been charged with sleeping with an enlisted man. She refused to accept nonjudicial punishment, and it appeared that the Air Force would court-martial her for adultery. The enlisted man was married. The secretary of the Air Force was a woman. The story filled the press. Then it was revealed that a dozen years before, Ralston had had a relationship with a female classmate at the National War College. That Ralston was separated from his wife carried no weight. Having a double standard in which lieutenants were court-martialed and generals were promoted was unacceptable to most administrations, especially those as politically vulnerable as Clinton's. Ralston removed himself from consideration. He stayed on as vice-chairman and went on to be assigned Supreme Allied Commander in Europe in 2000. That the administration did not stand up for him in the controversy was a disgrace.

A new chairman had to be found immediately. Neither brains nor brawn counted. Sadly, there was only one question: Is there anything in your past that could prove embarrassing? Many senior officers were offended or frightened by the question. More were unwilling to go through the confirmation process. Army General Henry H. Shelton was not.

A Special Forces soldier with several Vietnam tours, Shelton was serving as Special Forces commander in chief. He had led XVIII Corps into Haiti and had a fine reputation as a fighting man. He had also been a one-woman man since high school, marrying his childhood sweetheart. Shelton got the job. Given the rise of turmoil and terror, he seemed ideal.

In responding to the embassy bombings, the administration had many military options. Cruise missiles could strike with no risk to U.S. personnel. Special Forces could be inserted to seize or kill the guilty. Larger formations could be used to destroy the terrorists and their facilities.

Better than anyone, Shelton knew the risks and dangers associated with Special Forces. He feared that sending small numbers of elite forces such as the Army's Delta Force and the Navy's Seal Team Six deep into places like Afghanistan was a potential Desert One. He also worried that these forces could "go Hollywood," the pejorative

Army phrase for excessive and foolish risk tasking. A larger force would be difficult to deploy and retract. Hence, Shelton counseled restraint.

Burned in Somalia, the administration was terrified by the risk of casualties, both American and civilian. Shelton's caution was taken seriously. No one in the White House wanted to read in the *Post* or the *Times* that the military dissented from the administration. And the White House was incapable of imposing the discipline to prevent such leaks. The choice quickly boiled down to the antiseptic use of several dozens of Tomahawk cruise missiles.

Bin Laden's terrorist camps in Afghanistan were targeted and hit. A pharmaceutical plant in Sudan was also destroyed. The plant was alleged to be producing chemical weapons. It was not. Clinton issued an intelligence "finding"—that is, an executive order—to authorize covert CIA operations to hunt down and, if necessary, dispatch bin Laden. The administration had fashioned many of the weapons needed to eliminate bin Laden. It refused, however, to remove them from their holsters and pull the triggers.

As the administration grew more distracted by the Monica Lewinsky scandal, by late fall 1998 events in Iraq and Yugoslavia were becoming critical. Saddam had finally evicted the inspectors of the United Nations Special Commission team sent in after Desert Storm to verify the destruction of Iraq's weapons of mass destruction. In Serbia, Kosovo was becoming a potential holocaust. The administration was demanding that Serbian president Slobodan Milosevic withdraw his forces, in essence granting Kosovo quasi-independence.

To deal with Iraq, Operation Desert Fox was launched in December. U.S. and British warplanes carried out four days of strikes against military targets in retaliation and punishment for Iraq's ejection of the weapons inspectors. The extent of damage was never disclosed. Many observers saw this attack as a slap on the wrist. Allied aircraft continued to patrol the same no-fly zones and occasionally fired back after Iraqi provocation.

From the perspective of a television commentator, my reaction to Desert Fox was slightly different. Appearing on Rupert Murdoch's

Fox Broadcasting Network, I was asked what struck me most about the raid. I answered, "How did Murdoch have enough clout to have it named after his channel?"

Yugoslavia was more serious. Milosevic was using the terrible tool of ethnic cleansing on the Muslim Kosovars much as had been done to Serbs living in Kosovo. A bloodbath seemed inevitable. However, Kosovo was part of Serbia, itself a sovereign state. Therefore, a voluntary withdrawal from Kosovo by Milosevic was impossible to arrange. The sequence of events is interesting.

On December 19, 1998, the U.S. House of Representatives voted to impeach the president. On February 6th, 1999, the United States convened various Albanian Kosovars and Serbian representatives at the great chateau at Rambouillet outside Paris. On February 12th, the Senate acquitted Clinton. On March 18th, Albania signed the Rambouillet agreement. With NATO's deadline of late March for Serbian action fast approaching, the Clinton administration was finally free from the shackles of *la affaire Monica*.

On March 23, 1999, NATO launched Operation Allied Force, an air campaign designed to coerce Milosevic to leave Kosovo. There were many problems with the campaign. There was no strategic construct. The commander, Army General Wesley K. Clark, had been given little guidance. As Clark noted in his book *Waging Modern War*, at no time had the president, secretary of defense, JCS chairman, and the operational commander met together to discuss and plan strategy. Indeed, the only real guidance Clark received was after his remarks at a press conference in Brussels about Serbia's reinforcing its forces in Kosovo were misinterpreted. Clark's comments were taken by the administration as a rebuke of what the White House was saying. The order from Cohen relayed through Shelton was to keep his "fucking face" off television (no one recalled Mike Dugan's fate in 1990).

Clark would prove an irritant to the administration and his military colleagues in Washington. Intensely competent, Clark had graduated first in his class at West Point in 1966. Coincidentally, he was a Rhodes scholar with a fellow Arkansan, Bill Clinton, although they knew each other only casually. To his admirers, of whom there were many, Clark was the bravest of the brave and the man to lead in combat. To his detractors, of whom there were also many, his ambition and ego were overbearing and he was accused of treating subordinates badly. In reality, Clark was a brilliant officer who was battle wise and politically experienced. However, he did not tolerate fools or silly ideas, even when they came from the White House. The tension between Clark and Cohen and Shelton was palpable.

For seventy-eight days the bombing continued. Kosovo turned into a humanitarian nightmare. Tens of thousands of Muslim Kosovars were probably killed by Serbian army and police forces. Upward of a million fled as refugees. It was a cold, punishing winter. Clark insisted on the need for planning for ground forces, an option Clinton had publicly eschewed when he announced the commencement of Allied Force.

The administration believed (or perhaps just hoped) that Milosevic would yield quickly when the first bombs were dropped. As a result, contingency planning for ground operations was not considered by the White House. A ground war was thought unnecessary as well as too risky. But Milosevic did not relent. For eleven weeks, during which a subdued summit was held in Washington to mark NATO's fiftieth birthday, NATO attacked from the air. During those air raids, a B-2 bomber, the most expensive and modern in the inventory, dropped a precision weapon on the Chinese Embassy in Belgrade. The bomb exploded in a section of the embassy housing the intelligence offices.

China's leadership was infuriated and Chinese took to the streets to surround and pelt the U.S. embassy in Beijing with bottles and bricks. There was considerable doubt over whether the attack was accidental or a premeditated signal. Most Chinese still believe the attack was premeditated. It did not help that China opposed the bombing campaign against Serbia in the first place. America apologized for the accident. U.S.–Chinese relations were at a low point.

At the same time, the Atlantic alliance had never been closer to coming apart, even in the darkest days of the Cold War and in the face of Soviet threats. As bombs reined down on Serbia and Milosevic remained defiant, pessimism over the operation clouded NATO.

Fortunately, the threat of ground troops and, perhaps more importantly, not so subtle Russian diplomacy finally convinced Milosevic to fold. The crisis ended. It was, as a Washington pundit put it, "a win but an ugly one."

Milosevic was the biggest loser, although he would stay in power for nearly two years. Clark, whose strength of character and persistence helped carry the day, was never forgiven for his tough stands and his insistence on being given the tools necessary to achieve success. He retired early. Ironically, Joe Ralston, an earlier victim of Washington politics, replaced him in April 2000.

Unlike Saddam, Milosevic was booted out of office, not by force but by ballot box. Ultimately, Milosevic was turned over to The Hague for trial as an international war criminal. Still, peacekeepers remain in Yugoslavia.

Perhaps the most serious piece of unfinished business bequeathed by Clinton pertained to the Arab-Israeli-Palestinian conflict. Chapter 8 goes into this into greater depth. However, at the end of his administration, Clinton made a last-ditch attempt to resolve the intractable. In July 2000, he brought Ehud Barak, Israeli's prime minister and most decorated soldier, and Yassir Arafat to Camp David to broker a peace. Both sides seemed to be within inches of a just and fair settlement. The inches turned out to be miles. Pro-Israeli forces accused Arafat of walking away from the perfect deal engineered by Clinton and Barak. Pro-Palestinian groups blamed Barak for believing that Arafat had the authority to accept a negotiated settlement that did not fulfill all of the Palestinian aims. Still others accused Clinton of forcing an impossible situation to bolster his reputation.

Regardless, when Ariel Sharon, who replaced Barak after the failed vote of confidence, visited Jerusalem's Temple Mount, the Palestinians predictably rioted, spiraling the crisis to a more desperate state.

The truth is more complex. The sadness is that the next administration would have to pick up the pieces. As the intifada that began on July 29, 2000, rages and Israelis and Palestinians continue to kill each other, the situation has no obvious solution.

The last major overseas crisis Clinton faced was the bombing of the Arleigh Burke–class destroyer USS *Cole* in Yemen in October 2000. The stopover was less for fuel and more in support of the policy of engagement. The presence of U.S. warships and a sprinkling of dollars to pay for fuel and other staples were viewed as helpful in improving relations. Tragically, al Qaeda and bin Laden saw the opportunity differently.

In Aden harbor, a single person steered a small boat alongside the port side of the billion-dollar warship. The crew believed the boat was carrying stores. The bomb was detonated. Had the boat come alongside a few yards closer to the bow and the ship's magazine, *Cole* might have sunk. As it was, she was nearly ripped in two. Seventeen sailors died.

Anyone who has spent time at sea realizes how vulnerable any warship is in confined waters. A single patrol during the Vietnam War showed how easily and suddenly ambushes could be sprung. One night in late 1966, my Swift Boat—a Vietnam equivalent of the World War II PT boat—was patrolling close to the shore near Chu Lai, a small city in the southern part of South Vietnam's northernmost province. In support of a sweep by the 7th Marines ashore, we were the "blocking" force to cut off Viet Cong and North Vietnamese regulars from escaping by sea.

The sound and smell of a rocket-propelled grenade enveloped the boat followed, an instant later, by an explosion close aboard. In the machine gun turret above the pilothouse, my gunner's mate was momentarily stunned. The boat was obviously darkened so as not to give away its position (that worked well!). But the gunner's eyes were so dilated they turned into two white beacons. The grenade had flown through the pilothouse. Fortunately, both doors were open and no one was hit. Close to the shoreline, we were sitting ducks, even at night. So too is a ship in a harbor's restricted waters, whether moored to a pier or a buoy.

The Clinton administration responded to the *Cole* bombing with the now-standard package of cruise missile strikes. To most observers, this was minimal retaliation. And, outside the Navy and the Department of Defense, the tragedy was soon overtaken by the Flor-

ida electoral debacle, which would take six weeks to resolve before
Bush could be declared president.

In retrospect, while the Clinton administration had been chas-
tised by conservative critics for "engagement" in arguably nonvital
or relatively unimportant strategic areas such as Yugoslavia, Haiti,
Somalia, and southern Africa, that charge is unfair. Democrats since
the days of Wilson and later Kennedy have been taken to task for
excessive idealism. Walking away from Europe in 1918 was a blun-
der. Leaving Vietnam in 1961 might not have been were there the
chance. Today, the old debate between isolationist and interventionist is miscast as unilateral versus multilateral.

Regarding Somalia, Haiti, and Rwanda, the administration had
little choice. Television images of starving black faces and mutilated
black bodies provoked a justifiable backlash in the United States. For
Clinton, the combination of mitigating these human tragedies and
violations of basic rights and the issue of race demanded U.S. action.
So too in Yugoslavia. Genocide was something about which the
United States had a moral responsibility dating back at least to
World War II and Hitler's atrocities. And Clinton's constituents
demanded action. Thus, domestic politics joined foreign policy. But
the flaw was the failure to anticipate broader consequences and, in
essence, to think ahead.

In Haiti and Somalia, the United States intervened on the
ground with military force. The longer-term consequences were
largely ignored. Haiti remains in desperate straits. An attempted
coup in December 2001, another sign of instability, was thwarted.
Somalia remains a disaster area and a training ground for would-be
bin Ladens.

The dilemma regarding NATO and Russia is no closer to solution, although there appears to be an effort to bring Russia into
closer contact through a new consultation process. Despite all of the
rhetoric about protecting critical infrastructure and preventing terrorism, little practical progress was made.

In the Middle East, the Arab-Israeli-Palestinian conflict grows
bleaker and bloodier. The Arab world, particularly after September
11th and events in Israel, is in turmoil. No strategic framework with

Russia and China was put in place. And, after India's resumption of nuclear testing in 1999 and Pakistan's decision to explode its own bomb, South Asia has moved to a new and more dangerous level of rivalry.

Clinton and his advisers will argue that they did their best. And perhaps they are right. However, the forty-third president would have a different view. And he would also have less leeway in deferring or dismissing many of these pieces of unfinished business.

## Bush 43

Bush is unlike his predecessors, even his father. For one thing, the themes and promises of his campaign, from cutting taxes and improving education to embarking on national missile defense, are shaping his policies and actions as president. He appears unwilling to walk away from them. National security and defense are good examples. Well before he was nominated, Bush presented his blueprint for national security. In a speech delivered at the Citadel in South Carolina on September 23rd, 1999, Bush laid out his plans for his future administration. The speech was remarkably prescient.

Bush delivered a tough message. He observed that "for America, this is a time of unrivaled military power, economic promise and, cultural influence." Citing Franklin Roosevelt, a president whose style Bush would emulate in many ways, he recited the phrase "the peace of overwhelming victory." To use that power and influence, Bush saw the challenge to America "not as obvious, but just as noble" as defeating the evil empire. He identified the dangers of the "contagious spread of missile technology and weapons of mass destruction" along with cyber terrorists, car bombers, and unbalanced dictators.

Regarding other major powers, Bush spoke about "tough realism" in dealing with China and Russia and "firmness" in coping with regimes such as North Korea and Iraq that "hate our values and resent our success." Allies were singularly absent in the address. There was no specific mention of NATO, Japan, or any of America's longstanding friends.

The speech set out Bush's plans for the military. He talked about the all-volunteer force and called for "better pay, better treatment, and better training." Then he described his goals. He first called for an "immediate review of overseas deployments" with the aim of replacing "diffuse commitments with focused ones." His second goal was to "build America's defenses on the troubled frontiers of technology and terror." "Homeland defense," he said "has become an urgent duty."

Returning to the twin dangers of missile technology and the threat of biological, chemical, and nuclear terrorism, Bush issued a clear warning. "Every group or nation must know, if they sponsor such attacks, our response will be devastating." A strong response was not enough. Bush told his audience that the nation must do more to defend itself.

"At the earliest possible date," his administration would "deploy anti-ballistic missile systems, both theater and national, to guard against attack and blackmail. This would require amending or abrogating the 1972 Anti-Ballistic Missile (ABM) Treaty with the Soviet Union, "an artifact of the Cold War." All of this would be included under a strategic review undertaken by the secretary of defense if Bush were elected.

His third goal was to exploit "the revolution in the technology of war." That meant transforming the military's organization for Cold War threats so it could meet "the challenges of a new century" by changing structure while keeping the "same culture." Bush called for forces that were "agile, lethal, readily deployable" and with a "minimum of logistical support." And he specifically noted that "the best defense can be a strong and swift offense—including the use of Special Operations Forces and long-range strike capabilities"—a precursor of exactly how the war of Afghanistan would be fought in 2001 and beyond. However, no specific details were offered on tradeoffs and changes to alter spending priorities among the four military services—the Army, Navy, Air Force, and Marine Corps.

Unlike many political speeches, this one outlined the blueprint for what would actually follow. To a striking degree, Bush's policies have remained consistent with the plans outlined in the Citadel speech. And, as we will see, that speech, because of its implied unilateralism and even arrogance, became the grounds for substantial and continuing criticism both at home and abroad about U.S. policies.

During the campaign, national security played the smallest of roles. Candidate Bush was very critical of the Clinton administration's pursuit of the policy of engagement. Engagement, according to Bush, excessively committed U.S forces to peacekeeping and nation-building roles for which they were unsuited. As reports of failing military readiness surfaced, vice-presidential candidate Cheney boldly promised that "help was on the way."

The economy's health was questionable at best. Signs of a recession were growing stronger. The candidate therefore made his tax-cut program one of the centerpieces of his campaign. However, neither Bush nor Gore was prepared to risk "talking down" the economy and later be accused of provoking a downturn. The economy, which clearly was stumbling, was one of the immediate legacies from his predecessor. In a twist of fate, Bush the elder left Clinton an economy about to take off. Clinton did not return the favor. And there were other legacies.

## Rough Takeoff

As Clinton was bequeathed Somalia and Yugoslavia, Bush would have to deal with the unfinished business left over from the Clinton years. Fortunately, despite a number of early stumbles, there was no immediate crisis for the administration. Bush's Citadel speech remained the blueprint. Firmness was the hallmark of the U.S. attitude even though Bush had promised that the United States would act with great "humility."

The visit of South Korea's president, Kim Dae Jung, in February 2001 was mishandled. Secretary of State Powell believed that negotiations with the north, started by Kim and affirmed by Clinton, were the most sensible way to proceed. The White House objected. Kim was disappointed by the rejection and Powell told the press that perhaps he had "leaned a little too far forward" in his skis.

In April, a U.S. Navy EP-3 electronic warfare plane was struck

by a Chinese F-8 fighter well within international waters and forced
to crash land on Hainan Island. The plane and crew were interned
and a major crisis seemed imminent. China was still furious about
the U.S. bombing of its embassy in Belgrade during the Yugoslavian
campaign in 1999 and concerned about the Bush administration's
tilting toward Taiwan. The press reported serious discord between
the Pentagon and the State Department on how to handle and
defuse the incident.

It was good fortune that three very experienced military officers
were in important positions. Powell was secretary. The commander
of U.S. Forces Pacific was Admiral Dennis C. Blair, a seasoned and
brainy operator with extensive time in key Washington jobs as well
as a former Rhodes scholar. The American ambassador, Joseph
Prueher, was a retired admiral and Blair's predecessor. Prueher was
a distinguished naval aviator with many missions over Vietnam
under his belt. The Chinese had great respect for him and his ability.

The trio was able to negotiate a release of the crew. The incident
was played down and handled with deftness and skill. U.S.–Chinese
relations did not suffer. However, as reported in the press at the
time, unidentified senior officials in the White House and Defense
Department were not entirely pleased. Apparently, there had been
insufficient "firmness" in dealing with China.

Then came a series of seemingly unilateral actions by the United
States. The administration abandoned the Kyoto Protocol for environmental protection. The Senate had unanimously rejected the
treaty. However, the administration created the impression that it
opposed environmental issues. The United States also opposed the
International Criminal Tribunal and the Biological Warfare Convention. But most significantly, it indicated that the ABM Treaty, a strategic scantling of the Cold War, was an impediment to national
defense.

The fixation on national missile defense, soon to be renamed
missile defense, and abrogating the ABM Treaty created a firestorm
of concern in Europe, Russia, and China. Anti-American attitudes in
Europe increased as the Bush administration stood accused of unilateralism and abandonment of its key allies. Although the adminis-

tration won support of Congress for China's entry into the World Trade Organization, China was opposed to America's plans for missile defense. China saw the system as countering its own relatively modest strategic retaliatory capability of perhaps 30 InterContinental Ballistic Missiles. But China also feared that the United States would use such a system to protect Taiwan from attack or intimidation. The matter of missile defense and ABM is covered more fully in Chapter 7.

Bush's promised strategic review was started, but in several pieces mandated by law. One part was done as part of the congressionally required Quadrennial Defense Review (QDR). Every four years, Congress directed the executive to review its defense strategy and report back. The second piece dealt with strategic nuclear forces. The third was Rumsfeld's own assessment. However, in all of this, the secretary was severely handicapped by a lack of staff. Though Rumsfeld had been appointed and quickly confirmed, he was "home alone" in the Pentagon. Aside from his deputy Paul Wolfowitz, it would take months to fill the key slots.

The review did not get off to a good start. Rumsfeld convened some twenty-two separate panels. Many senior military officers on the four service staffs complained openly and bitterly about being cut out of the process. Two service chiefs and several four-star commanders in the field confided to me their disappointment in the effort. The QDR portion was actually completed on September 9th. It, of course, would be somewhat revised in just two days.

A senior Bush official in the Pentagon responsible for the QDR solicited my reaction. The briefing—delayed and rescheduled for October 11th and finally held on November 5th—suggested some of the turmoil caused by September 11th. My view was that the QDR was exceedingly well written, but it was eight years late in coming.

The new strategy was to deter, dissuade, and defend. The most significant difference was the concept of "deterring forward" within each region. This meant that the best defense was a good offense and the result was to extend the defensive perimeter for protecting America. This concept would require a different mix and deployment of forces. To most observers, it all made good sense.

The two biggest shortfalls in these reviews, in my judgment, concerned "transformation" and "reform." Bush and Rumsfeld were committed to transforming the military, but the question of "transforming to what?" was not clearly answered. General terms of more agility, lethality, and reach were too vague to drive programs and budgets.

As to reform, while Rumsfeld had sought "freedom" to manage the department and its resources, the administration had not identified clearly how it proposed to eliminate duplication and waste, much of which probably had been present when the Republic was formed. The dilemma Rumsfeld faced with this so-called fiscal-force mismatch is made obvious by a look at the secretary's career.

When Rumsfeld was a navy ensign flying off a carrier in the mid-1950s, the draft was in place. Little real annual growth in spending was needed to keep the forces trained and equipped. Then, "teeth"—that is, the forces that actually would do the fighting—amounted to about half the force. "Tail"—that is, the support—was also half.

When Rumsfeld became secretary of defense the first time, in 1975, 3 to 5 percent annual real growth was needed to maintain the current force. Teeth were about 40 percent of the force; tail was 60 percent. And the nation had moved to the "all-volunteer" force.

When Rumsfeld took the oath of office in 2001, 8 to 10 percent annual real growth was needed to maintain the current force. Teeth were as low as 20 percent; tail, 80 percent. The QDR had no real proposals for breaking this "death spiral," much of which was due to the jump in costs and capability of high-technology systems (B-2 bombers cost about a billion dollars apiece); the arcane manner in which annual budgets were submitted and approved by Congress, thereby guaranteeing inefficiency; and the extraordinary cost increases in keeping an all-volunteer force.

Early caricatures of Bush in European media made him out as an "impetuous cowboy." Despite its promise of humility, the administration was portrayed as "unilateral," indifferent to allies, and even arrogant. Controversy swirled over how to deal with Saddam Hussein. The issue seemed to be not whether but when. Debate was described between the "moderates," personalized by Powell, and the "conservatives," who seemed to be everyone else. The conservatives were reported as winning the battle for the president's heart. In early September 2001, *Time* magazine carried the story "Where Has Colin Powell Gone?"

The administration was stumbling. Support in Congress had waned. The defection of Republican Senator Jim Jeffords in July put the Senate into Democratic hands, dealing the administration a severe political blow. The budget was stymied and Bush seemed adrift.

Then came September 11th.

## Washington at War

As George H. W. Bush had said that "this aggression [of Iraq] shall not stand" in 1990, the younger Bush was equally determined "to bring the perpetrators to justice and justice to the perpetrators" of the bombings in New York and Washington. For obvious reasons, the administration began to move much as Bush had in 1990. The first step was to assemble a coalition. The next was to build the war plan.

Bush, perhaps based on his experience as a businessman, divided the responsibilities clearly. Powell took the diplomatic lead to build the coalition and to isolate the prime suspects—Osama bin Laden and his al Qaeda network. Rumsfeld was to construct the war plan. George Tenet, Director of Central Intelligence and a holdover from the Clinton administration, had responsibility for the intelligence and covert operations of the campaign. Attorney General John Ashcroft and Treasury Secretary Paul O'Neill were the leads in the judicial and law-enforcement effort to find the sources of money, cut off funds, and track down and arrest those who had a role in the attacks. Cheney provided counsel and wisdom and Rice was the White House coordinator for the president.

Bush in essence declared a war on terrorism and terrorists. There was concern over the word *war* and justifiably so. War technically requires a declaration by Congress. It is fought against a specific state and not a nebulous organization or social ills such as crime, drugs, poverty, and racism—all declared by earlier administrations in terms of "wars against. . . ." And a war imparts certain privileges and rules on the combatants stemming from the laws of war and the various Geneva Conventions.

During World War II, Roosevelt and Churchill waged war on Hitler and Nazi Germany. Nazism was to be destroyed. But all members of the Nazi Party were not to be hunted down. Bush went a step further. He committed his administration to "capturing or killing" all members of al Qaeda. Bush also declared that this war was not limited to "rooting out terrorists." Regimes and groups that supported terrorism and terrorists were also included.

Powell fashioned a global coalition. He began with NATO. Article Five of the founding Washington Treaty connotes that "an attack against one is an attack against all." Never, not once, during the Cold War, had Article Five been used. The Soviets had never attacked. For the first time, Article Five was affirmed by the alliance. It was invoked by a terrorist attack launched by a nonstate organization from a part of the world far removed from the old NATO boundaries. Yet the invocation was a stroke of diplomatic genius.

The coalition was expanded. The "stans"—Uzbekistan, Tajikistan, and Turkmenistan—were engaged and provided access and bases. An urgent mission was dispatched to Pakistan to assure the support of President Pervez Musharraf. Pakistan was rife with problems.

Musharraf heads a military regime that deposed Pakistan's last civilian leader. Elections are scheduled for October 2002. Musharraf has promised an orderly return to democracy and must make good on his promise. The powerful Inter-agency services Intelligence Directorate or ISI was strongly pro-Taliban. The Taliban provided training camps for mujahadeen to fight in Kashmir, the festering sore between India and Pakistan. Pakistan houses nearly 15,000 "madrasses." These are religious schools teaching Islam, in some cases from dawn to dusk, relying on strict memorization of the Koran as the only teaching method. Some have been turned into rabid anti-American and anti-Western propaganda machines. Children are taught to hate the United States and regard it as a great Satan.

As Chapter 8 will show, instability in Pakistan is real. Tensions with India have increased. As Taliban and al Qaeda members fled into western Pakistan, problems with terrorists and terrorism increased.

On October 7th, Operation Enduring Freedom began. The first day, about 25 air strikes flown from three aircraft carriers operating in the Indian Ocean and 15 from land bases in the Persian Gulf and the continental United States struck Afghanistan. The initial targets were the limited air defenses and the primitive command-and-control systems. The raids continued until the meager air defenses were destroyed. Then the strikes were directed against the Taliban and al Qaeda troops. Throughout, the United States operated with impunity, initially losing only a single B-1 bomber to a massive loss of hydraulics and electronics, not enemy action. The crew bailed out safely and was rescued. Several helicopters and drones were also lost.

By mid-November, Special Forces units and clandestine CIA paramilitary personnel were operating with the Northern Coalition in the "stans" and the northern parts of Afghanistan. The purposes of these forces were to train the Northern Alliance troops and to coordinate the air strikes. Secretary Rumsfeld proudly displayed a photo of horse-mounted, GPS (Global Positioning System)-equipped U.S. Special Forces troops riding into battle as the best example of "transformation."

These ground forces called in U.S. warplanes. Precise weapons could literally be guided into designated windows of a particular building. The resulting fires had a withering effect on the al Qaeda and Taliban forces. Flying with complete invulnerability, forty-year-old B-52s dropped thousands of pounds of bombs accurately on their targets.

In Vietnam, B-52s were used in so-called Arc Light strikes. After an attack, the ground resembled a deserted moonscape. All foliage and structures had been destroyed. In their place were countless bomb craters. Captured Viet Cong (and later, during the Gulf War,

Iraqis) would reveal how frightened they were of the B-52s and the devastation they unleashed.

By early December, the Taliban and al Qaeda were on the run. The Northern Alliance moved swiftly to recapture the northern part of Afghanistan, taking Kabul and then Kandahar, the center of Taliban activity. About two thousand U.S. Marines landed near Kandahar to seize the airfield. Units of the Army's Tenth Mountain Division were also deployed in country. The collapse of the Taliban was as sudden as it was unexpected.

In retrospect, the reasons for the collapse were clear. First, at no time were there more than seventy to eighty thousand Taliban among a population of roughly 25 million Afghans. For six years, the Taliban operated perhaps the most repressive society in the world, committing atrocities against people and things such as the priceless Buddhas they destroyed as being against Islam. The Afghans hated the Taliban. And, when Operation Enduring Freedom began, the number of Taliban actively engaged in the fighting was a small fraction of the total—possibly less than 10,000.

Second, the Taliban and al Qaeda had no idea of what American military force could do to them. With a surprisingly small number of American forces, including paramilitary, and only several hundred aircraft, the combination of precision and firepower created an extraordinary amount of shock, awe, and damage. The Taliban were defenseless no matter how well they were dug in. Two-thousand- and even fifteen-thousand-pound "Daisy Cutter" bombs destroyed or sealed off bunkers that were well underground. AC-130 gunships, armed with cannons and rapid-fire Gatling guns and able to see at night with an array of sensors, wrought havoc.

The Northern Alliance opposition forces helped bring such fire to bear. That they were armed, as were the Taliban, with Kalishnikof automatic weapons and rifle-propelled grenades and rode into battle on Toyota trucks was offset by this display of American firepower. Unmanned aerial vehicles such as Global Hawk and Predator provided continuous surveillance. As in Desert Storm, it turned out to be an unfair fight. In the initial stages, the United States lost ony one man as a direct result of combat, and he was a CIA operative. Since then, nearly 40 Americans died, most of them in accidents and air mishaps.

But as Bush was becoming a wartime president, he would also have to deal with serious pieces of unfinished business. The fact was that the nation was vulnerable to terrorist attack. A national commission on critical infrastructure laid out the facts in 1997. The only sector it chose not to include was food. With the poisoning of Tylenol and other drugs in the 1980s by still unknown parties, "Mad Cow" disease, and foot and mouth disease—the latter two limited mostly to England—the vulnerability of food to contamination is not new.

Terrorists turned jet liners into flying bombs and crashed them into the World Trade Center and the Pentagon. But consider how much more vulnerable those two cities were to a more massive and insidious attack. Trucks or cars laden with explosives could have been used to seal off bridges and tunnels. While the authorities did close down New York anyway, the panic from explosions in the Midtown, Holland, and Lincoln Tunnels and the Triborough and George Washington bridges would have been massive. Phone calls claiming biological attacks would have intensified the fear regardless of whether they were real.

As Chapter 4 will show, this vulnerability is inherent in an open society. Government will be dealing with this reality for as long as the nation endures. The risks and costs will appear in the effect of protecting against these vulnerabilities on individual rights and freedoms. Long lines in airports, restrictions on even getting up on short flights, and combat air patrols overhead with the responsibility of shooting down future renegade airliners were temporary measures. What happens when they become permanent?

Bush heads a government that still remains largely configured to deal with the Cold War. The National Security Act of 1947, amended in 1949 and 1958 and about which much more will be said, is the legal basis for government's national security organization. If the ABM Treaty was an "artifact" of the Cold War, what about the National Security Act?

The immediate limitations of the organization are exposed by the juncture of law enforcement and intelligence. The military and the Department of Defense have the largest resources, capabilities, and budgets. But posse commitatus, stemming from an 1878 statute to limit the Army's power of arrest, was designed to keep the military out of law enforcement. Terrorism raises the question of whether it is a criminal or a national security problem.

The CIA and the FBI have divided responsibility for counter-terrorism. The CIA is restricted from domestic activities. The FBI is expanding overseas. And the National Security Agency, part of the Pentagon, provides much of the electronic intercept and surveillance capacity. Determining responsibility and authority is not a simple matter. The difficulties of coordination are brought home with one story which the Bureau has not confirmed.

The story is this. The September 11th hijackers, including the apparent ringleader, an Egyptian called Mohammed Atta, had used Portland, Maine, as a stopover. Two FBI agents were sent to Bangor to find Atta's rental car and whatever other evidence might be present. The Portland police chief was told his help was not needed. When he protested, the FBI agents threatened to arrest him for "tortuous interference." Two weeks passed and the car had not been found. Finally, under great pressure from Washington for results, the agents sought help from the local police. It took them precisely eleven minutes to find the car.

The president has designated former Pennsylvania governor Tom Ridge director of Homeland Security. Ridge has "cabinet rank." He does not have, as yet, budget authority. He cannot hire and fire people in other departments. Nor can he change budget priorities. Only the president can. Whether this office will work or whether it will become the equivalent of the National Coordinator for Drug Policy, also known as the Drug Czar, with no authority or real power remains to be seen.

As Bush is finding out, there is no set organizational relationship with Congress. Each of the 535 members is constitutionally equal. Only the Speaker of the House and the President Pro Tempore of the Senate are specified by title in the Constitution as it pertains to elected legislators. The president of the Senate is the vice-president.

Thus, when Bush meets with the "leadership," it may only be five members (Senate and House majority and minority leaders and the Speaker). The other 530 can demand equal time. This is not new. However, under the circumstances of this type of crisis, the arrangement may not be helpful.

The Arab-Israeli and Palestinian conflict remains in chaos. The Camp David Talks of 2000 failed. Ehud Barak lost a vote of confidence in the Knesset. Ariel Sharon, a more confrontational and controversial prime minister, took office. An "intifada" (or uprising) began in September 2000 and continues. Violence and killing have intensified. The situation arguably has never been worse.

The autocratic nature of regimes in the Middle East, the Gulf States, and Africa has not changed. Saudi Arabia has been accused of paying off terrorists to keep them outside the kingdom's borders. As King Fahd grows frailer, Crown Prince Abdullah assumes a larger role. Abdullah is more independent than the king concerning the United States. At the meeting of the Arab League in Beirut in March 2002, the crown prince unveiled a new peace plan, leaked earlier to the New York *Times*. It is discussed later.

And relations with Russia and China, as well as with India and Pakistan, have been stressed by the abrogation of the ABM Treaty, among other events.

From every perspective, these pieces of unfinished business have become far more dangerous. The obvious question, as Lenin asked, is what is to be done?

# ★ 3 ★

# A World Transformed

### The Roots of Turmoil and Terror

To George H. W. Bush and Brent Scowcroft, the period from 1989 to 1991 was a "seminal" historical epoch that transformed the world. The Berlin Wall fell in 1989. Saddam was crushed in 1991. And then the Soviet Union toppled. Despite these watershed events, the question of whether this transformed world would prove to be a safer place for America lurked in the background like a socially suspect guest at a socially proper event.

Concurrently, "globalization" was exerting significant influence. Indeed, globalization would carry the transformation further and deeper than either Bush or Scowcroft could have imagined in 1991. In many ways, the consequences and forces of globalization are underlying causes for turning latent pieces of unfinished business in 1991 into full-fledged crises and challenges to the nation's safety.

To paraphrase Voltaire, statistics can be tortured into saying anything. However, to capture only a part of the great transformation that has occurred, consider a few isolated facts. After Desert Storm ended, the Dow-Jones index hit three thousand for the first time (April 17th, 1991). U.S. gross domestic product (GDP) was $5 trillion. Regular gasoline in Washington, D.C., was selling for about

$1.20 a gallon; milk for $1.22 (all current dollars). By best count, about three million people had access to the World Wide Web or the Internet.

As of December 31st, 2001, the Dow was at ten thousand, a more than tripling (although the purist will note that this amounted to an annual rate of increase of 12 percent, not spectacular). A gallon of regular gasoline in the District of Columbia still sold for about $1.20 (remember James Baker's explanation for the Gulf War). Milk sells for about $3.00, or about a 7 percent annual increase. U.S. GDP has increased to $ 9 trillion, a rate of increase between the Dow-Jones and the price of milk.

The biggest growth, of course, is access to the World Wide Web and the Internet. From virtually nothing a decade ago, best estimates suggest that nearly half a billion households and entities access the Internet. A similar trend understandably applies to personal computers.

The speed of this transformation, not only for 1989 to 1991 but over the last decade as well, was astonishing: a period so short it seemed measured in historical nanoseconds. Partly a function of the technology and science that have driven a genuine "knowledge revolution," the rapidity as well as rate of change was also accelerated by a virtually borderless world accessible to anyone with a cell phone, satellite dish, or computer. The latter is described as the phenomenon of "instantaneous communication." Its power comes from the literally billions of people who use or are exposed to this explosion of information swirling around the world whether through news or other media.

At the turn of the nineteenth century, a message could be transmitted around the world by telegraph. Underwater cables, first put down on the ocean's floors in the mid 1850s, linked the major continents and cities. In those days, it took about a day and a half for a telegraphed message to make a round-the-world trip, more time than it would take for the Concorde, an old technology by today's standards, to make the same trip flying at Mach 1.2. Invariably, messages were garbled, and, until Alexander Graham Bell's telephone

technology was improved, limited to the tedious process of telegra-
phy and the "dit dahs" of Morse code.

Today, "e-mail pals" correspond instantly even though they may
be many time zones and continents apart. A person in Virginia calling information for a telephone number in England may be connected to an operator in Colorado for the answer. Journalists report
live via "phone cameras" from al Qaeda caves in the Tora Bora
Region of Afghanistan to worldwide television audiences. Financial
markets run twenty-four hours a day. A day trader in the wilds of
Western China has nearly the same access to equity markets via the
Internet as a broker on Wall Street. Each of these is anecdotal evidence of the "shrinking" of the world in distance and time. *New
York Times* columnist Thomas Friedman presents a smorgasbord of
related insights into globalization in *The Lexus and the Olive Tree* for
interested readers.

The causes of the world transformation were not quite so instantaneous. Fontenelle's observation on this book's frontispiece that "it
takes time to ruin a world, but time is all it takes" is relevant. All
political systems contain certain weaknesses and contradictions.
Often, these prove terminal. Throughout history, every great power
achieving preeminence has fallen. Some have disappeared or been
absorbed. Others simply became lesser powers. Rome, Great Britain,
and the Soviet Union are among many cases of this phenomenon,
the theme of Oswald Spengler's *The Decline of the West*. The United
States has so far been exempted from this historical reality.

In Lenin's view, communism offered the promise of social just-
ness and economic equality. The Soviet Union, in practice, provided
neither. Centralized control and a system legitimized by terror and
force led to self-delusion and political variants of cognitive disso-
nance on a huge scale. The system was irrational. In its eighth decade, it imploded. The tensions between maintaining political control
and reforming the antiquated economic system exceeded the breaking point. Perhaps rulers in Egypt, Saudi Arabia, and elsewhere took
careful note.

The United States—as would any nation, particularly one with
such a high standard of living—has been inherently vulnerable to

those wishing to do harm. Two oceans and the limited reach of technology proved powerful defenses for nearly two centuries. However, only a hundred years ago, the country struggled with anarchists and terror. Two presidents were shot, one killed.

Bombs were anarchists' preferred choice of weapon. The infamous Haymarket Massacre in Chicago on May 4th, 1886, is a case in point, where dynamite led to a bloodbath between the police and protesting workers. The subsequent trial convicted eight anarchists, although who detonated the bomb remains uncertain. Wall Street was not spared. The J. P. Morgan bank was nearly destroyed by a bomb several decades later. Stemming this form of terrorism was a national priority. The threat would grow worse only two decades later.

The anthrax attacks of 2001 were called "unprecedented" acts of terror, but this was not the first time the U.S. mail was the purveyor of death. In May 1919 and then in June, nearly fifty bombs were mailed through the post office. The first wave targeted two cabinet officers (the attorney general and the secretary of labor); a federal and a Supreme Court judge; the postmaster general; the barons of industry J. P. Morgan and John D. Rockefeller; and other senior officials. In the second wave, Attorney General A. Mitchell Palmer's Washington home was bombed. Only the bomber was killed. The public was terrified by these and subsequent mail attacks. In response, Palmer launched a witch-hunt to root out the Communist, Bolshevik, and Red terrorists. The young director of the Bureau of Investigation as it was then called—J. Edgar Hoover—made his reputation heading the hunt for the Red Menace.

China, a hundred years ago, was partitioned. European imperialism and colonialism prospered. The British Raj controlled India and Pakistan and, along with Russia, played the "Great Game" in Afghanistan and what was called the "near east." The Saudi peninsula, as well as Palestine, was under the thrall of the Ottoman Empire. Pursuit of oil, to fuel the new "dreadnought" men of war coming off the line in Britain's shipyards, was the latest driving force for European states and foreign policy. From these roots, many contemporary realities have arisen.

## Legacies and Illusions of War

Force is the ultimate arbiter of dispute. Nearly a century ago, Sir Norman Angell wrote *The Great Illusion*. Angell's thesis was provoked by the globalization in the early years of the twentieth century. European economies had grown interdependent. Ruling elites were of a similar class often interelated across borders. Hence, in Angell's view, war was simply too destructive and expensive to remain a useful policy instrument. War would destroy economies. And no conquest would gain enough in reparations to make up the losses. Or so Angell argued until August 1914 evaporated his case.

Barbara Tuchman's *The Guns of August* analyzed in depth the causes of that war, collaterally exposing the flaws in Angell's thesis. She observed that nearly all the ruling families in Europe were related by blood. In Britain, the royal name was "Battenberg," from its German roots. Yet in 1914 political rivalries over power and colonies, nourished by arms races and secret treaties, exploded into World War I. From 1914 to 1918, the war raged in Europe. Millions were killed. And the royals were forced to change their name to Mountbatten, the English translation.

For the central powers and allies alike, prewar presumptions about strategy took their lead from Prussia's lightening victory over France in 1870. War would be swift and won by the side that mobilized first. Instead, war bogged down in the trenches of France and Belgium.

In many ways, the battles of World War I bore a resemblance to the U.S. Civil War but with losses that were orders of magnitudes higher. Thousands died to gain a few feet of ground in "no man's land." In battle, the internal combustion engine had largely but not entirely replaced horse transportation. Trains provided the heavy logistical lifting. Balloons flew in both wars. But aircraft made maiden voyages into battle even though weapons payloads were in the tens and single hundreds of pounds. Artillery ranges advanced considerably. The German's "Big Bertha" cannon bombarded Paris from a distance of forty miles. However, it was the "75" millimeter howitzer with a range of several miles and conventional artillery that were used extensively. The deadly Gatling Gun of the Civil War was replaced by the machine gun. One significant difference was the use of poison gas. Another was the transformation of navies.

At sea, battleships ruled the waves. These were not the primitive ironclads *Monitor* and *Merrimack*, which fought each other to a draw in Virginia's Hampton Roads, but behemoths displacing up to fifteen thousand tons with fifteen-inch guns and thick armor belts propelled by oil-fired boilers. There was only one major sea battle, at Jutland in 1916. England's Grand Fleet steamed into the English Channel to sink Germany's High Seas Fleet. The battle proved to be a standoff. Naval fleet actions would play no further strategic role in the war although Winston Churchill, England's First Sea Lord, tried to break the deadlock on the Western Front with the ill-fated expedition into the Dardanelles in 1915.

Submarines attacked on the surface. Cruising underwater was dangerous and limited in duration. But against unarmed or unescorted merchant ships, submarines were invincible. One consequence of Germany's strategy of unrestricted submarine warfare and the attempt to cut England off from commerce was to bring the United States into the war.

The other German strategy that had unintended consequences was the decision to end the war on the Eastern front with Russia. Lenin was sent back from Germany to Russia. It would be perhaps the most important train ride in history. In the Treaty of Brest-Litovsk, Russia paid a huge price to Germany for peace. However, it was to Lenin a price worth paying. The Soviet Union would emerge from Russia's ashes. Perhaps history does repeat. In 1996, after great pressure from the United States, Sudan evicted Osama bin Laden. Bin Laden went to Afghanistan.

World War I was to be the "war to end all wars." It was not. The peace conference at Versailles was abandoned by the United States. The Senate refused to ratify what admittedly was a bad treaty and Wilson was humiliated. Wilson was also incapacitated by a stroke.

Reparations and bitterness from the war exacted huge penalties on Germany. Every country had paid enormously in blood and treasure. Germany would attempt to make some financial restitution. Britain would never recover its status as the world's preeminent power. Socialism, communism, and fascism would thrive. Hitler and Nazi Germany, as well as fascist Japan, were the tragic dividends of the peace.

World War II was fought two decades later. War had been transformed. On land, mechanized war combined tanks, artillery, and close air support in formations that could move with speed and agility. Germany's *blitzkrieg* or lightening warfare was the precursor. The Wermacht swept through and around France's Maginot Line and the qualitatively and quantitatively superior allied forces, conquering Europe in six weeks in the spring of 1940.

Aircraft too had radically advanced. Powerful aircraft engines, high-octane gasoline, and strong materials such as steel and aluminum moved "strategic bombing" from a concept advanced by the Italian strategist Douhet to reality. During the First World War, Zeppelins terrified the English with limited bombing of cities. World War II brought virtually unlimited bombing. And tactics as well as strategy would be affected.

Fighter aircraft came into their own. In the fall of 1940, the Royal Air Force's Fighter Command Spitfires and Hurricanes (and the proud pilots who flew them) were lionized after the great victory in the skies over England against the Luftwaffe in the Battle of Britain. At Pearl Harbor, Japanese naval attack aircraft fundamentally changed the character of naval war. Eight U.S. battleships were sunk at Ford Island. The aircraft carrier and the submarine instantly became, by default, the new capital ships of the line. In the summer of 1942, the sea battles of the Coral Sea and Midway would be fought and won without surface ships engaging or even catching sight of each other. The fight was carried out at long range by aircraft alone.

Strategic bombing was directed at demoralizing the enemy and demolishing its military-industrial capacity. Tens of thousands died in firebomb raids over Hamburg, Dresden, Tokyo, Nagoya, and other Axis cities. Paradoxically, these raids had the opposite effect. Civilian resistance was stiffened on both sides. In Germany, which was poorly organized by the Nazis at the war's start, the bombing forced enormous efficiencies. By the fall of 1944 and at the height of the allied bombing campaign, German war production for aircraft, submarines, and other weapons was at its peak. Not until nuclear weapons were dropped on Japan did strategic bombing achieve its political end of forcing surrender.

Finally, while Napoleon began the *levees* for massing armies that turned warfare into battles between huge forces, the United States perfected industrial war. It simply outproduced the enemy. FDR termed this capacity the "arsenal for democracy." Industrialization became the American way of war. Whereas the Chinese and Russians could rely on raw numbers of troops, the United States was able to spend its way to victory by building more and better arms. Or so the nation thought until Korea and Vietnam came along.

The allies won the war. They also won a substantial part of the peace by reconstructing and democratizing Japan and the western half of Germany. The other part of the peace turned into the Cold War. The differences between East and West had been checked by the larger Nazi danger. That "war" persisted for six decades. It never deteriorated into a hot war. The cataclysmic prospect of nuclear conflict was a principal factor in keeping the peace. Ironically, the standoff validated Angell's discredited thesis. Angell had not been wrong, simply too early.

## Precision and Reach

By the time of the Gulf War, the United States had fought major wars in Korea and Vietnam and used force in hundreds of lesser instances. As World War II was a transformation from World War I, the Gulf War was a leap ahead in weapons' accuracy. Prior to Desert Storm, the history of war was linked by a common fact: Of every rock, arrow, bullet, and missile launched, fired, or shot, virtually every one missed.

In World War II, Korea, and Vietnam, bombing accuracies were measured in thousands of feet at best. The U.S. Sherman tank and its 75 mm cannon had an effective killing range of only three hundred to four hundred yards. When it was able to penetrate the heavily armored German Tiger or Panther tanks, up to ten rounds were needed for a kill. The vaunted Spitfire (and other fighters) calibrated its machine guns to hit a "sweet spot" some 270 yards away. Radar and electronic intercepts played key roles in combat and in code breaking. However, "the fog of war," as Carl von Clausewitz observed in his classic *On War*, was ubiquitous. Seeing over the next hill or sand berm, as General Fred Franks would note in Desert Storm, was still elusive.

The battle in Kuwait was an inflection point in war and absolute evidence of the military transformation taking place. Of all the ordnance expended by the coalition, only about 10 percent was "precision." Precision-guided munitions had fabulous accuracies because they were steered to their targets by a variety of means and sensors. Infrared, television, and laser guidance were the most common forms of ensuring this accuracy. Global Positioning System also allowed the soldier in battle and the pilot overhead to know with certainty and immediacy exact locations. This was a first in war. Extensive command-and-control communications were reliable and secure. To complement them, thousands of cell phones found their way to the troops. The combination was devastating.

Franks's VII Corps M-1 tanks were achieving first-shot kills at ranges of up to two thousand yards. After the war was over, the kill—not the hit—percentage of every main tank cannon round fired was an astonishing 90 percent. But Franks was still constrained by lack of information of what actually was lurking a hill or two away.

The air war had similar results. Horner's aircraft evaporated the rather complex and heavy Iraqi air defenses before unleashing their might on the army. With few exceptions, including a bomb dropped on an underground bunker in Baghdad filled not with senior Iraqi military but with civilians, "collateral" damage was limited (that was not true in the south, where "friendly fire" from the air and artillery caused about a third of all allied casualties). Horner complained that despite all of the intelligence-gathering systems, he never knew "where to stick the needle," as he put it, to collapse the regime and Iraq's will to resist.

Drones and unmanned aircraft achieved prominence in Afghanistan. In 1991, their potential was demonstrated. USS *Wisconsin*, one of four Navy battleships recommissioned in the 1980s, was on station in the Gulf. Her main battery of nine 16-inch guns fired the equivalent of a Volkswagen's weight of TNT twenty-five miles. She also carried an Israeli-made Pioneer drone. Her skipper and later Rear Admiral David S. Bill used the drone and big guns in tandem to deliver withering fire at long range. The combination was so powerful that the ship recorded televised tapes from the Pioneers of Iraqi soldiers trying to surrender to the unmanned aircraft. The concept of long-range fire was not new.

During the Vietnam War, Lieutenant General Victor ("Brute") Krulak, commander of Marine forces in the Pacific, invented Operation Sting Ray. Small squads of Marines were sent into the field to locate Viet Cong and North Vietnamese forces. When contact was made, "calls for fire" were radioed in. Some eighty thousand missions resulted. The problem was technical. The communications and fire-support units, whether artillery or air, were difficult to coordinate. Timeliness was poor. In some cases, hours and even days of delay were common. In theory, the operation was excellent. In practice, it had marginal results. As technology advanced, the merit of Sting Ray would prove itself in Afghanistan.

When Operation Enduring Freedom began on October 7th, skepticism about the outcome surfaced in the United States. The Taliban had successfully defeated the Soviet Army. They perhaps numbered up to 80,000. The terrain in Afghanistan was inhospitable. The cave complexes in Tora Bora and the White Mountains were seemingly impregnable. And bin Laden had invoked suicide as the modus operandi for his followers.

The United States relied on what turned out to be a minimal number of forces. Three aircraft carriers were deployed to the Bay of Bengal. Air Force F-15s and F-16s were deployed to the Gulf and nearby bases. B-52 bombers, relics from the Cold War, and B-1 bombers went to Diego Garcia in the Indian Ocean. KC-10, AWACS, and JSTARS command aircraft were sent as well for refueling and for controlling and coordinating the strikes. In all, only a few hundred aircraft were engaged. The adminstration has not released the actual numbers.

On the ground, there were perhaps several hundred CIA covert operators. Special Forces troops numbering in the hundreds joined selective Northern Alliance forces to train and equip them and ultimately to control the air strikes. About two thousand Marines were air lifted into Camp Rhino as a prelude to occupying the airfield at Kandahar. The four-hundred-mile assault from ships at sea was the longest in the Corps' history.

On a given day, about seventy to one hundred air strikes were flown. The difference was that upward of 90 percent of the munitions fired were precision. After the Taliban's primitive air defenses were eliminated, U.S. aircraft loitered at safe altitudes awaiting calls for fire from the ground. This was the twenty-first century equivalent of Krulak's Sting Ray. The effects were devastating. Imagine seeing from the ground the contrails of a B-52 lazily circling overhead out of range of anti-aircraft fire. Then, on command, a 500-, 2,000-, or even 15,000 pound bomb was dropped with pinpoint accuracy. That is shock and awe in the purest and most frightening form.

At some stage, analysis of this operation will be made public. No doubt, the remarkable military achievements from the Gulf War will be surpassed in degrees of effectiveness. In less than four months, the Taliban and al Qaeda were routed by the Northern Alliance on the ground and a few hundred aircraft directed by a handful of American Special Forces. While George W. Bush talked of "transforming" the military, Operation Enduring Freedom showed how this might be achieved in practice.

The videos of U.S. Special Forces personnel, dressed in full combat gear and armed with GPS, laser-imaging systems, satellite communications, and who knows what else, atop horses riding into battle made the point about transformation vivid. The crucial question however, is how these lessons will be translated into changing the force structure after this campaign ends.

An interim Afghan government under Prime Minister Harmid Karzai took office on December 22nd, 2001. The fight against terrorism is far from over. Rebuilding a nation that may well be at a pre–Stone Age level is a Sisyphean labor. Churchill's caution that "this is not the end or the beginning of the end but rather, it is the end of the beginning" should be taken seriously.

The magnitude of these transformations was brought home coincidentally at the celebration of the Marine Corps' 226th birthday at Washington's Hilton Hotel on November 10th, 2001. About one thousand guests, including Vice-President and Mrs. Cheney, took part. Our table was hosted by a bemedaled three-star Marine general. Present was Arnaud deBourchgrave (and his wife). DeBourchgrave was the last of the World War II generation of foreign correspondents. We had met in Vietnam in 1966. He had been wounded several times there. His rolodex ran from Anwar Sadat when he was alive to Jiang Zemin, China's president.

DeBourchgrave had reported from virtually every trouble spot in the world for fifty years. His ethic was that the role of journalists was to report history, not to make it. A profound change in the media had taken place. That respected and credible journalists such as Edward R. Murrow and Walter Cronkite were replaced by news celebrities earning tens of millions of dollars a year is a fact. The effects on the political leadership and the public of this media transformation have been profound. In some ways, the public affairs officer has become one of the most important members of any staff whether in the White House or with field commanders.

Seated next to me was a "twenty-something" Navy F-14 "Tomcat" pilot. Her father, a former congressman from California, sat across the way. She had just returned from a cruise to the Persian Gulf where she had flown thirty combat missions over Iraq. Her manner and conversation were those of a cool professional. She was petite and attractive and if it were not for her uniform had no outward signs of being a military officer. In that capacity, her assignment to the Navy test pilot school at Patuxent River, Maryland, confirmed her qualifications as an aviator.

Reluctantly, she talked about the strikes she had flown over Iraq. She was particularly impressed with the F-14, a fighter that had been around before she had been born. She called it, matter-of-factly and without the bravado associated with a "top gun pilot," the "most effective killing machine in the air." The reason, she said, was that the FLIR package—for forward-looking infrared—made ground attack target practice. The F-14 had originally been bought to shoot down Soviet bombers and missiles at very long range, not for close air support on the ground.

The combination of deBourchgrave, literally the old warhorse (who would go on to cover the war from Afghanistan at the end of 2001), and this new breed of fighter pilot made a striking generational comparison. If Bush and Scowcroft cast transformation in political terms, this was the most vivid example of change in a practical sense.

## Globalization: Two Revolutions

Globalization is an old phenomenon. Ancient Greece and Rome existed in a globalized world—but that world was bounded by space and time. The Greek and Roman empires extended across continents. They did not extend across the entire world. And it took days, weeks, or longer for news to reach Athens and Rome.

The eighteenth century likewise was globalized in the sense that most of the so-called civilized world was interconnected. Meanwhile, the intellectual underpinnings for the political, economic, and social systems that would empower the full force of globalization in coming centuries were being created. Adam Smith, Edmund Burke, and America's Founding Fathers were among the principal authors.

Globalization was not universally appreciated. In China, after waiting a long time for an audience, George III's envoy, Lord McCartney, was finally received by the Chieng Lung emperor. In 1793, China firmly held Middle Kingdom delusions of grandeur and power. McCartney was rebuffed. He was informed that China possessed everything she needed. Nothing from the world of the barbarian possibly could be of use. A half-century later, Western barbarians were preparing to carve China into colonies and cantonments.

The labor-intensive eighteenth century gave way to industrialization. The shift from agrarian-based economies where man and animal were the primary engines to an industrial age of machines was one of the true revolutions in history. As machines transformed society, political stability was imposed in Europe with Napoleon's final defeat at Waterloo.

For a century, an era of commerce and relative peace reigned on the continent. Capitalism was beginning to flourish. Democracy was moving from control vested in an elite to broader popular participation. However, industrialization and politics were breeding grievances for dissent and change. In a sense, these would become pieces of unfinished business in the nineteenth century.

In the United States, unfinished business of the revolution and the formation of the republic led to the Civil War in 1861. The dual system of federal and state governments left open crucial questions pertaining to fundamental rights of the state. The contradiction of inalienable rights existing alongside slavery had been deferred by the Founding Fathers. As the North industrialized and grew richer, the South remained agrarian and dependent on slavery for its economic well-being. Expansion west compounded these strains. As new states and territories joined the union, tensions over whether they would be "slave" or "free" snapped. Violence resulted. In the process, the southern states began seceding. Lincoln could not tolerate the threat to the Union.

After that war, the United States began a long process of political reconciliation and unprecedented economic and industrial expansion. Social issues over free and slave and black and white would take more than a century to set right. That transformation is still not complete.

Manifest destiny and the "winning of the west" created a nation three thousand miles from coast to coast with nearly limitless resources. The latter half of the nineteenth century created the foundation for economic superpowerdom. Much of this industrialization was financed by investment from England. A war with Spain in 1898 was spurred on by the "yellow press," which turned the sinking of the battleship *Maine* in Havana, Cuba, into a cause celebre. In winning, the United States became a global power, acquiring Cuba and the Philippines as colonies. Hawaii and a number of other footholds in the Caribbean and Pacific, including the Panama Canal, would become part of the de facto American empire. As it turned out, an internal explosion in its coaling bunkers sank the USS *Maine*, not an act of sabotage or deliberate mining.

As the twentieth century began, salons and institutes in London, Paris, and New York were filled with talk about the interconnectivity of much of the world in many of the same terms bandied about one hundred years later regarding globalization. A conference at the century's end was convened at London's Royal United Services Institute (established in 1842 by the Duke of Wellington to ensure broad debate and discussion on matters of military tactics and doctrine) on the topic of an increasingly interconnected world. In substance, the conference was not substantially different from what "think tanks" discuss today about globalization. The world then was connected neither globally nor instantaneously, but it was headed in those directions.

These trends continued throughout the twentieth century in conditions of war, peace, depression, and boom. Throughout, the United States has had enduring legacies around which its security and safety revolve and evolve. In Washington's Farewell Address, actually published well before he voluntarily left office after two terms as president in 1797, he warned the nation to steer clear of "permanent alliances."

Often mischaracterized as a call to remain aloof from foreign entanglements, Washington's proposal was for a policy of flexibility defined by national interest. In fact, this advice became polarized and misinterpreted. Interventionism and isolationism were used as rallying cries to make or oppose the case for unentangled policy. In the twenty-first century, they have been recast as "unilateralism" and "multilateralism." This is also a false dichotomy. Washington meant neither.

In the two decades between the world wars, the United States was indeed isolationist in a narrow security sense. It had not abandoned an internationalist outlook. Its businessmen and financiers operated globally. The House of Morgan, for example, was very active in Latin America and in helping Japan and Germany to industrialize. The United States convened the Washington Naval Arms Limitations Conferences. Because it rejected the League of Nations and refused to be drawn into the conflicts in China, Spain, and elsewhere that were about to explode into a world war, the United States was rightly regarded as isolationist. Pearl Harbor changed that forever. However, debate over the amount and extent of involvement abroad was never-ending.

When Japan formally surrendered in September 1945, the United States was the most powerful nation in the world and probably in all of history. The destruction of most of Europe, Russia, and Japan meant that the American economy, still on wartime steroids, accounted for about 40 percent of the world's entire GDP. The United States was undamaged by the war. Ruin was everywhere else. Russia suffered 20 million dead or missing, China perhaps as many. Less than a third of a million Americans died in the war.

The U.S. military, numbering about 12 million, was the best in the world. In addition to its lead in virtually every type of weapon, it possessed "the bomb." While it expended the only two nuclear weapons in its inventory on Hiroshima and Nagasaki, it would easily build more. Russia would need four years to develop their own; China nearly twenty.

So what did the United States do? It disarmed and demobilized. Roosevelt had expected that the United Nations Organization, led by the United States and Russia, would provide the vehicle for assuring the peace and stability that eluded the League of Nations. Sadly, Roosevelt died in April. The new president, Harry S. Truman, had limited experience in politics and foreign policy, having been plucked from his first Senate term in 1944 to run on the ticket with FDR. And FDR had not chosen to keep Truman "in the loop." The atom bomb and the Manhattan Project would be made clear to him only after he became commander in chief.

It was not until events in Europe turned nasty that the United States would reengage fully. From the Greek Civil War to the Berlin Blockade, the Cold War was taking form. As Churchill made famous in a 1946 speech in Fulton, Missouri, "an iron curtain was descending." The old ally was becoming the new enemy.

Eastern European states were falling under Soviet and communist control, part of the agreements Stalin thought he had been granted at the Yalta and Potsdam conferences in 1945. The United States put in place the plan for European reconstruction named for its creator and the general who helped win the war, George C. Marshall. Marshall served as secretary of state and then briefly as secretary of defense. An American of immense ability, Marshall frequently told his subordinates that "if you get the objectives right, a lieutenant can write the strategy." It is not coincidental that Marshall is one of two prior secretaries whose portraits adorn the wall of the current secretary's office. The other portrait Powell selected for his office was of Thomas Jefferson, not bad company.

The Marshall Plan was necessary but not sufficient to cope with the growing Soviet threat. In 1949, twelve states entered into the Washington Treaty creating NATO. In December, the Soviets exploded their bomb, engineered with secrets purloined from the United States and Britain. In June 1950, at the instigation of Stalin, North Korea invaded South Korea. The Korean War was underway. U.S. rearmament, something that Truman had avoided for four years, began in earnest. It would continue and continue and continue.

What differentiates this moment in history regarding globalization stems from two revolutions: knowledge and people. Without both, globalization would be a lesser phenomenon and one that had been evolutionary. There have been knowledge revolutions before. The "age of enlightenment" was appropriately named. At the turn of the century before last, the airplane, the radio, and the internal combustion engine as well as great advances in medicine and physics were about to make their mark.

Fifty years ago, thermonuclear energy, plastics, computers, and great strides in medicine and science were in place. Any era in the last several hundred years boasts of similar accomplishments. Today's knowledge revolution has simply compressed the time for these changes and progressions to take place. It is estimated that one consequence of this revolution is that in the coming decades, more new knowledge will be created than has existed throughout history.

This point is so crucial that I repeat it: More new knowledge will be created in the coming decades than has existed throughout the entirety of history. This will happen this century.

Again, evidence is anecdotal and intuitive. Forty years ago, Gordon Moore, one of the inventors of the computer chip and the giant company that exploited it (Intel), posited that every two or three years chip capacity doubles. Moore's Law, as it was called, has since been shattered. Molecular and parallel computing will enhance computer capacity and power even faster.

The human genome or DNA has finally been mapped. Nanotechnologies, operating on a microscopic level, rearrange molecules as the means for production. These and other technologies will combine to create still new technologies that at bare minimum will be revolutionary.

At a human level, many advances have already been achieved in communications, electronics, and computers. These result in products that are affordable and ubiquitous. In even what may seem the most primitive locales in South America, Asia, and Africa, satellite dishes, cell phones, and computers are common. One can recall visits to tiny villages in China and India where, despite poverty and remoteness, there was at least one satellite dish.

What this means is that billions of people literally have the ability to be in touch with the rest of the world. The unprecedented interconnectivity and accessibility are irreversible. That has all manner of consequences. The United States dominates the entertainment and telecommunications sectors. Its culture is on the Internet, in the skies, on CDs and the screen. It is everywhere.

With any culture, there are disciples and critics. McDonald's golden arches may be welcome in the United States. That is not the case everywhere. American wealth, opulence, and, to many, excess are not always well received, especially in states where the average standard of living is measured in hundreds of dollars a year—the cost of a cashmere sweater, a Hermes tie, or fancy dinner in the United States.

The positive gains from being "the sole remaining superpower" coexist with extraordinary resentment against the United States. The

U.S. Commission on National Security/21st Century report made this resentment explicit. It went further, concluding that this resentment would lead to parties' taking actions against the United States that could be catastrophic.

Any great power in history is subject to resentment and jealousy. The significant difference now is that the extent of this potential resentment and hostility is global and unlimited. At the turn of the nineteenth century, Great Britain was the primus inter pares among nations but by no means the predominant power. A condition of balance-of-power politics had persisted in Europe for nearly two hundred years. France, Germany, and to some degree Russia were able to play each other and Britain off in alliances and coalitions. There were also about sixty sovereign states around the globe.

In the twenty-first century, about 190 states exist. Of the total world GDP (and by extension wealth), the United States, with about 1/20 of the world's population, accounts for about ¼. By any standard, the United States enjoys an extraordinary level of economic power. That alone provokes jealousy and resentment. As the knowledge revolution continues, the United States maintains the most extensive university system in the world for both undergraduate and graduate studies, especially in the technical areas (ironically, many of the nuclear physicists working in China, Iraq, Iran, and elsewhere were U.S.-trained). This means that the U.S. economic advantages will only grow larger. As new technologies and products are created, even in a world with an accelerating growth in GDP, the United States, with a tiny proportion of the world's people, will increase its disproportionate slice of the world's GDP.

The second revolution is one of people. The combination of exploding technology and the creation of new states has enabled people to become more empowered and more able to draw on available resources through communications and the Internet. A century ago a sailor in the Royal Navy, or anyone else's for that matter, was powerless beyond the reach of his ship and its guns. The horizon, perhaps six or seven miles away, was very distant. A Chinese coolie or a farmer cultivating his flocks in Kenya was confined to a relatively tiny set of geographic and social boundaries.

Today sailors, along with everyone else, have global reach. The phenomenon of computer hacking illustrates how someone in St. Petersburg, Russia, routing his attacks through Rio de Janeiro in Brazil, could penetrate the computer firewalls of the Chase Manhattan Bank in New York. In Operation Enduring Freedom, there is little doubt that sailors sitting in operations centers at sea hundreds and thousands of miles away from the fight at CentCom headquarters in Tampa, Florida, have a firsthand and instantaneous view of the battle whether from drones and aircraft overhead or from satellites and other devices in space. The coolie or the farmer, noted before, is able to access the world's equity markets as if he were in London, New York, or Hamburg.

This empowerment of people has had a profound effect on innovation and change. Within the United States, despite the economic downturn of 2000–2001, unemployment dipped well below the famous Phillips curve's 5 percent floor, shattering several conventional pieces of economic wisdom. The reason was simple. Small, start-up companies with fewer than fifty employees were multiplying and creating the demand for labor that took unemployment to about 3 percent. This is the clearest signal of a people revolution.

This trend is spreading abroad. In large or relatively undeveloped states such as China and India, where there is enormous societal and cultural inertia, the effects will occur more slowly. But they will occur. In this process, the pressure for modernization will fall on both economic and political sectors. As the failed Soviet Union showed, economic progress without political change will not work. The upside is modernizing society and raising standards of living. The downside is also considerable.

As a result of these and other factors, globalization today is a relentless and mainly inexorable force. In a general sense, globalization will have profound effects on virtually every state and every society. But the precise effects will be uneven, uncertain in impact, and difficult to predict. Concurrently, globalization is both consolidating and diffusing power *and* creating forces of both integration and disintegration. Clearly, "strategic reach" has expanded in breadth and scope. And political, economic, legal, and cultural boundaries have been blurred and bypassed by globalization.

New security challenges have been created that are "horizontal" in character and cut across several or many boundaries. These will test basic institutional structures, from the international arena to national governments and other organizations that remain structured for "vertical" solutions.

The downsides of globalization arise from the inherent tensions noted above. In particular, globalization has intensified the traditional conflict between economic modernization and political control. This condition is as old as history. But globalization has touched all points of the world.

On a trip I made in 2000 literally around the world studying globalization, the conflict between modernization and control was striking. With many examples to choose from, consider just three: Japan, China, and certain Islamic states. The political and business elite in Japan readily understands the impact of globalization. Japan's economic bubble has long since burst. To produce a sustained recovery, Japan must make fundamental changes in its value and cultural systems. The strict hierarchical societal structure fails in business. Women and the elderly can no longer be excluded from the job market. And non-Japanese workers have to be assimilated if the economy is to flourish.

None of this is secret. The test will be whether the Japanese can respond to the pressures of globalization. If Japan fails in this endeavor, the unhappy history of Japan's transformation in the 1930s is a legacy that should not be entirely forgotten.

China faces similar challenges. Modernization is the first priority along with maintaining political "stability," polite jargon for keeping party control. China's leadership clearly recognizes the challenge. In Islamic states such as Saudi Arabia and Egypt, the clash between modernization and tradition Islamic values and culture must be resolved if future bin Ladens are not to run amok.

There is a further factor, one that Bush and Scowcroft view as the catalyst for transformation: one of the biggest strategic bangs in history.

## The Big Strategic Bang

Scientists believe the universe formed billions of years ago after a "big bang" created matter and the precursor elements that would become galaxies and solar systems. On December 25th, 1991, a strategic big bang took place in Moscow. The upshot was to create a new strategic universe in the detritus of the implosion that ended the Soviet Union. Over seventy years of revolutionary struggle between communism and capitalism and nearly fifty years of Cold War evaporated. Bush and Scowcroft were, of course, correct: the world had been transformed. The difficulty was that the consequences of that transformation had not been worked out. They remain a work in progress.

Not literally overnight but soon thereafter, the strategic consequences of the demise of the Soviet Union began manifesting themselves. The Cold War divisions between East and West and communism and capitalism disappeared. However, the social and political contradictions that had made the different ideologies attractive remained. Fundamental questions over how to modernize economies in the context of existing social systems were not dispelled by the fragmentation of the USSR. In tandem with this big bang, has been the power of globalization. It is this combination that is at the root of the transformations occurring.

## New World, Old Choices

For the United States, two administrations debated how to translate this new world order into practical policies. The chronic clashes between idealism and pragmatism and engagement and entanglement were no less fierce than when a genuine clear and present danger existed. The schizophrenic quality of these long-standing tensions proved no easier to deal with than before.

In a world where conflicts had become regional, such as India and Pakistan and Palestine and Israel, the absence of the prior global rivalry of the two superpowers limited leverage. Regional conflicts no longer were shaded in the context of the Cold War. For the

United States, the end of the Cold War sharpened the tensions between value and pragmatically-driven policies.

The United States could engage on the basis of policy driven exclusively by its principles and values. Human rights and democratic virtues dominated these considerations. Hence, with China, for example, such a policy would be intolerant of existing abuses and less concerned with promoting internal stability as the prerequisite for economic growth. Similarly, in the Gulf region, the defense of Saudi Arabia and other states would be conducted in the context of liberalizing and modernizing by those governments.

Pragmatism leads to other choices. Regarding China, in this view, the best means to promote democracy is through fostering an open market. Capitalism requires openness and freedom. Ultimately, the political system will accommodate itself to these characteristics and resemble them. A similar case can be made for the Gulf and other regions.

The crucial ingredient is leverage. The Clinton administration ballyhooed the value of being the "world's sole remaining superpower." It is difficult to determine what was derived from that condition and the rhetoric. Certainly senior administration officials could apply pressure and suasion to cajole or coerce states to take certain actions or, in more cases, to employ restraint. Promises and threats of economic succor or retaliation as well as other diplomatic tools were used. However, these tended to be more powerful when applied in the shadow of the Russian Bear. As Aristotle said, the main reasons for war are honor, greed, and fear. The same can be said of diplomacy.

The post–Cold War world had been variously described as "multipolar," "north versus south," "haves versus have nots." From an American perspective, each of these snapshots captures a facet. However, the mosaic is lacking. There is a broader strategic appreciation of the twenty-first century and its significance for keeping the United States safe. Much of the language has been descriptive, not analytic. There are analytical compass points. These are derived from the collision and collaboration of globalization and the strategic big bang. There are of course other causal factors that for ease of discourse are included under the broader headings.

## What Is Different Today

First and foremost, the physical survival of the United States is not at stake, the single biggest strategic difference of the past seven decades. Even with the biological and terrorist attacks of September 11th to underscore the proximity of danger, the nation will survive. Should a dreaded "rogue" state hurl a nuclear missile against an American target, the damage would be unprecedented. Still, the nation would survive. To be sure, panic or hysteria, such as the Great Red Scares of the 1920s and 1950s, will return in different form. There already has been concern over the "racial profiling" of Arab and Semitic-looking males in U.S. security checks after September 11th. Civil liberties may be infringed. However, the nation will not perish under multiple thermonuclear clouds and explosions.

Second, the political debate over ideology has been resolved. Fascism and communism presented ideological challenges to the value system and viability of democratic capitalism. Fascism is gone. Communism remains only in North Korea, Cuba, and China. There is no ideological challenge—quite the opposite. And China's "capitalism with a Chinese face" has moved to a market economy. Signs of democracy are improving. Local elections are predicted to spread to other political quarters.

Samuel Huntington, a distinguished Harvard political scientist, has predicted "a clash of civilizations" as the next ideological challenge. His argument, not universally shared, is that great cultures such as Islam will find themselves in growing competition and conflict with the West. To a degree, events have proven part of Huntington's thesis. Rather than ideology, it will be resentment and hatred, some of it from distinctions between rich and poor arising from the uneven impact of globalization, that will be the driving factors. Failure to apportion power and to empower citizens is also a significant factor in building resentment that leads to violence and terror. The unproven part of Huntington's theory relates to the next analytical reference point.

Third, in the hot and cold wars it has waged successfully, the United States relied heavily on alliances. NATO is the best example. NATO was and is a military alliance. The threat, Soviet military forces pouring west into Europe, has gone. NATO's newer *raison d'être* is to promote stability. In reality, this means serving as an insurance policy should instability or conflict reoccur and threaten Europe. Whether NATO will endure this shift from a military alliance to something different will be an important indicator of how security evolves in coming decades.

The new reasons for alliances in this transformed world are not for physical security against military attack, but to protect the security of partner states against a growing list of instabilities. Terrorism, economic default and stagnation, social injustice, pestilence, illegal drugs and crime, and the need for raising standards of living globally as perhaps the best means for keeping the peace have transitioned from idealized sentiments to practical policy aims.

Look no further than the AIDS crisis in Africa or the de facto international agreements to restrain money laundering as the best strategy for asphyxiating al Qaeda's financial breath. The basis for these agreements and alliances is mutual interest. That the United States is the most powerful partner in any of these is counterbalanced by the fact that the United States may have the greatest need. This reversal of the strategic formula of the Cold War is ironic. Need overshadows strength. This will force the United States to view these new alliances in a different light and enter them with a different attitude. Just as the United States became more sophisticated in appreciating that "free trade" could grow everyone's economy, alliances may incorporate the realization that stability can no longer be sealed off at various borders.

Fourth, globalization has transformed virtually all relationships. This applies to commerce, communications, culture, and conflict. For commerce to work well, there must be relatively unrestricted access and transparency among markets. Tariffs, barriers to entry, and protective pricing schemes harm the entire system. This was learned in the 1920s when tariffs helped collapse the economies in Europe and the United States and bring on the Great Depression. The other side of the coin is transparency. Free markets cannot work without rules and regulations that allow investors and consumers to understand what they are acquiring or buying. The collapse of the energy giant Enron was in part due to a failure to maintain sufficient transparency for management and directors to perform basic oversight.

As China joins the World Trade Organization (WTO), transparency is essential. Business law and codes, including a banking system, must be imposed, something China has never done. In this WTO environment, the term *foreign devil*, pejoratively applied two centuries ago to intruders, will take on new meaning. Lawyers descending on China in the tens of thousands triggered by the WTO and China's entry into the global economy, will be the next generation of foreign devil. And how China assimilates this intrusion into its social, economic, and political institutions will have a lot to say about China's future.

Part of globalization encompasses "instantaneous communications," often called the "CNN effect." News, flashed around the world as it happens, has a powerful effect. Governments must react after the fact and often learn of events in this manner. When Desert Storm began, Bush and Scowcroft were riveted to CNN. The reports of Peter Arnett and Bernard Shaw from the rooftops of Baghdad's hotels were essential intelligence indicators that the first raids started on time and were hitting their targets. The fact is that news is reported from regions in many cases well before government is alerted. Qatar's al Jazeera TV showing tapes of bin Laden is no longer a phenomenon. This is a result of globalization.

Globalization, along with the big bang, has redefined conflict. There are never exact historical parallels. However, the period in Europe following the Concert of Vienna in 1815 and ending in 1914 may be suggestive. Wars were still fought on the continent and in remote spots.

On the continent, the short Franco-Prussian War of 1870 interrupted a relative peace. The Americans had fought the bloodiest war in their history, the War Between the States from 1861 to 1865. Generally, conflict was found abroad where the industrial states chose to use arms.

The British were engaged in India, Africa, and China. The British and the Russians, were bloodied in the "great game" fought in Afghanistan and in the Crimean War. By century's end, the British had mounted the last cavalry charge in its history, at the Battle of Omdurman against the Mahdi in the Sudan (in retribution for the Mahdi's taking of Khartoum and killing the British Commanding General, "Chinese" Gordon, and the opportunity for Young Winston Churchill to make a name); embarked on a losing Boer War in South Africa; and joined or started the naval arms race with Wilhelmine Germany.

In the twenty-first century, there is still a chance of major war. India and Pakistan, Israel and her neighbors, and the two Koreas are flash points. The issue of Iraq looms. Where the United States takes the "war against terrorism," if it does move beyond Afghanistan, will influence the chance for war. However, it seems that as in the nineteenth century, violence rather than organized war between industrial states is the more likely prospect. This type of violence may prove more complicated. It entails elements of terrorism and criminality. The linkage with mass-destruction weapons raises its danger.

In this environment, nuclear forces and the doctrine of deterrence to prevent global war are less relevant. Thus far, India and Pakistan (along with China) have publicly promised not to use nuclear weapons first. Afghanistan has certainly cast doubt on the need for maintaining large numbers of conventional forces of the type that served well in the Cold War. If there are growth industries in the security business, it is in the intelligence, counterterror, and law-enforcement forces that are needed to deal with the dangers encountered in Afghanistan and in bringing the al Qaeda to justice.

Last are the cultural divides produced by globalization. As noted, Coca Cola, American movies and television, and the latest rock or hip-hop stars do not find favor everywhere. In traditional societies, whether Islamic or Asian, strong backlashes are common. The

National Security Strategy Commission captured these reactions in its report.

## Three Deficits

In this world transformed by a strategic big bang and globalization, the United States suffers from three chronic deficits. These are products of its political system, its culture, and its heritage. As the reader may know (or will read ahead in Chapter 4), a system of divided government requires consensus or a crisis to take major action.

Pearl Harbor and the Cold War provided purpose. But before September 11th, the United States was short on any purpose for rallying the nation. It remains to be seen how long the effects of September 11th will persist and how unilateralist (read isolationist) or multilateralist (read interventionist) the nation will become. These characteristics reflect a traditional deficit in purpose.

Second, there is deficit in organization for national security. The current structure remains very much a legacy of the Cold War. The National Security Act is still the organizing legal basis. That act put emphasis on defense, diplomacy, intelligence, and a strong economy as the best means of deterring and countering the threat from Soviet Russia. The threat has changed dramatically.

September 11th reinforced this simple truth. Security today is as much about homeland defense law enforcement and antiterrorism as it is about needing a strong military and diplomatic corps. Protection of a broader panoply of national goods, whether commercial aircraft or computer networks, is rightly receiving attention.

The establishment of the Office of Homeland Security and the pending reorganization of the Justice Department and intelligence agencies are clear signs of this organizational deficit. The question remains whether any reorganization can be made to work to solve the problems at hand.

The third deficit—in people—is the most serious. Attracting and retaining the nation's best for government service has been difficult. Job satisfaction, compensation, and prestige have been lacking. The appointment process has become exquisitely painful. The crucial reason for serving—-service to the country—has not been made appealing. As a result, before September 11th, manning the govern-ment from civil service employees to military and law-enforcement officers has been a challenge.

Before Colin Powell became secretary of state, for the first time in its history, the Foreign Service had been unable to fill its quotas for entry-level officers. Powell closed that deficit as much through increases to recruiting budgets and the publishing of posters with the general pointing a finger saying "I want you!" as through his cha-risma and record. However, people, the most crucial part of any organization, must be persuaded to serve if the nation is to be kept safe. This, along with the other two deficits, must be addressed.

## Keeping the Nation Safe

If turmoil and terror are adequate reflections of the dangers that lie ahead, what courses of action are open to the nation? No adminis-tration will dismiss or defer the overarching responsibility of provid-ing for the "common defense." The questions are how well or how badly the nation will be protected and whether the correct priorities are set to drive the allocation of resources. Unfortunately, General Marshall's guidance of choosing the right objectives is easier said than done, especially when the aims are likely to be ambiguous or hard to define.

Regarding "unfinished business," globalization has made the nation more vulnerable to potential disruption. In 1998, a relatively obscure "hedge" fund in Greenwich, Connecticut, had made a bad bet on interest rates and investments in Russia. Hedge funds were "unregulated," meaning that the Security and Exchange Commis-sion (SEC) and other federal agencies had no direct oversight as is the case with banks and all publicly traded companies in the United States. Suddenly, the fund was billions of dollars in debt. Investors, who had expected to make huge profits, had to dig deeply to make up the shortfalls. Overnight, the banking and monetary systems were in a state of shock. The systems could have collapsed. Because a number of large banks and investment houses intervened, a crisis was prevented.

This kind of vulnerability has always existed. The "crash" of the stock market in 1929 is a case in point. The difference today is that globalization has facilitated such relatively unknown and unseen entities to operate in ways that could cripple the larger financial system. And, given the heightened sensitivity to aircraft security, it would not be too far over the top to conceive of a future in which the potential vulnerabilities of an airplane to explosive decompression at altitude would require every passenger to board without anything on his or her person that could remotely be used to hide a bomb or weapon.

The matter of dysfunctional organization has been raised. It appears that the dysfunction is getting worse, not better. More will be said in later chapters.

The Arab-Israeli-Palestinian disputes grow fiercer and have been exacerbated by the effects of globalization. Instantaneous communication flashes news of every act of terror around the world. With Islamic populations numbering about a billion people, Israeli displays of force, regardless of justification, are not universally well received. While Israel recognizes this reality, it appears unwilling to subordinate its security to negative reactions to its use of force.

Within the Arab world and Egypt and Saudi Arabia in particular, the tensions of globalization between modernization and control have become fiercer. Bin Laden and others will continue to play on these tensions in an attempt to break them. They are real and the results will lead to greater turmoil and terror, further intensified by oil.

Meanwhile Russia, China, India, and Pakistan must cope with the impact of globalization and the tensions as well as opportunities that are created. One effect has been to complicate the policy choices. Another has been to induce great pressures on government to respond to the growing needs of a society that clearly knows what is happening around the world. Expectations grow. Standards of living must keep up.

# ★ 4 ★

## The Paradox of Freedom

### Bills of Rights and Other Ladings

Perhaps the most profound legacy left by America's Founding Fathers was the fundamental choice between individual rights and the role of government. The former were to be assured over the latter. As a principal safeguard for individual rights, government was purposely made inefficient. It was not by accident, for example, that in 2001 Congress and the White House could not agree on a national economic stimulus package after September 11th. Chapter 5 examines the organizational and practical national security consequences in detail.

The Constitution granted certain guarantees of freedom in writing to citizens in the Bill of Rights. Only in times of national emergency did government have the authority to override these rights. As a result, the fabric and texture of American society were grounded in the freedom of the individual. In the old days, that applied only to white, property-owning males. Today, barriers of gender and race have been largely breached.

Pursuit of life, liberty, and happiness is taken very seriously. As a result, the United States has become perhaps the most open society in the world. Access is taken for granted. And the Bill of Rights has even been extended to non-American citizens who are tried in our courts. This was one reason for establishing so-called military tribunals for trying the perpetrators of September 11th. An accused non-American should not automatically be extended the full rights of citizenship, particularly if the crime was as heinous as conspiring to kill some three thousand individuals.

Despite the occasional abutment of cultural aberrations such as "political correctness" on the workings of the process, a free, open society places fewer restrictions on its citizens than any other form of government. Of course, today, American airports are patrolled by armed National Guardsmen. Combat air patrol fly over the nation's skies to shoot down any aircraft that might have been hijacked and headed toward a lucrative target. However, beyond the skies, the United States possesses a treasure trove of vulnerabilities. Many can be protected or guarded, such as nuclear power plants. Others, such as buildings and monuments, can be made safer by guards and security checks at entrance points. But, unless the United States is turned into a police state, to paraphrase Abraham Lincoln, "you can't protect all of the people all of the time." And the more safeguards, the more restrictions on individual rights are imposed.

Whether bin Laden and his colleagues were aware of this legacy or not, in many ways, this is the fundamental danger posed by extremism and terrorism. In utilizing terror and violence to drive the United States back to its own borders, real damage is done not only to those innocents who are ruthlessly killed. The backlash and overreactions that can trample democracy, if allowed to do so, exact far worse penalties.

No matter how cynical or corrupt any single politician in power may be, virtually no American official in an important government post remotely wishes to fall prey to these excesses. However, the history of this nation illustrates that this has not always been the case. Vulnerabilities are not only physical. Good intentions are derailed by arrogance, power, and simple error.

The frightening question is not whether these inherent systemic and political vulnerabilities, with malice aforethought or not, will be exploited by extremists. They will. The issue is what can be done to

protect the nation's full spectrum of political and physical vulnerabilities from harm.

For those who dismiss this observation, *Six Nightmares* by
former Clinton National Security Adviser Anthony Lake is good
reading. Lake's sixth nightmare is what, in his view, has happened
to governance in Washington, D.C., and what he calls the reemer-
gence of the politics of "personal destruction." Clearly, Lake was
badly bruised by the bitter fight over his nomination to be Director of Central Intelligence in 1997, which forced his withdrawal.
However, Lake was not the only victim. The political culture had
become septic regardless of party affiliation. The confirmation
hearings for Republicans Robert Bork and Clarence Thomas for
the Supreme Court demonstrated that. The danger, according to
Lake, is failure of political culture. He concludes: "*The greatest
nightmare of all could be the further erosion of the democratic
compact* that had brought us through greater crises in our past
that we now face" [emphasis added].

## Siren Calls

Osama bin Laden has declared holy war on the United States. The
basis for this declaration is a bizarre mélange of radicalism, resentment, and revenge distorted by bin Laden's semi-psychotic interpretation of Islam. The logic is twisted. Islam is not a violent and
revolutionary faith anymore than Christianity and Judaism are. But
any religion can have zealots and extremists. By perverting Islam to
idealize martyrdom and with over a billion Muslims in the world
to proselytize, bin Laden's siren call has found a few ears. The
bin Laden message for a "crusade" against the United States goes
like this.

Because of its power and culture, the United States is racist and
repressive. Because of its continuing presence in Saudi Arabia, the
United States has contaminated Islam and desecrated three of its
most holy religious shrines. Because of its unyielding support for
Israel, its hostility to Palestinian rights, and its military strikes

against Arab Muslims, not only Iraq, the United States is an enemy to the Islamic faith.

The only course of action, according to the bin Laden mantra (a deliberately mixed metaphor), is to drive the United States out of the Islamic world. To that end, bin Laden has issued a number of *fatwas* or holy writs authorizing a *jihad* (a holy struggle) against America and Americans. The fact that bin Laden lacked the religious training and therefore the legitimacy to make these declarations has received little attention. He has other targets as well. His native Saudi Arabia and its ruling family are in his cross-hairs. Pakistan, a Muslim state, has a strong radical element and a military government that must balance this radicalism with its own hold on power. Its Inter-agency Services Intelligence directorate (ISI, about which much more will be said) was strongly in support of Afghanistan's Taliban. ISI has been a power unto itself.

Bin Laden's strategy for exploiting these opportunities—to create a Pan-Islamic regime extending from Saudi Arabia to Pakistan, replete with Saudi oil wealth and Pakistani nuclear weapons—will be examined in later chapters. However, his *fatwas* remain directed against the United States. What further danger he and, more probably, his formula for turmoil and terror present must be seriously assessed against the American vulnerabilities that could be exploited and the posture the United States may take in responding to this danger. Both physical damage and psychological damage are important to consider. And, it may prove that the political system and political culture will become the ultimate targets for these extremists and those who follow.

Sadly, while September 11th was a horrible surprise, there had been plenty of forewarning. On January 31st, 2001, the United States Commission on National Security Strategy/21st Century released its "Road Map for National Security." On the very first page of the executive summary, the fourteen distinguished commissioners sounded their warning about the vulnerability of the United States: "A direct attack against American citizens *on American soil* [emphasis in original] is likely over the next century. The risk is not only death and destruction but also a demoralization that could undermine U.S.

global leadership. In the face of this threat, our nation has *no coherent or integrated governmental structures* [emphasis added]."

One year earlier, the National Commission on the Advancement of Federal Law Enforcement reported that "global crime, cybercrime and terrorism in new and evermore dangerous forms will threaten the safety of Americans and the security of the United States in the next century. The Nation should move now on an urgent basis to prepare to detect these criminal activities at the source, counter them in all appropriate ways, and protect Americans to every extent possible."

Two years earlier, on October 13th, 1997, the chairman of the President's Commission on Critical Infrastructure Protection, retired Air Force General Robert T. Marsh, forwarded the commission's final report to Bill Clinton. His cover letter stated: "We did find widespread capability to exploit infrastructure vulnerabilities. The capability to do harm—particularly through information networks—is real; it is growing at an alarming rate; and we have little defense against it."

In addition to these formal commissions, there was a plethora of congressional hearings on the matter of U.S. vulnerability to terrorist attack and disruption. The "think tank" industry in Washington had unleashed barrage after barrage of warning. Clinton's Secretary of Defense, William S. Cohen, made an extraordinary appearance on television's Sunday morning talk shows. With him was a five-pound bag of sugar. Cohen told the viewers that if that innocuous bag had been filled with anthrax spores and properly dispersed, millions of Americans could potentially have been infected. The mortality rate was estimated to exceed 90 percent. Have a happy Sunday morning! Cohen published an op-ed piece with the same message in the Washington *Post*.

In the summer of 2001, the Washington, D.C.–based Center for Strategic and International Studies—in collaboration with other think tanks—ran a "war game" called Dark Winter. The scenario was a biological attack against the United States with the smallpox virus. After a few days of war game and an estimated 300,000 infected Americans, the exercise abruptly ended. The tension among the players was so great that the game had become dysfunctional.

With all of these warnings, September 11th came as a complete surprise. As a tactic, a surprise attack that starts a war invariably works, if only initially. From Operation Barbarossa, Hitler's invasion of the Soviet Union launched on June 22nd, 1941, to Pearl Harbor to the June 1967 and October 1973 Arab-Israeli Wars, surprise worked. Only in the June 1967 war did the attacker win; Germany, Japan, and the Arab coalition all were subsequently beaten. However, in the case of societal vulnerabilities, there is no question that the United States must be better prepared.

But has the United States grown so arrogant or complacent that it is unwilling to address the dangers of this transformed world with due gravitas? Or does its political system make it virtually impossible to anticipate these forms of catastrophe and take the necessary steps in advance, especially those needing substantial expenditure of political and fiscal capital? What are the nation's vulnerabilities that should concentrate the greatest concern and focus preventive priorities? Or is the extent of this vulnerability now so widespread that aside from basic precautions, the nation has no recourse except to await whatever fate has in store for the United States? Why were all of these warnings ignored, especially that of a serving secretary of defense who, after all, proved accurate in forecasting an anthrax attack that would occur less than two years later?

## The First Piece of Unfinished Business

What makes September 11th most frightening is that the disaster exploited the most fundamental strength of the United States: the openness of its society. This is the intractable contradiction. An open society is inherently vulnerable. Bin Laden and al Qaeda made this vulnerability real. He turned the strength of America against itself.

A democratic society such as the United States has no option. A democracy with long-established freedoms, basic inalienable rights for its citizens guaranteed by a constitution and laws of the land, and a free-market economy cannot operate in the atmosphere of a closed society for long. The inherent contradiction is clear. Success in an open society creates societal vulnerabilities, the other side of the coin to what happened in the Soviet Union.

The effects of globalization and the knowledge revolution as both pertain to information have inadvertently conspired to open American society to even more damaging forms of attack. But so too has the basic infrastructure on which American society depends become more vulnerable.

The airlines are an essential component of the transportation industries. Air travel was taken for granted. Airlines also affect many businesses, both directly and indirectly. After the rash of hijackings in the 1970s, airline security was enhanced. It was never, however, a painful inconvenience. The travel, entertainment, and transportation industries never suffered great economic hardship in mounting basic measures against hijackings.

Nineteen men armed with "box-cutters" who then hijacked four airliners have essentially put an end to this openness, certainly in the skies, and have probably done more damage to the travel and transportation industries than all the past recessions and depressions taken together. The negative effects on the Boeing Company, the sole American manufacturer of commercial airliners, have already been dramatic. Nearly half the orders for new aircraft were cancelled or delayed. And every large U.S. airline save one (South West) lost huge amounts of money in 2001 because of September 11th.

Few Americans will board an aircraft or open a letter for some time without thinking "what if?" Long check-in lines for security, requirements to remain seated for flights of relatively short duration, and plastic knives and bottles with meals are indicative of the more trivial impositions Americans must endure. Suppose similar constraints were imposed on all means of transportation and other forms of economic intercourse previously taken for granted—what effect might that have?

In the face of these events, neither George W. Bush nor anyone in Congress has made much of a dent in changing the "tone" in Washington. Talk about bipartisanship proved to be largely talk. As we will see, government divided by party ideology and balance of power may be incapable of sustained consensus even during crisis. And as for acting with greater "humility," with the war against terrorism in high gear, a humbler America is unlikely to register for some time to come.

In order to understand the full impact of this first piece of unfinished business, the reasons that have led to deferral or dismissal of each of the responsible warnings of attack against U.S. vulnerabilities are as important as the vulnerabilities themselves. There are characteristics of this system of government and its office holders that are neither unique nor aberrant. Arrogance (or complacency) is by no means the only symptom. But it is a good starting point. And there is no shortage of illustrations that provide insight and warning about the future.

The extraordinary wealth and inherent political stability within the United States certainly bred a sense of complacency. This sentiment was particularly relevant to the 1930s. "It can't or won't happen here" was part of the isolationist ethic. Appeasement, to prevent the horror of another world war, was the least unfavorable policy. Neville Chamberlain with his tightly rolled black umbrella returning to London from Munich in 1938 with "peace for our time" is a reminder of the perils of this course of action.

The Great Depression, Franklin Roosevelt's New Deal, and World War II changed the nation's character. Prior to the 1930s, federal government was meant to be and was kept small. A sign of the times was the White House. Through much of the war, the White House was directly accessible from Pennsylvania Avenue. Anyone could walk or motor up the driveway and park outside the northern entrance and under the portico to the White House. A single (unarmed) butler stood between a potential assassin and the president.

The New Deal increased the size and reach of federal government. Take one example: social security. With social security came the first of many new bureaucracies and government agencies to help the nation recover from economic depression.

World War II completed the transformation to big government. Government could no longer be part time and laissez faire. Winning the war was a full-time effort. Mobilization of the nation's resources and the creation of a defense-industrial base were essential for success. Hence, by 1945, for both domestic and national security reasons, the Founding Fathers' notion of limited government had been rendered obsolete. The Cold War would complete the process of making politics big business.

During that period, the United States developed a new self-confidence on the world stage. One of the recurring dilemmas prevalent throughout history has been the tendency for self-confidence to mature into arrogance. There is no known antidote, as Lord Acton succinctly observed: "Power tends to corrupt and absolute power corrupts absolutely."

The Vietnam War was, in many ways, a September 11th that lasted more than a decade. Fifty-eight thousand Americans died; at least a million Vietnamese also lost their lives. The experience was so searing and, in a strange way, caused by pieces of unfinished business that lingered from the Second World War that it, along with some of those pieces, provides important insights.

By the time the Kennedy adminstration came to town, arrogance was becoming a more permanent fixture of the political landscape. The Kennedy administration brought to power *The Best and the Brightest*, used by David Halberstam as a title for a book that chronicled America's Vietnam experience. Kennedy and his cabinet had all served in World War II in one capacity or another. They had the confidence of what would be called the "greatest generation." The war was fought against an evil totalitarian enemy. The United States had dusted itself off after the shock of Pearl Harbor. It had won the war. It also won the peace. The same effort was required in the Cold War against an equally dangerous adversary, now armed with thermonuclear weapons.

The test was to temper this idealism with reality. The best and brightest were highly talented and successful in their prior lives. Those qualities did not automatically translate into success in government, even though the label "Camelot" was affixed to the new adminstration. Camelot did, however inadvertently, convey the deviation between image and reality.

Kennedy was portrayed as the heroic skipper of a PT-109. He was injured when his boat was cut in two by a Japanese destroyer in the fog. Normally, skippers who collide with other ships get relieved. Not so with Kennedy. He received the Navy Marine Corps Medal, the service's highest noncombat award for heroism, for helping to rescue his surviving crew.

Vice-President Lyndon Johnson also served in the Navy. He received the Silver Star, the nation's third highest award for valor. Johnson would occasionally exaggerate his heroism, once claiming he was responsible for helping to shoot down twenty-two Japanese Zeroes. His citation credited him with extraordinary bravery as an observer in an aerial reconnaissance flight against Japanese forces in the Pacific. No one else in the aircraft crew was so decorated on that flight.

The other key national security officials had served largely in staff positions: Secretary of State Dean Rusk was an Army lieutenant colonel in the War Department; Secretary of Defense Robert McNamara was an Army Air Corps "whiz kid" working statistical analysis for Charles "Tex" Thornton, who would go on to establish Textron one of the nation's leading corporations; and National Security Advisor McGeorge Bundy, who admittedly had to cheat on an eye exam in order to join the Army, became an aide to a Navy admiral.

Two who had real wartime experience were Secretary of Agriculture Orville Freeman, a highly decorated marine who lost part of his jaw in an amphibious landing in the Pacific, and Secretary of Labor Arthur Goldberg, an OSS officer who help to organize and run clandestine guerrilla operations. Kennedy, however, knew nothing of their experience. And neither was part of the security team.

Kennedy had run for office alleging that a "missile gap" put the United States far beyond the Soviets in this measure of military power. Only in America could President and former general of the Army Dwight D. Eisenhower, the officer who defeated Hitler's Wermacht in Europe, be criticized for being "soft" on communism and running the military down. Candidate and Vice-President Richard Nixon lost what had been one of the closest elections in history. In fact, Nixon could have challenged the election due to voting "irregularities" in Cook County, Illinois, and in West Virginia. Nixon took the high ground and conceded gracefully. Eight years later he would win the Oval Office, in part on the promise to end the Vietnam War.

The Kennedy administration came into office sounding tough and looking regal. Kennedy's inaugural address soared with great rhetoric written by Ted Sorensen. "Ask not what your country can do for you but rather what you can do for your country," and the commitment to "pay any price and bear any burden" to preserve freedom attained immediate acclaim. With former Ford Motor Company president Robert McNamara at Defense, Dean Rusk at State, and McGeorge Bundy as the national security adviser, the team was adulated in the press. In reality, it had very little foreign policy experience.

The first foreign policy agenda item was the CIA plan for an invasion of Cuba. Cuban exiles and freedom fighters were being trained for a landing at the Bay of Pigs. The assumption was that once the anti-Castro force got ashore, Cubans by the thousands would flock to overthrow Fidel Castro. Eisenhower had grave reservations. However, he never shared them with Kennedy. After considerable and heated debate, Kennedy approved the assault for April 1961. It was a disaster. Air support had been promised by the United States. It was never delivered. The Cuban freedom fighters were killed or captured. The only good news was that no American forces took part.

After Kennedy assembled his cabinet to review the debacle, he was approached by the Secretary of Agriculture, Orville Freeman. Freeman asked Kennedy why he had not consulted him before the invasion. Kennedy was puzzled. Freeman, pointing to his jaw, asked, "Where do you think I got this?" Freeman was a veteran of amphibious assaults and, with Arthur Goldberg, had more real combat experience than anyone else in the cabinet.

The Kennedy team requested and received from Congress three defense supplementals, that is, additional spending. The strategic nuclear program was accelerated. The Kennedy administration had embarked on a major defense buildup. The Berlin crisis later that spring was Soviet leader Nikita Khrushchev's way of testing the new president. However, the administration was going to close the missile gap whether or not it was real and it was going to confront the Soviet Union ideologically in the battle for the hearts and minds of millions of people in the Third World.

The facts were otherwise. The CIA knew that Soviet First Secretary Nikita S. Khrushchev had literally forced a major series of defense reductions on the military and political leadership. During Eisenhower's eight years in office, the United States had adopted a strategy of massive retaliation. If there were to be a war, it would be nuclear. The United States had clear if not overwhelming superiority. Consequently, the Soviet Union would be deterred from any action approaching war. Eisenhower knew it. And, after seeing the changes unfold in the United States, by 1959, Khrushchev became a believer in mutual deterrence too. His problem would be convincing his Soviet colleagues of the benefits.

Khrushchev regarded Ike as shrewd, and respected his wartime record. The man who led the forces to victory in Europe did not see a clash with the Soviet Union as likely. It was avoidable. Military force could be put to other uses. Large expensive conventional forces were less important. They could be reduced. Ike led. Khrushchev followed.

The debate inside the Soviet Union was furious and lasted from 1959 to 1961. A disgruntled Soviet military intelligence officer, Colonel Oleg Penkovsky, kept the West informed about the entire debate. He managed to photograph copies of *Voenny My'sl* (Military Thought), a monthly publication of the Soviet general staff. The magazine was highly classified and published articles that spelled out the terms of the debate. Penkovsky passed the material to MI-6 through Greville Wynne, an English journalist in Moscow acting for MI-6. Britain passed the material to Langley, the CIA headquarters. There were other corroborating pieces of evidence.

The Penkovsky Papers ultimately had little impact. Inside the CIA, James Jesus Angleton, the agency's counterintelligence chief, believed there was a Soviet "mole" lurking within the agency. With good cause, he suspected that MI-6 had been penetrated too. The subsequent defection of Kim Philby and other British double agents in the fall of 1962 proved Angleton's suspicions. However, in that light, the Penkovsky materials were viewed as disinformation.

His plans derailed by Kennedy's military buildup and intent to confront the Soviet Union, Khrushchev desperately sought strategic leverage. The United States still maintained nuclear missiles in Turkey, on the Soviet border. Why not reverse the situation? After the Bay of Pigs, Castro was rightly worried about American efforts to dislodge and to assassinate him. Cuba would be a strategic island for shorter-range Soviet missiles. With these in place, the pressure for longer-range intercontinental ballistic missiles would be dispelled, or so Khrushchev thought. It would not have amused him to learn that Kennedy had ordered the Jupiter missiles removed from Turkey for precisely those reasons. To the president's chagrin, the order was ignored.

In October 1962, the United States had gathered indisputable proof of Soviet missile bases being constructed in Cuba. Missiles were en route via Soviet merchant ships. Within days, Khrushchev would have nuclear weapons only a few minutes of flying time away from the east coast of the United States. To Kennedy, this was an intolerable situation.

The history of the Cuban Missile Crisis has been well recorded. A movie called *Thirteen Days* released in 2001 glorified the crisis and distorted the record as Hollywood tends to do. However, it captured the sense of crisis and the realization that World War III was indeed a possibility. In the end, Khrushchev backed down. Russia would not base offensive missiles in Cuba.

In return, Khrushchev received the promise that the United States would not support or launch another invasion against Cuba. Unfortunately, Khrushchev's colleagues in the Presidium and the Central Committee were not impressed. Two years later, Khrushchev would be removed by a political coup. The new leadership under Leonid Brezhnev would be more conservative and less prone to such "hair-brained schemes" as Cuba. Russia would embark on a major arms expansion. The Cold War would get hotter and more expensive.

In later years, I had the opportunity to discuss Penkovsky and the early decisions of the Kennedy administration at length separately with McNamara and Bundy. Both reacted similarly. The administration came in promising a stronger defense. It made no difference whether Penkovsky was right or wrong. Both McNamara and Bundy said that the administration had made up its mind. It would proceed with an arms buildup. This type of attitude would come to dominate thinking about Vietnam.

Kennedy of course was killed in Dallas, Texas, on November 22nd, 1963. It is unknowable what would have happened in Vietnam if Kennedy had lived. His advocates asserted that the United States would never have been trapped in that "quagmire." Yet, after the Bay of Pigs, Berlin, and Cuban Missile crises, it is difficult to see what practical steps could have been taken to reverse the hardening of the Cold War. Kennedy was still prepared to "pay any price and bear any burden." The ideological struggle had shifted to Vietnam, where nearly seventeen thousand U.S. troops were serving as 1963 ended. Seventy had already been killed.

The new president committed himself to carry out Kennedy's programs for the remainder of the first term. Regarding Vietnam, in early 1964, he had his staff draft legislation for congressional support for a wider war. Mindful of the French experience and ignominious defeat and withdrawal after the fall of its stronghold at Dienbienphu in 1954, Johnson believed that those "little Asian boys were no match for Americans." When the Tonkin Gulf incidents occurred in early August 1964, Lyndon Johnson saw them as the opportunity for obtaining the authority to widen and win the war. He would not wait to corroborate the facts. His mind was made up.

On August 2, 1964, the destroyer USS *Maddox* was cruising in international waters off the North Vietnamese coast. She reported being attacked by three North Vietnamese PT boats and claimed to have attacked one of the vessels. Two days later, the destroyer USS *C. Turner Joy*, as consort, and the *Maddox* reported a second attack. Johnson had his justification. On August 7th, Johnson sent the Tonkin Gulf Resolution to Congress. It was a de facto declaration of war. It passed the same day. Only two senators, Wayne Morse of Oregon and Ernest Gruening of Alaska, voted against the resolution.

Clausewitz, that greatest of all military analysts, cautioned against the foolishness of starting a war without an idea of how it would end. Johnson now had his war. However, a more careful review of the evidence would have made congressional approval more difficult. There had indeed been an attack on the first evening. A local commander had mistaken *Maddox* as part of a clandestine raid made by the South Vietnamese naval units against the north. The raid had been part of Operation 34A, codenamed "Falling Rain," run by the CIA. Operation 34A was designed to raid the north, carrying the war to their homes and villages to show there would be no sanctuary.

There had been no second attack. *Maddox* and *Joy* were firing at imaginary targets. But the United States was in the war. Johnson ordered retaliatory air strikes and joked that he had just cut Ho Chi Minh's "pecker off." He was not quite right. The war would go on for eleven more years. Fifty-eight thousand Americans would have their names engraved on the memorial symbolically built below street level adjacent to the Lincoln Memorial in Washington.

Without stretching the similarities too far, Johnson was struggling in Vietnam with much unfinished business from World War II. The North Vietnamese brilliantly manipulated the openness of U.S. society. Ho Chi Minh and General Vo Nugyen Giap realized that the North could never stand up to American firepower. Hence, the strategy was to wear down by attrition the Americans in Vietnam and more importantly popular support at home. The North would win by not losing. The longer the war went on, the greater the discontent in the United States.

The North was not infallible. Believing that a conventional victory was possible, the Tet Offensive of January 1968 was launched. Viet Cong and North Vietnamese main force troops attacked throughout the south. Saigon was imperiled. Hue fell and had to be retaken at great cost.

The U.S. Military Command in Saigon was taken by surprise. Quickly, U.S. forces recovered and took the offensive. Tens of thousands of North Vietnamese and Viet Cong were killed. The offensive became a rout. But the American public was buying none of it and seeing much of it on television. In the spring, Johnson told the nation he would not seek another term. He had been broken by the war.

The United States had not been well organized to fight the war either. McNamara tried commanding the war from the Pentagon. Johnson literally redirected air strikes while they were en route to targets. Generals William Westmoreland and later Creighton Abrams commanded U.S. forces in the country from Saigon. Admiral John S. McCain commanded U.S. naval forces operating off the North Vietnamese coast.

There were four different ground wars in the South, none coordinated with the others. The Marines were assigned much of what was called I Corps by the Vietnamese, that stretched from the Demilitarized Zone dividing the two countries to Chu Lai in the south. The Army meanwhile had much of the rest of the country as its tactical area of responsibility. In the Delta, a third war was fought—a combined riverine task force of Army ground troops and Navy sailors. And the CIA was waging a fourth, secret ground war—the Phoenix program, which targeted suspected Viet Cong and North Vietnamese agents for termination with extreme prejudice, the code words for assassination. An estimated fifty thousand Vietnamese were killed by Phoenix. The CIA also operated in nearby Cambodia and Laos, part of the secret war.

There were five air wars. The Navy and the Air Force had separately assigned target areas in the North and conducted air operations independently. The Navy and Air Force also operated independently in the South. The Marines had their own air forces. The lack of interoperability was manifest. Air Force and Navy units had different radios (uhf and vhf) and could not communicate. There was virtually no coordinated planning.

The chief rationale for waging the war in Vietnam was to stem the spread of communism. This was the unhappy legacy from World War II. Americans still bridled at "losing" China to the communists in 1949. The vile senator Joe McCarthy and his anticommunist crusade had overly sensitized Americans to the "dangers." Soviet Russia

and China were erroneously viewed as united communist allies acting to subvert the rest of the world.

The "domino theory" prevailed. If Vietnam fell to communism,
so would Southeast Asia. Australia, Japan, and the rest of Asia could
topple like dominoes in a row. The perception of a monolithic Soviet
and Chinese communist threat had a firm hold on Washington. That
perception proved wildly wrong. It would take President Richard
Nixon (and an opening to China) six years to end U.S. presence in
Vietnam. And Nixon would be gone in 1975, resigning to escape
impeachment over the Watergate scandal.

Vietnam has passed into history. Six administrations have
labored to avoid the mistakes and misperceptions that created that
quagmire. Perhaps the Kennedy/Johnson years will prove the anom-
alies. However, there are inherent reasons why arrogance may be
impossible to limit despite the promises of every administration not
to repeat the mistakes of the past. And if arrogance is restrained,
complacency still is a lurking danger.

## Arrogance and Naiveté

Winning the nomination and then the presidential election is heady
stuff. Incoming presidents have every reason to believe that electoral
success legitimizes the programs and policies that were promised or
inferred. Outside help need not apply. In many cases, loyalty during
the campaign led to important positions in the administration. This
was necessary to ensure that the agencies of government, manned by
civil servants not necessarily beholden to the new team, would follow orders.

Especially for candidates will little experience in Washington, the
power of the presidency, the pomp and circumstance of the White
House, and the awesome responsibilities of the job have to seem
overwhelming. Literally overnight, the incumbent inherits a huge
bureaucracy to look after every need from hundreds of Secret Service
men and women sworn to protect the first family with their lives to
having Air Force One, the most famous airplane in the world, at his
disposal.

As the leader of the "free world," the new president instantly becomes the most important politician on earth in terms of dispensing power, influence, and favor. The famous "football," that is, the nuclear release codes, is kept only paces away from the president at all times, reminding him of his responsibilities. Invariably, the president is the most socially attractive guest at any function, the first name on any "A" list. He and his family are subjected to continuous and total media scrutiny in which every word uttered is recorded. It would be unreasonable to believe that any individual would be unaffected by these realities and trappings of power.

With few exceptions, new administrations turn out to be very inexperienced in the ways of Washington. This was true with Carter, Reagan, and Clinton. Bush senior had eight years as understudy. And while Bush junior picked a very capable team, each of them had been out of power for a minimum of seven years. Things change considerably in far less time.

At the same time, the process for selecting and confirming government officials becomes more drawn out. Bush suffered not only these delays, but the six weeks it took to determine the winner of the election—an inexcusable although unavoidable situation. No matter how well intentioned, the combination of power, success, and process has therefore contributed to a sense of arrogance in viewing the world. In this environment, fact and reality too easily are trumped by ideology or political expediency. And when they are not, as in the case of Bush 41, reelection is not automatic.

Susceptibility to arrogance is not limited to the White House. Government bureaucracies both in the executive and in Congress share this penchant. It is trite to describe the congressional staffer who assumes the power of his principal. However, while Congress passes laws, members do not write them. That is up to the staffs. As a result, in virtually every piece of spending legislation, amendments and "earmarks" are inserted after the vote. This de facto legislating clearly bestows power. With power there is the risk of arrogance.

Bureaucracies also have the responsibility for carrying out their duties. For most of them and those who serve in them, they intend to do their level best. Since Washington is built on a double adversarial system—the chronic battle between and among agencies and offices over power, turf, and dollars and the presence in government of many attorneys raised in a system of adversarial jurisprudence— toughness and intransigence go hand in hand. This too leads to arrogance. No one who believes he is working responsibly wants to be told how to conduct his job. Outside criticism is invariably unwelcome, whether justified or not.

Examples are the stuff of thousands of books. In 1995, a colleague and I put together a small group of retired admirals and generals for the purpose of taking the lessons of Desert Storm and the revolution in military affairs (or RMA as it is called) to produce an alternative strategic concept for the United States. Among the senior retired military were veterans of Desert Storm: Admiral L. A. (Bud) Edney (who commanded the Atlantic Command and NATO Atlantic forces); General Fred Franks (who led VII Corps); General Chuck Horner (who commanded the air war); Admiral Jonathan Howe (who commanded NATO forces in the Mediterranean and had been deputy national security adviser); General Gary Luck (who commanded XVIII Corps); General Thomas Morgan (who had been Marine Corps assistant commandant); and Admiral Leighton W. (Snuffy) Smith (who later commanded NATO forces in Southern Europe). This group spent three years and developed a concept based on "shock and awe" called at the time Rapid Dominance.

The idea was simple. To be most effective, military force should be directed at affecting, influencing, and controlling the will and perception of the adversary, not only at destroying military forces and supporting facilities. The notion was Clausewitz taken to his logical but understated conclusion.

Clausewitz argued that, in war, the purpose of military force was to break the will of the enemy to resist. Clausewitz believed that will could best (and only) be broken through disarming the enemy or threatening to do so. Shock and awe were derived as the mechanisms to bypass or compress that interaction. In essence, the broad application of shock and awe, properly administered, answered Horner's question of "where to stick the needle." Affecting, influencing, and controlling enemy will and perception became the center of this doctrine.

The operational method to accomplish this task was called "effects-based" targeting. This concept is not new. Combined with precision munitions and advanced means of collecting timely intelligence and battle information, effects-based targeting focuses first on the outcome or effect that is to be achieved.

Suppose that a power generation facility is the target. The effect is to eliminate the production of power for a certain period, not necessarily destroying the entire facility. In World War II, Vietnam, and even Desert Storm, normally this target would have been physically destroyed. But there are other vulnerabilities. If the generators, power distribution lines, transformers, and switching systems are neutralized, the net effect is the same. And, with a known time for estimating repairs, the length of outage can be calibrated.

With current technology, individual generators, power lines, transformers, and switches can be targeted with relatively small, precise munitions. Replacing generators, lines, and switches is a long-term process taking, in some cases, a year or more. In the past, it might have taken hundreds of munitions to eliminate a generating plant. Now, one or two weapons can accomplish the same effect without imposing much collateral damage or excessive casualties.

Resistance to this concept of shock and awe inside the Pentagon and military was strong. Four former secretaries of defense (Brown, Carlucci, Rumsfeld, and Schlesinger) signed a letter to Secretary Cohen endorsing the concept. Despite high-level support among senior civilians, the bureaucratic realities were too strong. The notion of shock and awe was too threatening to the conventional wisdom and, more importantly, to the current and planned conventional force structure. Fewer tanks, ships, and aircraft could well be the result since destroying the enemy's entire military might was secondary to controlling will and platform. In those circumstances, these platforms would be subordinate to the weapons and electronics systems they carried.

Only the Air Force, which commandeered the name, showed any interest. Rapid Air Dominance became the new slogan. Whether shock and awe offered an effective alternative or not, the inertia of a huge bureaucracy could not be deflected. Despite the huge sums spent on experimentation, most of these experiments would be driven internally by the services. An outside idea, no matter how much merit it may carry, faces these obstacles. And even when Rumsfeld became secretary, Rapid Dominance would not arise as a central part of any of the twenty-two panels and strategic reviews. Making change is not easy in part because of huge bureaucratic resistance. There is also a predictable arrogance toward outside intervention that extends across government.

## It's the Economy, Stupid

In the second of two videotapes carried by al Jazeera television, Osama bin Laden offered chilling direction to his followers: "There is another way [to strike America] through hitting the economic structure, which is basis for the military power. If their economy is destroyed, they will be busy with their own affairs rather than enslaving the weak peoples. It is important to concentrate on hitting the U.S. economy through all possible means."

Bin Laden probably arrived late at this view. It is doubtful that anyone in al Qaeda realized the extraordinary economic impact September 11th would have. Bin Laden himself did not envisage the complete destruction of the twin towers. He sought instead to have them standing partially destroyed as a grim reminder to the United States. However, hundreds of billions of dollars of damage were imposed. The warnings of prior commissions, studies, and war games can no longer be ignored given the risks and the likelihood that someone will carry out bin Laden's orders after he is long gone. This danger intensifies if future extremists adopt the concept of effects-based targeting in attempting to disrupt, terrorize, and demoralize the United States.

Economic warfare is as old as war. Generally, economic warfare was the weaker adjunct to military forces engaged in conflict with the enemy. Embargoes and sanctions formed a part. Both took time to have effect. Those effects were rarely decisive.

Germany twice used submarine warfare to impose economic damage on its enemies. With its navy bottled up in home waters, Germany found that submarines were the principal means available to carry the fight to the allies. The allies applied economic warfare as well. But, even with strategic bombing campaigns, economic warfare did not force Hitler to quit. And while Japan was being strangled and starved by an almost airtight blockade imposed by the unchallenged U.S. Navy, two nuclear weapons were needed to end the Pacific war.

More recently, during Clinton's second term, planning for different forms of economic warfare was carefully and quietly done. The commander of the Atlantic Command with headquarters in Norfolk, Virginia (to be renamed Joint Forces Command [JFC]), Marine General John J. Sheehan, was wrestling with two problems that had proven intractable: Cuba and drugs. Castro, the last remaining communist leader in this hemisphere, was a continuing nuisance. Drug trafficking, emanating largely from Latin America and Colombia, was increasingly difficult to control.

Sheehan pondered how economic warfare methods could be applied to states such as these to coerce or produce policy outcomes that had proven impossible to obtain otherwise. On a frequent basis, the most senior national security officials of the Clinton administration at the deputy secretary level met at the National Defense University at Fort McNair in Washington, D.C., to consider Sheehan's provocative idea. The discussions were highly classified.

"Follow the money" is one of law enforcement's best means for attacking crime. Following the money to include money-laundering activities and ways to circumvent legal banking and financial systems was an obvious topic for discussion. Both Attorney General Janet Reno and, later, Treasury Secretary Robert Rubin were opposed. Reno thought that it would be impossible to change the laws sufficiently to follow the money without compromising the rights of average citizens. Rubin, formerly the co-head of what then was the largest private banking institution in the world, also demurred. He knew too well that international finance required trust and confidence. Rubin was concerned that going after the money on a state-to-state basis could shake confidence in the financial system.

The planning effort remained just that. It turned out to be a precursor of the economic warfare and closing down of money supplies waged against bin Laden and al Qaeda. It would be naïve to believe that this approach, in concert with economic effects-based targeting, would not occur to extremists wishing to do grave harm.

## How Vulnerable?

How vulnerable is America? The question must be answered in several pieces. With a nation of 280 million people spread across a continent, only selective portions of the population are really vulnerable to attack. With a GDP of about $10 trillion and more than double that figure in the value of infrastructure, real estate, and investment, the United States is unlikely to face an economic collapse. A brief overview of the probable vulnerabilities establishes the range of threat. But the more likely problems will arise from means to protect these vulnerabilities from being exploited and the infringements that will have to be imposed on daily life and even on constitutional rights. For the clever and cynical terrorist, these latter targets are likely to produce the greatest harm to the nation. Using the openness of a democratic society against that society attacks the most precious value—freedom. As the North Vietnamese recognized, by adopting a strategy of winning by not losing and bringing the war into America's living rooms with the evening television news, they succeeded in eroding the will of the United States. The use of terror and other means to attack U.S. vulnerabilities for the purpose of destroying American will is the damage a cunning adversary will try to employ.

Before September 11th, there may have been a natural reluctance to cite publicly all of America's more obvious potential vulnerabilities for fear of creating new temptations no one had considered. The worlds of Hollywood and fiction harbored no such restrictions. Nuclear and biological attacks were routine. The trick was to raise the level of spectacle to attract more viewers and readers. And, while no one foresaw airliners crashing into New York's World Trade Center, Tom Clancy managed to fly a fictional commercial 747 jetliner into the Capitol Rotunda, killing the president and many members of Congress in the process so that the hero of most of his novels, Jack Ryan, would be elevated to the presidency.

In simple terms, this country is inherently and fundamentally vulnerable across its entire length and breadth. The proof is for the reader to take a short walk around his or her neighborhood asking a single question: With the right tools, whether bombs or computers, how much damage could be done to the community? Or, after viewing the nightly news from the Middle East following the latest suicide bombing, answer the question of how much terror a string of suicide bombers could inflict on the United States.

The Presidential Commission on Critical Infrastructure Protection identified eight national infrastructures "so vital that their incapacity or destruction would have a debilitating impact on our defense and economic security." These included transportation, oil and gas production and storage, water supply, emergency services, government services, banking and finance, electric power, and telecommunications. These eight were compressed into five "sectors": information and communications, physical distribution, energy, banking and finance, and vital human services.

Readers who find the five sectors self-explanatory are invited to jump ahead. The information and communications sector is largely the public telephone network and the Internet, to include telecommunications and computers. The largest non-natural threats to this sector are deliberate physical and electronic attacks to destroy, disrupt, confuse, deceive, and cause systemic failure. In 1999, two Chinese colonels wrote a provocative book called *Unrestricted Warfare* that elaborated how these attacks might occur and what targets they would strike.

Physical distribution entails the "vast interconnected network of highways, rail lines, ports and inland waterways, pipelines, airports and airways, mass transit, trucking companies, and delivery services" for moving goods, services, and people. Vast is an understatement. There are over 4 million miles of public roads, nearly half a million interstate trucking companies, 25 million trucks, and over 200 million personal vehicles. For air transport, there are some 400 airports. About 6,000 transit entities, 1,900 seaports, and 1,700 inland river terminals complete this picture. Each is potentially vulnerable.

Before September 11th, outside aviation, there were virtually no security safeguards except for Customs and Immigration and Naturalization Services at border checkpoints. Figure 5 on page 29 of the report suggests the possible threats. One is downing bridges. On the chart, the collapsed bridges shown are those crossing the Mississippi River. This is significant, because, while there are nearly 90 road and rail bridges spanning the river, closing only a few down would disrupt most cross-country surface transportation.

The report makes reference to the Global Positioning System or GPS. The vulnerability of GPS has been no secret. Dependence on GPS has increased from JDAM's (joint direct attack munitions) so successfully employed in Afghanistan to car navigational systems. Former Secretary of Defense James Schlesinger has often used GPS vulnerability as something that the government must address for both military and commercial security reasons.

The energy sector ranges from power generation and distribution to storage and exploration. Energy shortages and blackouts have been rare but newsworthy. The problems with deregulation of California's electrical utilities were man-made. Through disruption, destruction, or deliberate attack, great damage and panic could be achieved. A recent study examining this vulnerability in Mexico concluded that a cyber attack could take down virtually all of Mexico's electrical generating capacity. U.S. and Mexican grids are connected. So too are borders and flows of people across them. These vulnerabilities can no longer be limited to what happens in the United States.

Banking and finance are as central to America's security as blood is to a human. Lessons from life are illustrative. So-called unregulated hedge funds preyed on weak currencies. Runs on currencies from pounds sterling to Thai bhats have cost governments billions of dollars. When Long Term Capital Management failed, it nearly took a number of large banks with it. And this was business, not terror or purposeful assault. Shaking the confidence in the money and banking system, as Rubin worried, would have potentially catastrophic effects. Hence, despite the safeguards from armed guards in banks to discourage robberies to the most advanced crypto and cyber protection to prevent electronic theft, the vulnerabilities remain.

Finally, there is the vital human services sector. Water supply systems; police, fire, rescue, and medical emergency services; and government nonemergency services from mailing Social Security and benefits checks form this infrastructure. Much has been made of poisoning water supplies. While this is physically more difficult than people realize, if the aim of terror is to terrorize, the actual effects are less important than the immediate reactions that are created. Similarly, an overload on emergency services would help build panic and fear.

Elaborating on further specific vulnerabilities is a delicate matter. Some will suggest that the mention of any scenarios or possible crises gives information to potential enemies. Yet, without greater public awareness, action is not automatic. Remember all of the previous warnings and the image of the secretary of defense with his bag of mock anthrax.

Unfortunately, the Critical Infrastructure Commission failed to mention one sector of fundamental importance: food. Over the years there have been attacks on the food sector, from nature and from man. In 2001, Britain suffered from an outbreak of foot and mouth disease. Animals with cloven hooves—cows, sheep, and pigs—were infected. Millions were destroyed. Meanwhile, Mad Cow Disease (BSE) still lurks. It is taken so seriously that blood from anyone having set foot in Britain in the past twenty years is disqualified from giving blood in the United States. These were acts of nature.

Manmade attacks could be worse. In World War I, German saboteurs unsuccessfully tried to infect American herds with anthrax. Killing off America's food supply seemed a good idea as part of the program of economic warfare. Seven decades later, Americans found Tylenol and some food products contaminated by poisons and ground glass. One response to the understandable panic was tamper-proof wrappings.

Food production and distribution, especially in an age of unprecedented genetic engineering, are potential targets. Taken together with the vulnerability of the other sectors, the opportunities for mischief, terror, and even death cannot be discounted. Think about just three possibilities for future bin Ladens (each of these has been publicized elsewhere).

The United States is dependent on paper. Consider a day in the life of most Americans. The paper arrives first thing. Mail is delivered. Cash changes hands multiple times to buy both the simplest of goods and services and the most expensive. Who can survive without checks and check books, all paper? Invoices, reports, and publications, despite the paperless electronic age, are still ubiquitous. Now suppose the paper supply had been contaminated or impregnated with dangerous biological or chemical agents.

Worse perhaps than contaminating the water supply is to attack the supply of milk. Multiply the Tylenol problem by several orders of magnitude to estimate the panic and disruption. And, as noted, there are other foodstuffs that are as ubiquitous, including bread, eggs, meat, and poultry.

Finally, suppose suicide bombing really came to America. Even if there were only a hundred suicide bombers determined to do harm, the results would be disproportionately large. The nation has already experienced waves of bombing from the 1919–1920 outbreak to the Southern churches and schools that were destroyed on the basis of skin color. And, in the name of God, so-called Christians attempt to blow up abortion clinics on the grounds that it is immoral to take human lives. Perhaps bin Ladenism arrived on these shores a lot sooner than Americans realized. And perhaps his tortured views of religion cannot be isolated to a single denomination.

## After All, We're Dead

The above was the realistic and accurate view of the father of Keynesian economics. Given all of these vulnerabilities, most made more so by the freedom and access routinely enjoyed by Americans, can anything be done? Or are only resignation and the long view required? The full list of answers and recommendations follows in due course. There is, however, one set of ideas that must be laid out first. Otherwise, there will be no means to assess the magnitude of the dangers that lie ahead if and when these vulnerabilities are challenged and to create the necessary remedial and preventive measures.

During World War II, allied code breaking helped win the war. The Battle of Midway in the Pacific in June 1942 was won by a much smaller American fleet with only three serviceable aircraft carriers against a much more powerful Japanese naval force that numbered twice as many units because the Americans knew the "when and where's" of the Japanese plan. The Japanese ciphers had been cracked.

In Europe, the code-breaking operation was centered around Bletchley Park in England. Many of the most brilliant minds in the kingdom in mathematics, physics, and related subjects were assembled under Alan Turing. Bletchley broke Enigma, the German code, as well as other ancillary ciphers. The advantages were enormous. One of the residual benefits was the invention of the large computer to assist in the code-breaking exercise.

Today, the United States needs the equivalent of Bletchley Park. The "codes" that require breaking are substantially different. Penetrating the thought processes, motives, and intentions of extremists such as bin Laden is one of two priorities. The second is to use these broken codes as the basis for conducting a vulnerability assessment of where and how extremists might strike. From these analyses and assessments, plans of action can be made and taken.

A new Bletchley Park is necessary but not sufficient in this campaign against extremism. There are profound organizational challenges. Former national security adviser Lake is not correct in dismissing these problems as part of the "institutions of our democracy." However, he is absolutely right in sounding an alarm over political culture and the dangers that arise from destructive democracy. Whether or not bin Laden has read Lake's book or any of the clarion calls cited above, someone wishing this nation ill will avail themselves of this open and available literature. Therein rests a real danger.

# ★ 5 ★

# The Tyranny of Government—
# Overly Checked and Out of Balance

## The Second Piece of Unfinished Business

Bin Laden and company may have stumbled onto a powerful lever for moving the United States. During the Cold War, the Soviet Union combined a massive military with an irrationally organized society and an ultimately flawed ideology to challenge the West. It failed.

North Vietnam was shrewder. It prevailed over the United States ultimately by not losing the war while relying on the impact of nightly American TV delivering that message to millions of American homes. Now, bin Laden has perfected an even cleverer strategy. With nineteen men and box cutters, he killed over three thousand people and erased nearly a half trillion dollars from the world economy.

Will the United States be up to the task of keeping the nation safe? Is a political system derived from the experiences and the best intellects of the eighteenth century capable of responding to the rigors of the twenty-first century? Can this huge and vastly complex government, with so many centrifugal forces and competing agendas, be organized to deal with this fundamental assault on American freedoms and values? And can enough good people be persuaded to serve to ensure enduring solutions?

The government of the United States is an enormous enterprise overseeing annual expenditures of about a trillion and a half dollars and employing literally tens of millions of people directly in its endeavors and indirectly because of them. It has the power of life and death. It makes the laws and regulations that govern the nation. It can declare war and raise or lower taxes. It has the power to arrest and to punish wrongdoing. Its second most important task after ensuring domestic tranquility is providing for the common defense. And, by virtue of its Constitution, it has ensured that power, authority, and responsibility are spread across the broadest reaches of its government.

## Checked and Balanced?

Every high school student should know that the government of the United States and its institutions are based on two sets of checks and balances. The reason for this division of political power was to provide the ultimate safeguard for the rights of individuals by limiting the efficiency and reach of government. Individual freedom and liberty were assured by inefficiency of government. No Americanized versions of George III or Parliament would be tolerated.

Power was first divided between and among the three branches of government—the Congress, the presidency, and the judiciary. Authority and responsibility for each branch are defined by the Constitution, the laws of the land passed by Congress and signed by the president, and libraries full of rules, executive orders, and regulations.

Second, the federal system apportions power between national and state governments. This system of checks and balances was created to protect individual freedoms from the whims of government. Against any number of dangers, from war to depression, this system and the institutions of government have served the nation well for two hundred years.

But it was not by accident that the Constitution made no mention of political parties. Indeed, among leaders as great as Washington and Adams, the sentiment was pronouncedly against them.

Parties, these wisest of the Founding Fathers believed, would produce "factionalism" and dissension. Washington and Adams also believed that campaigning, especially for the presidency, was demeaning and unbecoming.

Just after World War II and the hardening of the Cold War, the National Security Act of 1947 was passed into law. The purpose of that legislation was to provide for the common defense against the Soviet Union. The act was amended in 1949 and 1958. It remains in full force, modified by other legislation such as the Goldwater-Nichols Department of Defense Reorganization Act of 1986.

The Soviet Union of course is gone. The national security structure is not. The crucial question remains: Will these institutions, grounded in events and ideas of the eighteenth century and last modified for a Cold War that has ended, withstand the rigors and tests of the twenty-first century? The exquisite danger that bin Laden and his particular brand of extremism pose should cause Americans to regard this question very seriously.

## Good Morning, Mr. President

In February 2001, the Commission on National Security Strategy/21st Century released its findings. After hearing the conclusion that in the face of new threats, "our nation has no coherent or integrated governmental structures," a few alarm bells might have been triggered in government. They were not. The reasons included timing, personality, and the inherent resistance of American bureaucracies to serious ideas and thoughts from the outside world.

Because of the contested election, the administration was off to a late start. At State, the new secretary, Colin Powell, faced a department with the lowest morale and budget shortfalls since World War II. At Defense, the new secretary, Donald Rumsfeld, was home alone. It would take six months to bring in the better part of a new team. A huge fight over the confirmation of Attorney General-select John Ashcroft had embattled the new administration. Besides, the president had his own views on foreign policy. But personality counts too.

# US ORGANIZATION FOR SECURITY

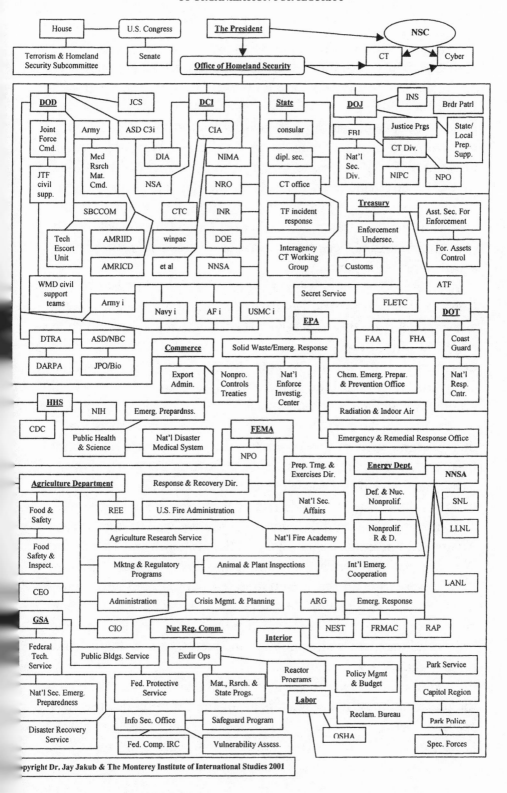

The co-chairs of the commission were former senators Gary Hart and Warren Rudman. Hart had made a run for president in 1988. His candidacy ended abruptly after he was confronted with irrefutable evidence of an extramarital affair he had tried to conceal. As a Democrat, he had no particular clout with the White House. Rudman, a combat commander in the Korean War and a tough prosecutor before coming to Congress from Maine, had been John McCain's vocal campaign manager in the Republican race for the nomination. After the McCain challenge subsided, Rudman had no friends in the Bush camp. Furthermore, Lynne Cheney, wife of the vice-president, had been an original commissioner but withdrew shortly after being appointed.

In the end, the commission leadership briefed Condoleezza Rice, Colin Powell, and Donald Rumsfeld. Neither the president nor the vice-president could be scheduled. Hart, Rudman, and commission executive director retired Air Force General Charles G. Boyd expressed disappointment. At best, the administration was neutral about the study even though many of its recommendations would eventually find their way into policy.

Broader forces were also at work. As noted, the organization of the government in providing for the common defense has several foundations. The Constitution is the most important. The law, in particular the National Security Act of 1947 (as amended) and the various titles of the U.S. Code (i.e., Title 10 for the Armed Forces, Title 18 for Crimes and Criminal Procedures, Title 22 for Foreign Affairs and Intercourse, Title 32 for National Guard, and Title 50 for War and National Defense are among the most relevant), provides the statutory basis for the organization. Executive orders and regulations add further direction. The annual congressional authorization and appropriation bills approve spending and often give specific orders and mandatory direction. Finally, precedent and politics continually shape these institutions.

As this chapter will show, this system of divided government and the organization of that government for the common defense have become overly checked and out of balance. Some people such as Colin Powell will argue that ultimately it is people who make any system succeed or fail. Certainly Powell is correct. But good people can go only so far in making an imperfect system better. At some point, systemic and organizational flaws must be corrected. Otherwise, an external force may expose those flaws and failure.

This is precisely what happened in Vietnam and after. In military operations, organizational flaws helped lead to disasters such as Desert One and Beirut. The same syndrome also affected intelligence and law-enforcement agencies. The FBI failures at Ruby Ridge and in Waco, Texas, in dealing with the Branch Davidians and the bungled investigation of Los Alamos nuclear physicist Wen Ho Lee for allegedly passing secrets to China are examples. The CIA was damaged by mole Aldrich Ames (the FBI had Richard Hanssen) and the unfortunate bombing of the Chinese Embassy in Belgrade during Allied Force did not help. One of the difficulties is that the successes of both agencies generally are unreported. Failures manage to leak out. As a result, the public tends to believe what is public, not what actually happened.

## The First Article

The United States is the most litigious society in the world. There are more lawyers in Washington, D.C. than are practicing in Japan. China's entry into WTO will ultimately bring more attorneys to Beijing. With all of these lawyers, it is a wonder that the legal bases for providing for the nation's common defense are largely missed.

Most Americans do not recall what the Constitution has to say about the structure of government. It was not serendipity that Article I was assigned to the legislature. The Founding Fathers believed that this branch would do the governing through the passage of laws. The president, defined in Article II, would be vested with the "executive power" and was responsible for implementing the work and the will of Congress.

Section 8 delineated Congress's powers. Among them were the power to "lay and collect Taxes, Duties, Imposts and Excises"; "provide for the common Defence"; "declare war"; "raise and support Armies"; "provide and maintain a Navy"; "make Rules for the Government and Regulation of the land and naval Forces"; "call forth the Militia . . . [and] . . . provide for organizing, arming and disciplining the militia and for governing such Part of them as may be employed in the Service of the United States."

The president was designated "Commander in Chief of the Army and Navy of the United States and of the Militia of the several States when called into actual service." With "the Advice and Consent of the Senate . . . provided two thirds of the Senators present concur," the president can make treaties. Also with the Senate's advice and consent, the president appoints ambassadors, public ministers, consuls, and other officers established by law.

It is important to understand these specific powers and responsibilities fully. As we will see, the power of the presidency grew. In the often partisan battles with Congress, Congress's ultimate power set forth in Section 8 tends to be downplayed. But it is a truism of American governance that while the president proposes, Congress disposes.

Finally, regarding the federal and state divisions of power, Article X specifies that "powers not delegated to the United States by the Constitution nor prohibited by it to the States, are reserved to the States respectively or to the people."

## The National Security Act

The National Security Act established the National Security Council system. Originally called the Act of Unification because it married the old War and Navy departments under a single national military organization, the act also created a third service—the Department of the Air Force. In 1949, the Defense Department was formally named, the authority of the secretary of defense expanded, and the role of chairman of the Joint Chiefs of Staff created.

Under the president, the role of the NSC was to advise, assist, and coordinate the making of national security policy. Membership varied. Harry Truman, the first president to serve with the act, ignored it. Since then, its statutory members have included the president, vice-president, secretary of state, secretary of defense, and attorney general. The newly established director of central intelligence was a pro forma member as was the assistant for national security, a position not mentioned in the act. Others have been added by presidential preference, including the secretary of the treasury and, in the Clinton administration, the ambassador to the United Nations. After 1986, the chairman of the JCS normally attended as a member.

The National Security Act also made no mention of the newer threats and the agencies of government charged with national security responsibilities. In 1947, Soviet power and not terrorism, proliferation of weapons of mass destruction, drugs, and crime were the clearest and most present dangers. The National Security Agency (responsible for electronic eavesdropping), the Drug Enforcement Agency, the Federal Emergency Management Agency, and the new Homeland Security Agency (about which much more will be said) all exist outside the act. And each is vital to the nation's security.

## The Clash of Branches

Ambiguities regarding the authority and responsibility vested by the Constitution appeared almost immediately and have been part of the nation's history since. Despite the attitudes of Washington and Adams that it was "undignified" to run for the presidency, political parties were gaining purchase. Candidates would have to run for office and publicize their campaign even though, then as now, the president was elected not by the popular vote but by the Electoral College. Thomas Jefferson was the first person to campaign publicly for the presidency. His election was settled on the eighty-sixth ballot. Not long after, his serving vice-president, Aaron Burr, would be tried for treason. Those were exciting times.

The flaws that would cause the imbalance of power over states rights could not be contained. The Civil War ended this piece of the nation's unfinished business. After the bloodiest war in the nation's history, the federal government's authority had been irreversibly established. The progression in increasing presidential power and the size and reach of government has already been cited. For those less familiar with history and perhaps believing that the "good old days" were more halcyon regarding government, the humor of two of America's greatest observers adds context.

Mark Twain said of a particular member of the House, "The congressman is an idiot. But I repeat myself." In the "gay" and roaring twenties, when the term could be used without sexual connotation, Will Rogers observed about Congress that every time they passed a law it was a joke. And every time Congress made a joke, it turned out to be a law.

## The Big Bang and Government

During the Cold War, the organization of government regarding national security was basically "vertical." That meant that individual departments generally had clearly divisible lines of authority and responsibility. The State Department handled diplomacy and foreign policy. The Department of Defense provided the forces to deter the Soviet military and, should deterrence fail, fight and prevail over the enemy on the battlefield. The CIA provided intelligence and covert or clandestine operations to recruit informers and prevent the Soviet KGB from doing the same. If a secret war had to be fought in Latin America, the Middle East, or South East Asia, the agency could do that. The FBI meanwhile went after the spies and counterspies. It was all relatively neat and orderly—or so it seemed.

In fact, the world was never quite so vertically organized. But the massive nature of the Soviet threat and Soviet military strength certainly sustained that impression. And the clear and present danger of the Soviet Union helped to maintain a sense of political bipartisanship that lasted for nearly two decades. As Senator Arthur Vandenburg, one of the architects of the nation's Cold War security, declared, "Partisanship stops at the water's edge."

Then two circumstances changed. First, power continued to accrue to the presidency. The executive branch had grown considerably since the New Deal. World War II had turned Washington into a major city with politics and government the leading industries. By the early 1950s, military rearmament was well underway. Nuclear weapons numbered in the thousands and many were kept on instant alert. This meant that the president in essence could declare war by virtue of ordering a nuclear strike. Eisenhower was in office, and people had confidence in the general who won the war in Europe. For two terms, Eisenhower's steady hand kept the nation on a safe course despite the growth in Soviet power.

Congress had many veterans of World War II and Korea. The seniority system existed in both houses. Committee chairmen were powers unto themselves and were largely determined by time served in Congress. With Eisenhower and then Kennedy and Johnson, it took only a few members of Congress to strike a deal with the White House. The seniority system imposed a certain discipline. It also restricted full debate. However, by virtue of common experience and common threat, regarding national security there was a genuine sense of nonpartisanship. And politics had not become so bitter. Republicans and Democrats could regard members of the opposition as friends, not constant adversaries.

Vietnam ended many things. The Imperial Presidency, as it was called, was one of the first casualties. The Watergate scandal and then revelations of CIA wrongdoing turned Congress into an investigatory body highly suspect of the executive branch. Democrats ended the seniority system. The House of Representatives became far less disciplined, the Senate less so. However, more oversight, investigation, and regulation emerged as principal means to control "rogue elephants" whether at Langley or in the White House.

There were further political complications. Over time, the expense of running for office increased dramatically. Television advertising was considered the major culprit. In 1970, the average House race cost less than $25,000. A Senate race averaged about half a million dollars. In 2000 and in real terms, campaign spending increased many fold. Jon Corzine, a former head of the investment firm of Goldman Sachs, spent $50 million of his own money to win the Senate seat from New Jersey in 2000. For better or for worse, politics was increasingly becoming a continuous campaign for office rather than the practice of governing.

As the most successful journalists had moved from reporting the news to making it, successful politicians were turning into celebrities. A walk around the Senate provides interesting evidence. Virtually every senator wears makeup today. The reason is the constant need to appear on television and to present the best face possible.

Worse, politics turned destructive. In the 1980s, an insidious tendency to "criminalize" political differences began to take root. Instead of political disputes being resolved by voters, the police and the FBI became surrogates. The impeachment of Bill Clinton set a new standard in that regard.

Instead of trying Clinton for real crimes and violations of his office, sadly, his sexual peccadilloes were surrogates. The irony, after his acquittal in the Senate, was the report of dalliances on the other side of the aisle. Former Speaker Newt Gingrich admitted to having an affair with a young staffer, whom he would marry. His chosen successor, Bob Livingstone, had to stand down for a similar reason of infidelity. And Henry Hyde, chairman of the House Judiciary Committee that led the impeachment, admitted to fathering a child out of wedlock—a "youthful indiscretion" he declared, although he was 43 at the time.

House Democrats epitomized this progression of criminalization. Rallying against Majority Whip Tom DeLay in 2001, the Democrats sought to indict him on violation of RICO—the Racketeer Influenced Corrupt Organizations Act. The act was designed to prosecute organized crime, not political opponents. In fairness, there was certainly payback for the way the Republicans had hounded former Democratic Speaker of the House Jim Wright out of office for taking kickbacks. However, criminality became the latest tool in the political bag of dirty tricks.

The second circumstance was the dramatic change in threat. Monolithic, militarized communism that could be dealt with by a largely vertical national defense structure was gone. Instead, new threats appeared. These were largely "horizontal," cutting across many agencies and departments. For example, countering the proliferation of weapons of mass destruction, drugs, crime, disease, political instability, and failing nations could not be the responsibility of only one agency or department. This same organizational reality was true in Congress. For decades, Congress was organized around committees and a budget process that presented thirteen appropriations bills for approval. The changing security environment and the basic organization of the U.S. government were badly "out of sync" with the clear and present dangers facing the nation.

Law enforcement and intelligence are two vital areas that make this point. Take terrorism. Where does law enforcement start and stop? What is the role for intelligence? Since the CIA has no legal authority to operate in the United States and the FBI has no basis for an intelligence finding approved by the president for terminating enemies with extreme prejudice (i.e., killing them) how should these matters be handled? And, given the routing of global telecommunications through the United States, what does this mean for electronic eavesdropping, which requires warrants for tapping into communications by American citizens?

Another example reinforces the complexity of overlapping jurisdictions. In the District of Columbia, there are about thirty different police forces. Even the Mint and the National Institutes of Health have separate federal police forces. Suppose someone were to attack the White House. Who would have jurisdiction? Is this a terrorist act? Is it an assassination attempt? Or is it some other motive, perhaps that of a mentally impaired or deranged individual? Which police force is in charge?

The Metropolitan Police could have jurisdiction. If this were a terrorist incident, the FBI has authority; an attempted assassination, the Secret Service; if committed on certain federal grounds, the Park Police. If automatic weapons or explosives were involved, would the Bureau of Alcohol, Tobacco, and Firearms have a responsibility? If a long-range weapon were fired from, say, across the Potomac, would Virginia authorities have jurisdiction?

Almost certainly, the FBI would be given the responsibility for the investigation. However, that assignment would cut across many other jurisdictions. The point is clear: In a world in which horizontal security threats and dangers will emerge not only from states but other actors and causes that cut across many jurisdictions, an organization designed vertically is at a huge disadvantage.

While the first phase of Operation Enduring Freedom, almost entirely military or "paramilitary" in character, appeared to work well, the test of the national security organization will come in the many subsequent phases. Rebuilding Afghanistan, dealing with the causes of extremism in the region, keeping India and Pakistan from each other's throats, and finishing old pieces of business are daunting. Each will require unique and varied skills that cut across virtually all levels of government. That is the challenge.

## Just Say No

All bureaucracies have inherent strengths and weaknesses. A century ago, the British civil servant J. Northcote Parkinson invented his law: The larger bureaucracies grew, the more inefficient they became. Inherent strength lies within this inertia. Instant decisions are normally impossible. Issues can usually be examined from different directions. Recklessness and fecklessness can be avoided.

On the other hand, innovation and objectivity can be stymied. Interests that serve bureaucratic and not broader purposes often prevail. Compromise can dull precision and inhibit action. And these characteristics persist across government and the agencies and departments that comprise it. If competence and subtlety are needed, bureaucracies are not guaranteed to deliver both.

This book is not a study of bureaucratic politics. However, in terms of overly checking and unduly unbalancing the processes of governing, the bureaucratic and cultural characteristics of the many varied agencies of government take their toll. Because the Defense Department is the largest of the agencies and probably the one most covered by the media outside the White House and Congress, more about it is known publicly.

In simplest terms, the department's purpose is to be prepared to fight and to win the nation's wars and battles. The most precious human and material resources are intimately involved. Life-and-death decisions are often taken even when the nation is not technically at war. As a result, the "corporate culture" of the four military services and the uniformed side of the department is very competitive and focused on winning. This culture is also "conservative" and can be overly cautious. It is reluctant to take undue risk, particularly in abandoning what have been successful policies and what has worked in war. The old expression "if it ain't broke, don't fix it" surely applies.

The elemental dilemma is that this need for "winning" is applied to most activities, including those where it does not fit. Both the earnest cries of service academy cadets and midshipmen "to beat Army or Navy" at every sporting event and the budgetary battles waged in the Pentagon, OMB, and Congress reflect this attitude toward winning. The military services, despite the impact of "jointness" to overcome certain rivalries and the understanding that wars are won by the nation and not by individual services, are wedded to their weapons platforms, doctrines, and esprit that makes each the best in its particular business of waging war on land, sea, air, and space. There is a certain bureaucratic "equity" in that each of the four services is entitled to a more or less constant share of the resources and the credit.

Furthermore, since Vietnam, the uniformed military, largely under the persuasive arguments of Colin Powell, has become more discriminating by "just saying no" to arguments for using force. Terms such as "exit strategies" and "precise objectives" are used to begin discussions on whether to use force, not the other way round. This is largely commendable. Because of short turnarounds in civilian leadership and less experience in Congress in foreign policy and war and peace issues, posing the proper questions before force is committed is eminently sensible. However, too often, this just-say-no attitude prevents change and stifles innovation.

Since World War II ended and the military was drawn down in 1945, there has been only one case of a service unilaterally imposing drastic reductions on itself. In 1970, Admiral Elmo R. (Bud) Zumwalt, at age forty-five, became the youngest chief of naval operations in naval history. The fleet numbered about 950 ships, most relics of World War II. In the first two months of his tenure, Zumwalt set about cutting the Navy almost in half. His argument was that given the threat of a modernizing Soviet fleet, the U.S. Navy could not afford to defer its own modernization simply to keep a huge number of obsolete ships in service. Zumwalt's decision evoked controversy. However, he won. In many ways, Zumwalt rightly deserves the title of father of the modern Navy.

When Rumsfeld entered office the second time, he was charged by the president with "transforming" the military into a force for the twenty-first century. He was rebuffed by the services. The reasons were due to neither disloyalty nor insubordination. Instead, it was bureaucratic sclerosis at work. In simplest terms, why change what is proven simply to meet political promises for transformation? The difficulty in providing answers to the question of "transforming to what?" was not lost on the services.

While the four services clearly have different ethos, missions, cultures, and histories, there are common characteristics. They are organized, trained, and equipped for operations in the way that each service has specified, not some outside authority. They believe in that organization and the particular weapons and platforms they employ. And, since the so-called war-fighting requirements—that is, how each service intends to fight in combat—are the ultimate "trump cards" in assessing programs and systems, the military is not going to forgo exclusive authority over them without a substantial bureaucratic fight.

Numbers also count. Because services are bureaucratically positioned against reductions, cutting the numbers of personnel and systems has always been difficult. Carter and Clinton found cutbacks difficult. Reagan was better received because of huge defense increases. Building up from a Pentagon perspective is bureaucratically far easier than building down. Hence, while the younger Bush was initially perceived as pro-defense, his directions for transformation were met with skepticism and resistance.

Examples abound. Several years ago during the Clinton administration, a conversation with the Army Chief of Staff, General Dennis Reimer, on qualitative and quantitative tradeoffs made this point. I had observed that Desert Storm had been a remarkable war for several reasons. The Army's M-1 Abrams tank had set an incredible standard for land warfare. None were lost in action. It had a 90 percent probability of a kill on the first shot. And it killed Iraqi tanks at seemingly unprecedented ranges of a mile, occasionally shooting its antitank rounds through sand berms before hitting enemy targets. Reimer appreciated the discussion.

Then I asked why the Army had not exploited this capability in its battle organization and war plans. Reimer grew less comfortable. The argument was this: each M-1 carried about forty rounds of 120-mm cannon ammunition. Assuming only a 50 percent first-kill probability instead of 90 percent, each M-1 was capable of "killing" twenty enemy vehicles. By that logic, one hundred M-1s could account for two thousand enemy vehicles just with the ammunition on board. After Desert Storm, Iraq possessed about twenty-five hundred tanks, armored personnel carriers, and other vehicles. Why then would more than two hundred M-1 tanks be needed in Kuwait in the event of another Iraqi attack or in the event of an attack into Iraq? And why did the United States need to maintain about seventy-six hundred M-1 tanks in its inventory? Surely, we could do well with far fewer. This argument did not go any further.

The same argument and logic applies to each of the services and specific systems. The Air Force's new F-22 Raptor fighter is the world's best air-superiority machine in the world by a huge margin. Why then are so many needed? The Navy's nuclear submarines are the world's best. With the end of the Soviet Union, there really is no potential adversary. Why then are so many needed? These arguments and questions generate the same response: bureaucratic shock. No service or service chief will regard them as serious. The reason is that each service needs the best in sufficient numbers. No one wishes to take the chance that numbers may not count.

Compounding this resistance is the defense-industrial-congressional iron triangle. Defense is a monopsony in that there is a single buyer—the U.S. Government. Defense is the most regulated and oversighted sector in the free market. All of the large defense companies—Boeing, Lockheed-Martin, Northrop-Grumman, General Dynamics, Raytheon, and, since January 2002, United Defense—are publicly held. This means that they are responsible to shareholders and dependent on Wall Street analysts who assess share value. Each is in business for the old-fashioned reason—to make money.

In these circumstances, large programs are vital to each company. While the department may elect to cut back programs for strategic or budgetary reasons, companies are not so driven. There is nothing wrong in this tension. It is the ultimate paradox of a free market. Companies stay in business by making money. They are responsible to shareholders and employees as well as to the government and the nation.

One solution is to nationalize defense, as had been the case until the First World War. Today, nationalization is too expensive and is politically unacceptable. Hence, a "hybrid" of public companies reinforced with government-owned facilities such as the National Laboratories and other research organizations results. Clearly, this structure leads to "checks and balances" over what any adminstration and the Defense Department can do in making changes for the future. It must rely on a largely civilian industrial base. Congress, of course, is on both sides of this: it appropriates all defense expenditures. And it represents its constituents.

Finally, the just-say-no defense was very much alive in the preliminary planning for Operation Enduring Freedom. The senior military and the Joint Chiefs of Staff produced a plan that was a variant of the air campaign originally designed to counter Soviet air defenses in Europe and then refined for Desert Storm against Iraq. It was a methodical use of air and missile power to destroy the Taliban defenses. Then air power would focus on "preparing the battlefield" by targeting Taliban ground forces.

Rumsfeld was not satisfied with the first plan. It was too ponderous in his view. It did not take into account what Rumsfeld saw as the extraordinary technical advantages the United States possessed in intelligence gathering and precision strike. Why not employ more Global Hawk and Predator drones to saturate the battlefield? Why not use Special or Marine Forces as forward spotters for air power? Why not compress the timetable and collapse the morale of the Taliban through the advantages of overwhelming firepower, precision, and battlefield surveillance?

That is what happened. While no evaluation of this operation has been released yet, senior sources within the Pentagon confirm Rumsfeld's direction and leadership in forming the strategy and plans. The big winner was innovation. The aircraft carrier *Kitty Hawk* was stripped of virtually its entire air wing to carry Special Forces troops. Unmanned aircraft proved their worth. And the B-52, an aircraft with nearly six decades of service, became the tactical weapon of choice because of its ability to loiter overhead and its carrying capacity. Finally, to the consternation of the Army, the U.S. Marine Corps was the first major ground force sent into action because of its flexibility and forward sea basing.

The command and control was also extraordinary. The CinC, Army General Tommy Franks, could keep his headquarters in Tampa, Florida, while fighting a war half a world away. Information could be flashed in real time from the battlefield literally anywhere in the world with the proper communications and decryption systems. The secretary of the Air Force, Dr. James G. Roche, literally a captain of industry and a former captain in the Navy, took pride in noting that the Joint Forces Air Commander (JFAC), in his command headquarters at King Khalid Military Air Base in Saudi Arabia had a real-time, accurate and comprehensive picture of the entire battle taking place over Afghanistan hundreds of miles away.

Roche also was surprised when entering the facility to hear an officer cry "attention on deck," a naval, not an air force, term. The reason was that the JFAC was joint and manned by personnel from each service. A Navy lieutenant commander had sighted the secretary and responded accordingly. To Roche, this was a sign of the times and of transformation. A headquarters hundreds of miles from the battle was fully capable of commanding the fight. Technology was that good.

There is an interesting footnote. When Roche was in the Navy, he was early selected for a destroyer command, authorized by the policies of the navy's head, Admiral Zumwalt. Zumwalt was far ahead of his time. He would go on to tell his subordinates that in the not too distant future fleet commanders would run their forces from command posts in the Rocky Mountains. Tampa, Florida, and

Saudi Arabia were not the Rockies. However, this picture was not all
that different from what Zumwalt had foreseen thirty years before.

## Candidates for Change

A surrogate for institutional reform has been increased oversight and
regulation. Instead of needed organizational change, the alternative
has been greater scrutiny. In the Pentagon, for example, congressional opposition to the large Reagan defense spending increases of
the 1980s entailed finding instances of "waste, fraud, and abuse." In
an organization as large and complex as the Department of Defense,
that was not difficult. Toilet seats for a P-3 aircraft that reportedly
cost $6,000 and hammers at $500 each made news. Unfortunately,
the tyranny of the accounting system was at fault. The total cost of
the P-3 antisubmarine aircraft was spread through individual sub-
components including its toilet seats. The facts made little difference. No "ordinary" person could understand why these items that
were part of daily life could be so grotesquely overpriced.

At hearings and press conferences, critics called these offenses
outrageous wastes of taxpayer resources and worse. This verbal lashing was in essence punishment for political disagreements over
defense spending increases. Commissions and panels were convened
to examine these allegations of wrongdoing. Regulations were
rewritten. But there was no fundamental reform.

Congress would not relax what it saw as its prerogatives under
Section 8 of the Constitution. And no president would tolerate any
interference in his role of commander in chief. As a result, a cumbersome and overly regulated process was made more so. Taxpayers
continue to carry the burden of institutional excesses that cost tens
of billions of dollars a year. And that is without the so-called pork
that is inserted by Congress for constituents at home.

Consider three seemingly minor examples that paint a broader
picture. Each represents an institutional failure. During the Gulf
War, General Schwarzkopf had an urgent need for several thousand
cell phones. A Japanese company had the right phones in the proper
numbers. The problem was that even in war with an expedited pro-

curement process in place, the cell phones could not be purchased. Domestic-content laws prohibited the Defense Department from using products that did not contain a certain percentage of U.S.– furnished material even in time of war. The impasse was resolved when Hitachi donated the cell phones, bypassing the need for procurement.

In 2001, Congress appropriated no funding for the MX Peacekeeper Missile. Nor did it appropriate any funding to decommission the weapons. So here was the folly of a major weapons system that was in the inventory but had no funding to support it or get rid of it. You are the Secretary of Defense. How do you deal with this issue?

The same year, the Defense Department decided to consolidate bases for the B-1 bomber. Unfortunately as it turned out for the department, B-1s from bases in Georgia and Kansas would be transferred to bases in Texas and South Dakota. Texas, of course, was the president's home state; Senate Majority Leader Tom Daschle hailed from South Dakota. There are few issues more volatile than military bases and constituent jobs. The Senate responded to the request rather dramatically passing by a 98–0 vote a binding resolution forbidding the transfer of a single Air Force aircraft from one base to another without Senate permission.

There is a fine line between tragedy and satire. These instances reflect both. They also suggest some of the major institutional problems that confront the new Homeland Security office. No matter how well intended, one of the dividends of divided government is to produce action that is often irrational. No sane person would permit these situations to occur given the authority and a smattering of common sense. Yet, they did happen and will again.

## Congress

It is tempting to place a great deal of blame on Congress for many of these problems. For decades, American public opinion has usually held Congress in low regard. Mark Twain and Will Rogers would be pleased. Paradoxically, Americans tended to hold individual members who represent them in high regard. The institution and not the individual was the cause for complaint.

The Constitution has little to say about the organization and structure of Congress. Only three officers are specified: the Speaker of the House of Representatives; the President of the Senate—who is the vice-president, and the President Pro Tempore of the Senate. Each house is authorized to make its own rules. Each senator and representative is equal in standing with his peers. (Women did not have the vote when the Constitution became law and were not elected to Congress.)

Congress organized itself around a committee system in both houses. Committees are where the bulk of work is done, from drafting bills to holding hearings. When Congress reorganized itself in 1947, there were fifteen full committees and fifty-nine subcommittees in the Senate and nineteen and eighty-nine respectively in the House. In 2001, there were twenty committees in both chambers, sixty-nine subcommittees in the Senate, and eighty-eight in the House, virtually no change given the current fifty states.

The largest and most significant change has been in the number of caucuses and unofficial political committees. This increase reflects the strength of campaign-centric politics and the pressure to raise money. In 1947, there were virtually no caucuses and committees. In 2001, there were twenty-two of these organizations in the Senate, from the Bipartisan Senate Task Force on Fatherhood Protection to the Western States Coalition. In the House, there are ninety-nine, starting alphabetically with the African Trade and Investment Caucus and ending with the Upper Mississippi River Task Forces. There are also forty-one of these bicameral organizations. The reason for this upsurge in "unofficial" caucuses and committees is obvious. Each one attracts funding. Money has become more than the life's blood of politics in the United States.

Before 1974, the budget process in Congress consisted of an authorization and appropriation process. The authorization phase determined what programs would be recommended for actual expenditure of funds. The appropriation phase approved the funding through thirteen spending bills. In 1974, the Budget Reform and

Impoundment Act added a budgeting phase, meant to establish the general spending limits for expenditures as the basis for the authorizing and appropriation process. No business or other government uses a similar process. It is simply too cumbersome, time consuming, and wasteful. Congress prefers this convoluted process in order to give more members access to some of the purse strings if not the purse itself.

Meanwhile, the traditional thirteen spending bills work their way through this laborious process every year. While Congress has modified some of its committees to reflect changing realities, it remains a historical curiosity that business is still done in this manner.

Finally, there are quaint rules that govern both houses. In the Senate, secret "holds" can be placed on nominees, preventing their consideration. Senators also are allowed "the courtesy" to pass judgment on judicial nominees from their respective states. But these rules are not always open to the public and remain jealously guarded. No public corporation or entity would be permitted to work in this manner. In essence, while there is great oversight of the executive branch by Congress, the only real oversight of Congress, outside of media reporting, is the ballot box and elections. In fact, Congress was not made subject to the equal-opportunity laws, since that would have given the executive branch and the Equal Opportunity Commission oversight over Congress, something strictly prohibited by the Constitution.

## The Pentagon

The five-sided configuration of the Pentagon aptly applies to the five main centers of power inside the Department of Defense. In overseeing the biggest enterprise of its kind in the world, the department has an annual budget in excess of $350 billion (growing to $380 billion in 2003), an active duty force of about 1.4 million, and another 2 million civilian employees and reservists. The Pentagon buys everything from ice cream to nuclear submarines and maintains what is probably the largest system of day-care centers in the world. It must be ready to transition to war in a heartbeat. And it must be prepared to cope with public relations nightmares from losing troops because of friendly fire to the latest sexual scandal or misconduct.

The person in charge is the secretary of defense. To assist him, in the office of the secretary of defense, there are two thousand staff members. The military is overseen by the chairman of the Joint Chiefs of Staff and the five other members—the service chiefs of the Army, Navy, Marines, and Air Force and a vice-chairman of a Joint Staff. Limited by law to under a thousand, the Joint Staff in fact numbers much more and has become the most influential in the Pentagon due to the Goldwater-Nichols Act. That act mandated that the services detail the best and brightest to joint duty. The services have complied and the results were self-evident. Assignment to the Joint Staff is now essential for promotion.

The fourth center of power in the Defense Department is the services themselves headed by a civilian secretary and staff and a uniformed chief and his staff. The services have jealously guarded their unique institutions and force structure. This has led to interservice rivalry. This competition is good when it produces. Too often, however, it has created redundancies. For example, each service has its own separate air force. In Vietnam, none of the services could communicate easily with the others in combat. Fortunately, the services have since become truly "joint" in operations if not in competition for budget dollars.

By Title X, the civilian service secretaries are assigned the responsibilities for training, organizing, equipping, staffing, and disciplining their service. The military have virtually no Title X or legal authority in law. By custom and practice, the uniformed military have been permitted to turn blind eyes to that distinction.

The fifth center of power is the unified commanders or "CinCs." These are geographic (Europe, Pacific, Atlantic, Latin America, Korea) and functional (Space, Strategic, Transportation, and Special Forces) commanders. Working for each are staffs jointly manned by representatives from each service. The CinCs report by law directly to the secretary of defense. By custom, the chairman of the JCS is usually placed in the chain of command and the CinCs report to the secretary through him. The CinCs were empowered by Goldwater-Nichols. Indeed, when Special Forces Command was created in 1986, because Congress believed that the services had little time for these elite troops, the CinC was given his own budget and a separate assistant secretary of defense was established. This is the only CinC that has a separate budget line (Program XI) and an assistant secretary of defense to look out for his interests.

As with the organization of Congress, no sensible business or rational entity would operate this way. Five power centers in essence constitute a system of checks and balances that stymies efficiency and, often, decisions. Each power center has particular needs. These needs may not contribute to the greater good. A case in point is the shift in focus to military forces that are more "expeditionary." Expeditionary means the ability to deploy quickly and efficiently.

The Navy–Marine Corps for years has been the nation's prime expeditionary force. By virtue of sea basing, these forces cover the globe without needing basing rights and other land-based access. As in Afghanistan, their reach inland can be considerable—in that case, over four hundred miles. The Air Force, recognizing the need for expeditionary forces, reconfigured its organization in the late 1990s. Operations in Afghanistan that have been principally Navy, Marine, Air Force, and Special Forces demonstrate the application of expeditionary-type capabilities.

The Army meanwhile is forming Interim Brigade Combat Teams (IBCT) to make these forces more deployable. The difficulty is achieving that result without building a second Marine Corps. Too often, redundancy has resulted. In war, this is not necessarily a bad thing. The dilemma is ensuring that redundancy is premeditated and not the result of bureaucratic competition.

Additionally, defense agencies have sprung up like Topsy. These agencies are designed to provide services for the entire department and not for single services. There are a number of defense agencies for communications, auditing, logistics, and intelligence. Taken together, these agencies account for nearly a third of the total defense budget. The problem is that these agencies are inefficient. A review team commissioned by then Secretary William Cohen found, for example, that the Defense Logistics agency routinely added a surcharge, often as high as 17 percent, to what it charged the services to cover its overhead. In other words, instead of costing less, the opposite was the case.

When this complex Department of Defense organization is matched with Congress, constituencies are created. A particular committee or member fashions an alliance with an agency or office. Breaking the iron grip on budgets and programs becomes difficult if not impossible. The consequence is that defense costs at least a quarter or a third more than it should if it were sensibly organized. It is irrationality of organization and not "pork" that is the real driver of unneeded cost. Military bases are the poster children for this dilemma.

Secretary Rumsfeld states that the Department of Defense has 20 to 25 percent more bases and infrastructure than it needs. These bases are enormously expensive to maintain. Environmental and workplace laws require strict enforcement and remediation. The department is not funded for them. So there is a double hit—many more bases than are necessary and greater expenditures just to keep going.

The political sensitivity of bases is as old as the republic. In the 1980s, as the Cold War was winding down and the United States had a huge excess of bases, after terrific birthing problems, a procedure for closing down unnecessary facilities, called the Base Realignment and Closing or BRAC process, was enacted into law. Every few years a commission appointed by the president and Congress would convene. This commission would survey the bases and make recommendations for realignment and closure to the president. Once that was completed, the list would go to Congress for a single up-or-down vote in each house. The intent was to remove politics as much as possible.

The last round was in 1996. Politics could not be excluded and the Clinton administration buckled. With an election pending, California was too important. Hence the administration removed an air force base from the list of bases to be closed. The upshot has been that despite the strong recommendations of the last two secretaries of defense and threats to veto the defense budget unless a new round of base closings was authorized, the next round will not take place until fiscal year 2005.

As with any political issue, there is substance as well as rhetoric. In fairness to members of Congress, bases at home mean jobs and revenues. As bases consolidate, it is clear that states such as California, Virginia, Texas, the Carolinas, Florida, and Nevada—which have the largest military populations and installations—have the advantage. For example, naval forces must be on the coastlines. The Army and Air Forces need large training areas. These cannot easily be moved. So dealing with the need for efficiency and savings clashes with political realities.

Similar problems of organization apply to law enforcement and intelligence. In December 2001, the president sensibly directed the new FBI director to reorient the agency to countering terrorism. Unsurprisingly, crime rates are increasing. The intelligence community, reduced in so-called human intelligence or humint, assets, has been ordered to get back into the business. However, all of this will take years. It is not simply a matter of signing a directive and then expecting an immediate reaction. How long does it take to train a professional in any field? Lawyers, doctors, and architects have at least three years of postgraduate studies. Why should that be any different in the law-enforcement and intelligence fields?

A further organizational problem is that no matter how often coordination is mandated, the disconnect between federal, state, and local authorities remains huge. The Clinton administration began a program in over one hundred cities to cope with what is euphemistically called "consequence management" of a terrorist attack with weapons of mass destruction. Emergency services such as those that performed such heroic work in New York on September 11th were to be coordinated, trained, and linked. Yet basic tests of local capabilities to respond to possible terrorist incidents show that the program has a long way to go.

National Guard forces report to state governors until they are nationalized. The role of the Guard has always been politically charged for that reason. And since the federal government picks up the tab after the Guard has been nationalized, states are anxious to use that route as much as possible. The problem is one of efficiency and cost. The Guard is a terrific resource, but putting that resource to good use is constrained by these organizational difficulties.

## The Office of Homeland Security

The continental United States has been directly attacked by an external enemy only a handful of times. During the War of 1812, the British burned the White House. In 1916, Pancho Villa sallied into New Mexico. December 7th, 1941, was the day that FDR remarked would live in infamy. September 11th brought home the reality that ocean barriers no longer assure the nation's safety.

Because of these historic and geostrategic realities, homeland security and defense have not been top priorities even during the Cold War, when nuclear attack was at least a distant possibility. Over the last few years, homeland defense has become more fashionable. The Hart/Rudman Commission, among others, called for establishing a cabinet position charged with homeland security. George W. Bush, having promised such a measure during the campaign, has now made good on that.

On October 8th, 2001, George W. Bush issued the executive order establishing the Office of Homeland Security and the Homeland Security Council. The mission of the office is to "develop and coordinate" the implementation of a national strategy to secure the United States from terrorist threats or attacks. Within that order, terms such as "coordinate, review, and assess," and "work with" are the verbs. And the office is meant to work with virtually all of the other departments (Treasury, Defense, Justice, Health and Human Services, Transportation, Management and Budget, CIA, FBI, FEMA) and to coordinate with State, Interior, Commerce, Labor, Agriculture, Energy, Veterans Affairs, and EPA).

But the director of Homeland Security is given no budgetary control or authority over the other departments. Nor is there any authority to discipline or hire and fire outside his immediate office. In that regard, this assignment could follow the pattern of the so-called Drug Czar or Director of the Office of National Drug Control Policy, an important but largely powerless position. As a start, eleven Homeland Security/Policy Coordination Committees (HSC/PCC) have been established (Detection, Surveillance, and Intelligence; Plans, Training, Exercises, and Evaluation; Law Enforcement and Investigation; Weapons of Mass Destruction Consequence Management; Key Asset, Border, Territorial Waters, and Airspace Security; Domestic Transportation Security; Research and Development; Medical and Public Health Preparedness; Domestic Threat Response and Incident Management; Economic Consequences; and Public Affairs).

There are three important it be assigned questions that will determine the value of this office. First, will it be assigned sufficient authority and power? Second, can this office deal with the full range of national vulnerabilities? Third, can this office resolve the basic bureaucratic obstacles that preclude full exchange of intelligence and information and assignment responsibility and accountability?

At this stage, these questions cannot be answered. However, the challenges can be illustrated with two examples. Regarding vulnerability assessment, will this office produce meaningful recommendations? Currently, airport security is transfixed with safeguarding aircraft. What happens on the far side of the metal detectors and gate security has captured attention. But to a potential terrorist intent on terrorizing, the lucrative target may no longer be the aircraft.

From curbside to check-in, lines have grown larger. There is no security check of people who are getting on line to buy tickets and to check in for flights. In some cases, these lines have hundreds and thousands of people waiting. Furthermore, security is being provided by National Guard troops. Some carry ammunition. Some may have been trained in close combat. However, who has looked closely at these contingencies?

At Atlanta's Hartsdale Airport, a man racing for a flight went up a down escalator to reach his gate in time. The result was near panic. Security overreacted. The individual was considered a possible terrorist. Virtually all air traffic on the east coast was shut down.

Suppose two terrorists entered a major airport carrying suitcase bombs. They would not be inspected or checked until they got to the ticket counter. With perhaps a thousand people in line, the effects of several suitcase bombs would be horrific. It would be made worse if the bombers were suicidal and if simultaneous attacks took place at multiple locations.

National Guardsmen would respond. For those with ammunition, the .223 caliber bullets for M-16 rifles are jacketed. Traveling in excess of twice the speed of sound, bullets are likely to penetrate and pass through what they hit. In other words, in a confined space such as an airport, collateral damage could be extensive.

Second, sharing intelligence and information will be difficult. The former head of counterterrorism for the FBI, James Kallstrup, is now head of security for New York City. After September 11th, Kallstrup has been vocal in criticizing the reluctance of the FBI (or for that matter any intelligence agency) to share intelligence even with someone who had a senior position within the organization. This difficulty of coordinating and sharing, especially in law enforcement and intelligence, is a major challenge. The need to maintain sources and methods and to protect sensitive information is clear. However, sharing is essential. Negotiating this bureaucratic reality will be one of the Office of Homeland Security's greatest challenges.

Of course, since coordination with the fifty states is essential, the selection of Governor Tom Ridge of Pennsylvania could be a deft stroke. One of Ridge's functions will be to serve as an ombudsman and facilitator with his former colleagues. As we will see, coordination among federal, state, and local authorities is likely to be the single most effective activity that can be undertaken to defend against domestic attacks.

## A Bottom Line or Two

The hard-nosed critic can look back over the past decade (or longer) and assert that the United States has not done badly. Perhaps there is nothing wrong in the way it is organized. It does the best that it can. Since the Constitution will not be rewritten to form a parliamentary or other form of representative government, debate is at the margin. Surely more efficiency and effectiveness are needed. However, even profound institutional change is unlikely to produce either.

For better or worse, that argument is short-sighted. The inherent dilemma is that the problems facing the United States are crosscutting and not nicely lumped under a single threat. The basic structure of government is purposely organized to preclude efficiency and often delicacy. Blunt instruments abound. Authority and responsibility are so finely parsed and dispersed across government that even obvious decisions are difficult to make. Against a threat such as the Soviet Union, these constraints were workable. Against box cutters and new threats to America's way of life, it would seem that such a cumbersome and convoluted organization lacks the flexibility and agility to respond. Furthermore, politics have become increasingly aimed at elections—campaigning and raising money. Governing seems a lesser priority. Campaign-centric politics are but one symptom of this failure to govern. Destructive personal politics are another.

The upshot has led to a people deficit. Fewer and fewer Americans are interested in government service. Before September 11th, virtually all agencies and departments were scrambling to hire and retain quality individuals in sufficient numbers to make up shortages. Through an unfortunate quirk in the law regarding retirement, the civil service will have a huge exodus of senior people over the next few years. There are no replacements in the pipeline because acquisitions were so few. This is particularly true in the Department of Defense.

One reason for this personnel deficit is a failure to empower people. The inhibitions on authority and responsibility throughout government are fatal when aggressive and dynamic people look at a career of service. They don't apply. This was the case in the Foreign Service until the new secretary of state came aboard. Whether this is a matter of his charisma remains to be seen.

The second cause for concern is that the current organization does not appear up to the task of reacting to these threats. To be sure, Operation Enduring Freedom has proceeded far better than anyone anticipated. However, when addressing the pieces of unfinished business—from the inherent vulnerability of an open society to keeping the two bookends of the current region of crisis from disintegration, it is not certain that the current structure, including Congress and the executive, will work.

The flaws are in the organization of both the executive branch and Congress. Unless or until the executive branch has the authority assigned to the appropriate agencies and departments—and that means reprioritizing budgets and people—and Congress is able to reduce some of the restrictions and impediments that block sweeping action, there is no guarantee that the future equivalent of nineteen men with box cutters will not do even greater damage.

# ★ 6 ★

## The Crescent of Crisis

(Note that the statistics come from the CIA World Fact Book;
and IISS, World Bank and OECD publications)

### Jihads and Chronic Conflict

Of the many causes of the violence, turmoil, and terror that currently afflict the crescent of crisis, two deserve special mention. The first is bin Laden's pathological and grotesquely skewed philosophy of religion, politics, and revolution manifested in his jihads or holy war against infidels and enemies of the faith. The tactics of this holy war are to punish and coerce. The United States and Saudi Arabia were the early targets, but more have since been added to the list.

The broad ambition is to create some form of a radical pan-Islamic regime. This entity, perhaps an al Qaeda organization writ large, would be loyal to the death to this perverted interpretation of Islam, funded with Saudi petro-dollars and armed with Pakistani nuclear weapons but not necessarily confined to one country or locale. Bin Laden's brazen disregard for Afghanistan as simply one battlefield on which to wage his jihad conveys the extraterritoriality and cynicism as well as the danger of his variety of extremism.

The second cause is the unyielding and quintessentially tragic political struggle over territory, sovereignty, resources, ambitions, and even survival, intensified by the centuries-long accumulation of historical animosities, jealousies, hatreds, and resentments, many of

175

which now seem uncontrollable. Despite pauses and relapses in this cycle of struggle, the trend is decidedly negative. Violence is not declining—quite the reverse. What is particularly frightening is the growing linkage between these two separate causes of turmoil and terror and the potency for disaster this interaction of powerful forces creates. These dangers, passions, and motives, filled with hatred and revenge, extend from the Eastern Mediterranean and the Arab-Israeli-Palestinian conflict to the Bay of Bengal and South Asia's India-Pakistan rivalry.

The center of this crescent includes the Gulf States, Syria, Iraq, and Iran. With religious roots of conflict as old as Judaism, Hinduism, Christianity, and Islam, political enmities and grievances have been supercharged by the impact of globalization, the reach of modern technology, and the fanatical perversion of religion directed toward violence, terror, and destruction. Given these and other harsh realities, it is difficult to overstate the potential for disruption and disaster that is present. Not only historical feuds are at work. Martyrdom through suicidal attack and jihad has become a weapon of choice.

With the demise of the Cold War, the threat of nuclear war that could end society as we know it disappeared. That is not true in this region, where the likelihood that weapons of mass destruction will be used is probably growing. War as it has usually been waged in the past century, with armies battling other armies, is not the principal fear, although India and Pakistan could certainly alter that calculus. Instead, the larger danger is the direct threat posed to the existing political order and to ruling regimes whether autocratic or democratic by the interactions of bin Laden's version of jihad and the chronic causes of conflict in this crescent of crisis.

It is extremely difficult for Westerners in general and Americans in particular to understand how young people anywhere could so enthusiastically embrace bin Laden's jihad and seek martyrdom in the fervor to inflict destruction on America. Hence, the videotapes discovered in Afghanistan during Operation Enduring Freedom of followers of bin Laden gleefully calling for death to all Americans are especially shocking and revealing. From a Western perspective, the hatred and the irrationality of the indoctrination and mind control needed to motivate such fanaticism are likewise difficult to comprehend. Yet, to an acolyte and would-be follower, the reasons for martyrdom are appealing and seductive. This is not a historical idiosyncrasy confined to this conflict or to parts of the crescent of crisis.

There are many instances of recent suicidal fanaticism. Japanese kamikazes during World War II as well as mass suicides of Japanese civilians fearing American captivity and Chinese "human wave" attacks in the Korean War are gruesome reminders. The distinction is that those were "traditional" wars. The conflict today is far from traditional by any Western standard.

Regarding the second cause, a great tragedy is that many grievances spring from equally legitimate reasons that now constantly clash in near-permanent and seemingly unresolvable conflict. Palestinian aspirations for sovereignty, particularly the return of their homeland, abut Israeli preoccupation over immediate safety and security and even the survival of the state. Long-term resolution of these disputes has been close to impossible. The new reality is that compromise may be even further away.

There are no satisfactory answers to the questions of who is in the right and who is in the wrong. More perplexing is what, if anything, can be done to mitigate the vicious cycle of violence, reprisal, revenge, and death that has become part of daily life in the Middle East. And what are the reasons that have escalated this violence and terror over the past few years to the point that negotiation, let alone lasting peace, seems a fruitless pursuit?

It is also difficult for most Westerners and especially Americans to picture life as a Palestinian or Israeli-Palestinian, all second-class citizens, under an increasingly harsh Israeli occupation in one's very own country. It is equally difficult to imagine life as an Israeli. Almost every Israeli has extended family that suffered horribly during the Holocaust and possibly since. Surrounded by vastly superior numbers of neighbors who seek the destruction of Israel, existence is not an academic question.

Similarly, it is difficult for a Westerner to conceive of life as a modern Saudi, Iraqi, or Iranian anxious to share in the governing and improving of society but denied any and all access to the levers and perquisites of power. What is not unimaginable is the reality that these conflicts have become increasingly intertwined and perhaps inseparable. Bin Laden has learned that his cause is advanced by widening jihad, not constraining it. The increase in the level of turmoil and terror on virtually all fronts is clearly to bin Laden's advantage.

This perception gap exists because of often profound cultural differences between American and non-Western societies and the American tendency to assume that others should or will act as we would. This was one of many reasons why the United States failed in the Vietnam War. Recent U.S. interventions in Panama, Haiti, Somalia, and Serbia show that this gap still exists. In the first three, each state is worse off than before. But other than in Yugoslavia in 1999 where NATO's future was at risk, these interventions had relatively little significance outside the region. That is decidedly not the case now. Dealing with these diverse and different cultures and ideologies in ways that are intelligent and informed and use common sense will be crucial to resolving many of the pieces of unfinished business that confront the nation and much of the world as well.

## Unfinished Business: Five Conflicts

Five intra- and interstate conflicts are of particular interest to this analysis. Moving from west to east, the Arab-Israeli-Palestinian is the first and perhaps the most publicized. By and large, it is difficult to separate this conflict from the others that exist in the Arab world.

Second are the internal conflicts in the Arab and Islamic worlds over leadership and unity, and within Islam itself. Leadership of a collective pan-Arab regime, dating back to Egyptian president Gamal Abdul Nasser, pits the larger and militarily more influential states of Egypt, Syria, and Iraq against one and another and against the wealth of Saudi Arabia. Iran plays an important and complicating role because it is a non-Arab, oil-rich, and fundamentalist-based regional power. And the Islamic sects of Sunni, Shi'a, and Wahabi are often in direct conflict.

Third is the struggle between modernization and the autocratic demands of traditional Islamic society, exacerbated by the tensions between Arab and non-Arab Islamic states and within Islam itself. Issues such as peace and stability, extending well beyond the forces of "Islamic fundamentalism" and the historical rivalries between secular leaders and clerics for power, are at stake. The future fabric of Islamic society will be largely determined by these tensions, although the impact and outcomes will vary from state to state.

Fourth is the India-Pakistani conflict. While Kashmir is the flash point, cultural, religious, and political differences are powerful components in this ongoing standoff. Although nuclear weapons provide one reason why the dangers of confrontation are more serious, the new strategic importance of South Asia as a bulwark in the fight against terrorism and instability also raises the stakes. The United States is deeply involved in both countries and Pakistan and India have become important potential strategic partners. For the United States, strategic necessity may compel strategic choice. However, politics create a huge obstacle to choosing any clear-cut or single policy direction.

The alternative of selecting either India or Pakistan as America's principal ally in the struggle to capture or kill bin Laden and his associates is untenable. Adverse reactions would be fierce and counterproductive. Believing it could "select" a single partner would label the United States as arrogant. Adopting the policy of strategic aloofness, often cast as "unilateralism," cannot engage the necessary cooperation for neutralizing extremism. And a policy of working both sides concurrently requires extraordinary delicacy and skill and therefore is inherently fragile. This is not a rich menu of choices for U.S. policymakers to contemplate.

Finally, the bin Laden model of conflict that perverts and turns Islam against both Islam and much of the rest of the world, principally the United States, must be delegitimized and disassembled. Not only must the head be severed. The body must be rendered impotent. Hence, attacking the legitimacy as well as the structure of bin Laden's jihad and supporting base is a prerequisite for success.

Put another way, bin Laden's jihadism is not simply Islamic fundamentalism run amok or a hijacking of a religion. Nor is it merely terrorism put to political use. Drawing from the European extremists and revolutionaries of the nineteenth century, there is a deeper ideological and political conviction present that drives strategy. Therein lies the cancer. From proper diagnosis will come a cure.

Bin Laden and his jihad are determined to disrupt and overthrow the political order much as the revolutionaries and extremists of an earlier century attempted. His sermon, while not intellectually well honed, relies on a combination of religious fervor, legitimacy, and reward in the afterlife for stirring conviction and ensuring loyalty to his extremist cause. Despite the vastly different cultural universes that separate bin Laden from most of the rest of the world, with perhaps a billion practitioners of Islam as potential followers, even the tiniest percentage of success in recruiting will yield thousands of possible converts.

The first four conflicts can be considered old news that still requires careful attention. The fifth conflict is very different and more dangerous than the others because it is highly exportable, as the United States discovered on September 11th, 2001. And it is this conflict created by bin Laden that creates the potentially explosive link with the others.

There may be little that can be done to reeducate the extremist bent on martyrdom. And it is clear that many Egyptians, Syrians, Lebanese, Israelis, Saudis, and other Arabs harbor deep emotional resentment and reasons for reprisal and revenge as do Sunnis, Shias and Wahabis against the others. In this case, the human condition is color and racially, if not gender, blind. But beyond basic explanations for turmoil and terror, it is true that the specific causes and roots vary greatly from state to state and conflict to conflict. Hence, there is no silver bullet or single policy that will address all of these conflicts.

The crux of the security challenge facing not just the region but much of mankind as well is that unless or until profound change for the better is instituted, turmoil and terror in this crescent of crisis can only get worse. The old protective barriers of geography and space that safeguarded the United States no longer will work quite so well. America's physical security is now directly affected by what happens in this region.

Washington's advice to steer clear of permanent alliances may or may not be relevant in the twenty-first century. However, the United States has no choice but to be engaged as the first line of its own defense. Engagement for reasons relating directly to physical self-defense is what makes this security challenge profoundly unique and different from that of the Cold War.

## The Bookends

The image of a simple bookshelf is clear. Each book is a separate entity, dependent on adjacent books for stability. What keeps the row standing are the bookends. Without either, the books will obviously collapse. And, if there are gaps in between, the books are also unstable. This image applies to the entire region.

The ingredients of oil, religion, politics, ideology, history, animosity, resentment, and weapons of mass destruction comprise part of the bookshelf and are a formula for inherent instability explosively volatile. Use of mass-destruction weapons by several belligerents is possible for the first time in history. And the impact of the information and knowledge revolutions has been to bring the world closer by breaking down the barriers that have isolated societies from outside influences.

One of this book's theses is that each of the points of conflict in this crescent is connected to the others. A second is that jihad and long-standing political points of conflict are commingling and overlapping. An explosion or spark in one locale can no longer safely be assumed to be isolated from the others. Given the extraordinary leverage that bin Laden has uncovered through attacking the openness of American society, it would be folly to believe that no one else will ever make use of this ploy. Hence, breaking the explosive links, in essence defusing at least one of these crises points, may be the only means that the United States will have at its disposal to keep the nation safe for the long term.

## The Roots

The roots of extremism and terror are ancient. Messianic views of religion, martyrdom, assassination, tyrannicide, regicide, and terror are not solely phenomena of this decade or century or of the current crises. The reason for a brief review is to cast light on means to mitigate their impact and on potential solutions. What will prove of particular interest is the similarity between the motivations of bin Laden and al Qaeda and the extremist movements of the nineteenth century. A little history illustrates the broader landscape.

It is a historical irony that one of the first known terrorist organizations was active in the Zealot struggle in Palestine from about A.D. 66–73. The struggle was shrouded in religious mysticism and carried out through a campaign of targeted assassination. The terrorists known as the *Sicarii* favored short knives and daylight hours to kill their enemies. Despite the often-contradictory literature describing the times, the *Sicarii* appear to have been extremist and anti-Roman (the imperial occupying power). Many of their victims were moderate Jews of the so-called Peace Party. This combination of messianic ambition cloaked in extreme religious garb, despite the question of whether the *Sicarii* were patriots or robbers, and a reported inclination toward martyrdom is not unique to bin Laden.

Messianic expectations mixed with terrorism defined a later sect—the Assassins. In today's jargon, the Assassins were a spin-off of the eleventh century Ismalis plying their trade two centuries later. The dagger was the weapon of choice and held a sacramental quality. The body counts grew steadily and included the Crusader King of Jerusalem, Conrad of Montferat. Two unsuccessful attempts were made on Saladin's life.

As is now well known, the word *assassin* comes from the Arabic for "hashish" or the marijuana-like substance the Assassins used to steel their nerves much as rum was administered for years to the British forces to bolster spirits and induce liquid courage under fire. Assassins of the thirteenth century used terror as a means to defend religious autonomy, a struggle that became ultimately fruitless. Throughout history, there have been many other terrorist groups, from the Thugees in India to the secret societies in China during the latter part of the nineteenth century.

American revolutionaries were regarded as terrorists and criminals in the quest for independence. The French Revolution, with its murderous excesses, led Edmund Burke to invent the term "reign of terror." However, it was the aftermath of both revolutions and the huge political transformations that were sweeping through Europe that created nearly two centuries worth of fodder for revolutionaries and extremists.

Monarchs and aristocracies ruled Europe in the early years of the nineteenth century. Britain was the exception, with the monarch balanced by an unwritten constitution and the beginnings of real democracy. For much of the post–Congress of Vienna century before World War I, turmoil and conflict within Europe were intrastate. The divine right of kings to rule was losing legitimacy and therefore political authority. Politics in European states were focused inward, one reason why major wars were largely avoided.

Europe was being transformed by the industrial revolution and by political revolutions such as those in 1830 and 1848. Italian and German unification led to the formation of the modern state system in Europe. Meanwhile, industrialization flourished. Political and economic modernization was sweeping throughout most of Europe.

Intellectual ferment over these transformations along with the struggle for political power produced ideologies of both left and right, each proposing an alternative form of government. In that regard, interestingly, communism and fascism were two sides of the same ideological coin. Both inherently were idealistic. Each sought to impose a better form of government.

Fascism called for a dictatorship by an elite who would provide the necessary discipline for society, which inherently was unruly. Communism envisaged a dictatorship of the proletariat in which, ultimately, government would disappear. And along the political spectrum were anarchists and social revolutionaries who looked on violence and terror as the means to achieve their political ends. In this last category bin Laden's predecessors resided.

Mikhail Bakunin is one representative of revolutionary enthusiasm with relevance today. His *Principles of Revolution*, published in 1869, and his "Revolutionary Catechism" were textbooks for terrorism and extremism. Bakunin believed that the cause of eradicating evil, that is, destroying Russian Imperial rule, was holy. Merciless destruction and reliance on terrorism were essential ingredients in cleansing Russia by sword, violence, and fire. Walter Lacquer's seminal work *The Age of Terrorism* provides further insights.

The relevant point is that Bakunin packaged his brand of extremism in a religious-like appeal and fervor. The ultimate aim was to foment a revolution that would drive out the ruling leaders and replace them with the revolutionaries. In Bakunin's bizarre logic, terrorism was actually seen as humane. Because terrorism was highly selective, it harmed far fewer people and brought far less destruction than a war that could kill tens of thousands and turn cities into rubble. Hence, terrorism, to paraphrase Lenin, became the weapon of terrorists with the object to terrorize.

It would take nearly four and a half decades before these extremist philosophies would find the operational means for seizing and consolidating power. Lenin and the Bolsheviks provoked the Russian Revolution and through it were able to establish the Union of Soviet Socialist Republics. Terror, violence, and revolution were essential parts of the tool kit. Trotsky, ultimately assassinated by order of Stalin in Mexico just prior to World War II, argued for "permanent revolution." Regardless of the tactical or permanent nature of revolution, in Europe, extremism fathered communism. A decade later, another form of extremism based on economic crisis, racial hatred, and the resentment of the accumulation of too many grievances from an unjust peace would produce the Third Reich, Nazism, and Adolf Hitler.

At this point, it is unknowable where the danger posed by bin Laden and his form of extremism will lead. Bin Laden apparently has escaped the vengeance of Operation Enduring Freedom. His whereabouts remain unknown to those who want to bring him to justice. Whether he will remain elusive or surface in a more virulent form remains unclear. But bin Laden has the potential of a Lenin, armed with a different ideology and revolutionary motive, to change the world to fit his version of jihad.

Bin Laden also could be a Pancho Villa who, after a foray or two, is forced to remain on the run. Regardless of bin Laden's staying power and endurance, it is perhaps inevitable that someone or something will replace him and assume his mantle. Indeed, in January 2002, the *Wall Street Journal* reported a possible contender in Southeast Asia: the *Jemaah Islamia*, an extremist Islamic group, announced its intent to establish a state dedicated to the destruction of the West.

From an American security perspective, therefore, the analogies of bin Laden and others like him with nineteenth century extremism are useful reference points in making the case that the danger may be broader than simply al Qaeda. States in the crescent of crisis, like Europe of that earlier time, are under intense pressure to modernize. These pressures are constrained and even repressed by the nature of the largely autocratic regimes, many legitimized by a hereditary succession system, whether Saudi Arabia or Syria.

The largest threat that emerges from bin Laden's extremism is the formula that followers or other revolutionaries can plagiarize. Bin Laden's initial version of a "revolutionary's catechism" stemmed from a distorted interpretation of Islam and enormous resentment against the Saudi ruling classes as the basis for revolution, vengeance, and religious cleansing. The clarion call is to establish a pan-Islamic regime, crossing through much of the crescent of crisis and funded by oil and strengthened by access to nuclear weapons. Others could well answer this clarion call. Keeping America safe means preventing that eventuality.

## Unfinished Business: The Arab-Israeli- Palestinian Conflict

The "bookends" that define the current zone of battle politically and geographically are obvious and have had long, bloody, and violent histories. Three of the states—Israel, Pakistan, and India—became independent at about the same time, just after World War II. Israel's creation and the subsequent Arab-Israeli conflict led to four full-scale wars in three decades and chronic bouts of violence and "inti-fada." The first war, in 1948, assured the survival of the infant Jewish state.

Today, Israel is a regional military superpower with 163,000 mili-tary personnel under arms, 425,000 reservists, and mandatory national service. Its intelligence service is regarded as one of the world's best and Israel is pathological about internal security. El Al is the only airline not to have had a hijacking. Israel's population is 6.4 million of which about a fifth are Arab Muslim, mostly Sunni. Israel has 18,000 settlers in Gaza and the West Bank; 217,000 in East Jerusalem; and 15,000 on the Golan. Life expectancy is seventy-eight and per capita GDP is $20,000.

There are about 3 million Palestinians in the autonomous areas of Gaza and Jericho. Estimates of GDP and life expectancy and other economic data are not reliable but are certainly substandard. The Palestinian Authority has a paramilitary of fifteen thousand includ-ing police and other security forces equipped with small arms and clearly no match for any trained military opposition, especially the formidable Israeli Defense Force (IDF).

This history of Palestine and Israel is well known. After World War I, the British controlled Palestine. The earlier Balfour Declara-tion authorized settlement by Jews. For the next three decades, Pal-estinian Jews went about creating the means for establishing a Jewish state. Unfortunately, history and geography were unkind. Palestine and its capital of Jerusalem are the holy of holies for three of the world's great religions. Judaism, Christianity, and Islam share com-mon heritages and sacrosanct territory from the Dome of the Rock, a holy Islamic place, to Nazareth and the birthplace of Jesus to the Wailing Wall.

Pogroms and holocausts against the Jews in Europe created streams of refugees fleeing to Palestine and the promise of a perma-nent Jewish homeland. Palestinian Jews relied on terror to force British withdrawal. The *Irgun* and *Palmach* were Jewish terrorist organizations conceived for those purposes. Indeed, Menachem Begin, later an Israeli prime minister, was part of the cell that bombed the King David Hotel in Jerusalem, wounding and killing a large number of British soldiers. To the Jews, the targets were British occupying forces. And wounding rather than killing was the preferred tactic since it meant that more soldiers would be needed to deal with the injured. This selective use of terror was clever and efficient. It was terror, nonetheless.

The British, under a UN mandate, finally agreed to withdraw, creating the state of Israel. The first war broke out almost immediately. Israel of course defeated its Arab neighbors. While much has been made of American support for Israel, in 1948 it was on political rather than economic and financial levels that such succor was provided. France was Israel's closest ally.

Israel is a tiny state, the size of New Jersey. It is less than ten miles wide at its narrowest point and is surrounded by hostile Arab neighbors. To the Arab world, Israel was an unacceptable irritant thrust down its collective throat by the British and the "Zionist conspiracy." Israel's presence was an affront. Destroying Israel and driving Israelis into the sea were not lunatic intentions.

Israel and its citizens, however, could not forget the Holocaust. The vivid image of tens or hundreds of thousands of Jews passively submitting to Nazi dicta and orders that consigned death warrants and horrible incarcerations at concentration camps never would disappear from Israel's psyche. Israel might not fight to the last woman and child, but it would never delegate its survival to anyone else.

The second war was fought in October 1956 concurrent with the Anglo-French attack and intervention in Egypt in the Suez Crisis. Britain and France had intended to occupy and hold the canal. Israel attacked west into the Sinai. However, international opinion including that of both the United States and Soviet Union ran so strong that the ill-fated attackers were forced to withdraw from Suez. The Soviets also used Suez and the temporary siding with the United States as cover for their bloody repression of the Hungarian Revolution in November.

Seven years later, the third war, named the "Six Day War" for its duration, ended with Israel seizing and occupying Jordan's West Bank, Syria's Golan Heights, Jerusalem, the Gaza strip, and much of the Sinai east of Suez that was Egyptian. Israel had launched a preemptive attack and overwhelmed the Arab forces arrayed against it. Until that time, the bulk of Israel's support and armaments came from Europe and not the United States.

The magnitude of the defeat and the loss of territory were unacceptable to the Arab states. Indeed, foreign observers viewed Arab forces very much as a joke, with little fighting capacity. The Soviet Union, which after the Suez Crisis had increased its presence in the Middle East, saw the opportunity to cultivate Arab allies, particularly in Syria and Egypt. It is probably forgotten that until 1972, the Soviets stationed over twenty-five thousand military advisors in Egypt. The Egyptian and Syrian armies had been tailored very much in the Soviet model and used Soviet equipment, for which they had paid top dollar or shekel equivalent.

Anwar Sadat realized that ultimately peace with Israel was in Egypt's best interest. Sadat also despaired of Soviet presence and influence. As a result, by 1973, Sadat had expelled most Soviet forces from Egypt. The Soviets still maintained a small naval presence. Meanwhile, in part as a counter to Soviet influence and in part due to increasing pressure from domestic politics and pro-Israeli lobbies, the United States evolved into Israel's strongest supporter as well as its main supplier of arms and foreign assistance. Sadat realized that no progress toward peace could occur as long as Israel still occupied the Sinai and Egyptian territory.

For months, Sadat secretly planned for a war to regain the Sinai. Syria, too, was engaged, as was Jordan. The war was to be launched in October 1973 during Ramadan and Yom Kippur, two of the holiest times for Muslims and Jews. Egypt attacked and successfully crossed the canal into the Sinai. Syria mounted its charge south of the Golan Heights and nearly succeeded in cutting Israel in two. Surprise was complete. Israel was literally fighting for its life.

The United States mounted a major resupply effort of military equipment to Israel. Time was critical as the battles raged, so the bulk of the shipments had to be delivered by air. America's NATO allies, save Portugal, fearing OPEC and economic retaliation from the Arab states, refused permission for overflight and basing rights.

Virtually every gallon of gasoline the United States flew into Israel required seven or eight gallons to fuel the aircraft.

The Israelis recovered from the surprise attack. After desperate fighting in the north, the IDF forced the Syrian Army to retreat and ejected them from Israeli territory. In the south, counterattacks were mounted against the Egyptians in the Sinai. An Egyptian army corps in the Sinai was cut off and surrounded. It was not a virtuoso performance for Israel throughout the first stages of the war but neither was it a loss. Having regained the initiative, the IDF was able to beat back the Syrian and Egyptian attack and regain most of the territory it had occupied since the 1967 war.

The Soviet Union could not remain silent and allow its allies to be so ignominiously defeated. First, the Soviets threatened to intervene with its forces. Since it already had a substantial number of warships in the Mediterranean as part of its naval *eskadra*, a naval intervention if only to show political support was perhaps the less risky option. Soviet warships had been purposely interpositioned among ships of the U.S. Sixth Fleet. The situation was growing critical. A single incident between naval forces, including an encounter by accident, could have had grave and unintended impact.

The tension was so palpable that the Sixth Fleet Commander, Vice and later Admiral Daniel J. Murphy, sent for his son, who happened to be stationed aboard a frigate escorting the fleet flagship. Murphy wanted a brief visit "just in case," as he later put it. The younger Murphy, who went on to become a vice-admiral and command the Sixth Fleet twenty-seven-years later, recalled that he greeted his father with the stern admonition "I hope you know what the hell you're doing."

As with Operation Allied Force in 1999, there was an extraordinarily serious crisis at home. The Watergate scandal had exploded and criminal and congressional investigations were homing in on the White House and Richard Nixon. The president was reported to be in such a desperate physical condition over Watergate that, after the Soviets threatened to intervene, there was concern that Nixon might order the use of nuclear weapons. And the United States was still fighting a war in Vietnam even though it had begun reducing its forces several years earlier.

The Yom Kippur or Ramadan War and the subsequent U.S.–Soviet crisis are not all that well remembered. Responding to head off possible Soviet intervention in any form, especially ground forces, the White House ordered that "Defense Condition Three"—that is, a military alert condition of readiness short of wartime but higher than in normal peacetime—be set. The media reported this as a "nuclear alert," which technically it was not, even though the strategic forces did set a higher degree of readiness. Nixon and his national security adviser, Henry Kissinger, would later write that this superpower nuclear confrontation was a more dangerous threat to peace than the Cuban Missile Crisis a decade before.

Both men knew that the Soviet nuclear inventory was fully capable of destroying the United States in 1973, something it could not have done in 1962. Along with much of the American public, the Soviets were taken aback by this response. The strength of the reaction in America probably reinforced Soviet concerns. A nuclear standoff, given a politically wounded American president, must have frightened the Politburo as much as it did many members of Congress, already concerned with Nixon's behavior. Fortunately, the Soviets were either bluffing or never intended to escalate this crisis after Israel had regained the military initiative.

Had the Soviet Union sent ground and air forces to Egypt, the prospect that they might engage the Israelis in conflict was real. It was also likely that, given no time to acclimate to or train for battle in the Egyptian desert, the Soviet forces were at a severe disadvantage. The IDF was also a better force and there was every chance it could have badly beaten Soviet forces. The Soviets understood these risks and the potential consequences of having thousands of Soviet soldiers as potential Israeli prisoners of war. The Soviet Union did not press forward. Meanwhile, Israel remained firmly encamped in the Golan, the West Bank, and the Sinai. Despite "a close run thing," the combined Egyptian-Syrian attack had been beaten back. The Soviet Union did not intervene, the United States stood down from "DefCon Three," and years later the elder Admiral Murphy (who would go on to be Vice-President George Bush's chief of staff) would be present at the change of command when his son took over the Sixth Fleet.

As noted earlier, Sadat used the war to launch the peace. He ultimately would go to Israel and later would sign the Camp David Accords with Menachem Begin, formally establishing peace between the two states. However, Egypt was the only Arab state to do so. Israel remained at war with the others.

Under the leadership of the two heads of state and President Jimmy Carter, peace in the Middle East was no longer an impossible dream. The key to future success was engaging the other Arab states. Unfortunately, Iran, one of America's major allies in the Gulf, experienced its revolution. The shah was out in part because his reform effort failed and he did not take the threat of his potential successor as seriously as he should have. The Ayatollah Khomeini and strict cleric rule were in. And, in 1980, Iraq marched against Iran.

For twenty years, the Arab-Israeli-Palestinian conflict had had moments of peaceful interludes and promise and years of turmoil and terror. The Israeli occupation of Lebanon, the massacres in 1982 of Palestinians in camps near Beirut in which Prime Minister Ariel Sharon played a crucial role and for which Arabs accuse him of committing war crimes, strikes against Syria and Iraq, and terrorism against Israel are reminders of the violence that is never far removed. But after the Gulf War and orchestrated by Norway's then foreign minister Dr. Johann Holst, who sadly died at a very young age shortly after, the Oslo Accords between Israel and what would become the Palestinian Authority (PA) under Yassir Arafat were negotiated in 1993.

Oslo was based on a land-for-peace swap. Over the next decade, both sides agreed to Israeli withdrawal from the bulk of the occupied territories. In return, the Palestinian Authority would ultimately recognize Israel and reject all means to destroy her. Sovereignty would gradually be returned to the Palestinian Authority, ultimately leading to an independent Palestinian state. Agreement over Jerusalem's final status, perhaps the thorniest problem, was deferred.

At the time, the Israeli Labor party enjoyed a majority. Prime Minister Yitzhak Rabin, former minister of defense, was personally highly popular and strongly in favor of reaching a just peace with the Palestinians. A formal peace treaty had been negotiated and signed with Jordan in October 1994—what should have been a major landmark.

Tragically, a fanatic Israeli, an ultraorthodox Jewish student who believed that any concessions to the Palestinians threatened Israel's existence, killed Rabin in 1995. His assassination was one of the worst disasters to affect the peace process and the Middle East. His immediate successor, Shimon Peres, would not retain office as political power shifted to the right-wing Likud party.

Prime Minister Binyamin Netanyahu was and remains highly conservative. A most articulate spokesman for his country, Netanyahu had served in the government and as ambassador to the United States. His brother Jonathan had led the famous commando raid on Entebbe Airport to rescue Israeli citizens taken hostage by troops responsible to Uganda's psychotic president, Idi Amin. Netanyahu's brother was killed by a stray bullet, the single Israeli casualty. As prime minister, Netanyahu actively distrusted Arafat and the peace process. Given his history, that distrust was predictable. It did, however, impede the peace process.

Under Netanyahu's administration and the slogan "peace with security," Israel began moving its citizens back into the West Bank, defying the UN Security Resolutions that forbade new settlements. The Palestinians of course retaliated with protests and violence. When Netanyahu was replaced by Ehud Barak, Israel's most decorated soldier, in the 1999 elections, hope for restarting the peace process was rekindled. Like Rabin's, Barak's distinguished military service gave him the legitimacy to embark on energizing the peace process.

Barak was prepared to swap land for peace. However, no real progress was made. The Middle East peace process was threatening to spiral in the wrong direction. In the summer of 2000, as his term was winding down, Bill Clinton summoned Barak and Arafat to Camp David for a last-ditch effort to bring peace to the Middle East.

The reasons for this effort went beyond any ambitions Clinton may have harbored for leaving a legacy. The Oslo Peace Process was in its final stages. Arafat threatened to proclaim an independent Palestinian state in September. Israel found that unacceptable. A crisis was in the making.

The negotiations were intense and went on for just over two weeks. Clinton was present for most of them, facilitating and cajoling both sides. In the end, Camp David failed. Barak believed that he had gone further than he should have in agreeing to return virtually all of the occupied territories to Palestinian control. Barak saw Arafat as the villain in not accepting what to Israel was a generous and bold offer in the extreme. Israel had gone, in its view, more than the additional mile.

To the Palestinians, the issue was not about percentages of territory where the battle was drawn over relatively tiny slices of land but entirely over sovereignty. Palestine demanded full authority for self-rule, independent of and not subservient to Israel for its security. These two diplomatic ships were not just passing each other in the night. The ships were not sailing in the same ocean. Despite his charm and force of personality, Clinton could not close these differences. To some critics, Clinton's initiative exacerbated the conflict because there was no obvious solution. False expectations were created. Failure was inevitable in this view as was the return to violence. Sadly, both happened.

In late September, Ariel Sharon, then defense minister, took a controversial stroll on Temple Mount, a holy place to Islam. His entourage of bodyguards and politicians was large. Palestinians and Arabs were deeply offended by what they believed was a purposeful affront by Sharon. Riots and violence followed in protest, a repetition of what had happened eleven years earlier during Desert Shield when violence broke out following a Palestinian gathering on Temple Mount. Palestinians declared an "intifada" or uprising in protest. Since then, the cycle of violence has worsened dramatically.

Following the Camp David debacle and an unsuccessful attempt to get the talks back on track at a conference held in Taba, Israel, in January, Barak was humiliated and routed in the February election.

Sharon became the new prime minister, heading a coalition government. Given a choice between talk and action, Sharon clearly favored the latter. Israel resumed adding new settlements in the West Bank. Palestinian violence increased first with stones and then with guns and bombs. There was a series of bitter attacks and escalation by both sides.

Palestinian suicide bombers from the terrorist groups Hamas, Egyptian Islamic Jihad, and Hezbollah targeted innocent civilians at restaurants, on buses, and in shopping malls. Israeli soldiers were shot dead in ambushes. The Israeli military counterattacked. Israel adopted a policy of preemptive or targeted killing, namely assassinating Palestinian agents and terrorists before they could perpetrate terrorist acts. A vicious cycle of terror, reprisal, counterreprisal, and terror again has become the norm. In this killing, Israeli and particularly Palestinian civilians did the dying, the latter comprising the bulk of the casualties.

Despite peace missions led by CIA Director George Tenet, former Majority Leader George Mitchell, and, for the Bush administration, retired Marine General Anthony Zinni, there is no end in sight to the violence. In the fall of 2001, George Bush called for an independent Palestinian state, the first American president ever to do so. In a speech in Louisville, Kentucky, Secretary of State Colin Powell repeated the proposal. Unfortunately, violence in Israel and Palestine has postponed further negotiation and the unprecedented U.S. declaration in favor of an independent Palestinian state has had little impact. Sharon has demanded seven days of peace as a prerequisite before Israel will resume talks with the PA. Over the past months, it has proved impossible to restrict violence for as long as seven days.

In December 2001, an Israeli Army helicopter destroyed a building next to Arafat's office. Arafat was not harmed in the attack. Since then, Arafat had been largely trapped in his office, with Israeli tanks and armored vehicles parked outside his office. The message is unmistakable. In January 2002, Israeli commandos intercepted a ship in the Red Sea carrying some fifty tons of weapons for the Palestinian Authority. Since then, violence has continued from Palestinian suicide bombers and machine gunners and strong Israeli military reprisals.

Excerpts from *The Strategic Survey*, an annual publication of the highly regarded International Institute for Strategic Studies in London, describe the state of the Arab-Israeli-Palestinian relationships over the last half-decade. For 1996–1997, the first year of Netanyahu's prime ministership, the *Survey* reported: "The intransigence of the ideologically driven Likud government in Tel Aviv and . . . Arafat's weakness combined . . . to cast the once-promising Arab-Israeli peace process in doubt. . . . The result was a return to rock-throwing street demonstrations against Israeli soldiers and suicide bombings against Israeli citizens. . . . Negotiations have stalled and threatened to break down, leaving the area on the verge of yet another wave of extremism and violence."

The report for 1997–1998 was bleaker: "A long year . . . left the Israeli government, the Palestinians and neighboring Arab states further apart in early 1998 than at any time since the signing of the Oslo Accords in 1993. The stalemate . . . has become dangerous." The 1998–1999 *Strategic Survey* was even worse: "Despite the continued efforts of the United States . . . the end result was dismal." Netanyahu's policies had alienated many Israelis and his government lost a vote of confidence.

With Barak's accession to the prime ministership in May 1999, the *Survey* reflected optimism by not reporting any negative changes. Barak, as noted, was the peace candidate. On his broad shoulders expectations rested and ran high. The failure to negotiate a peace cost Barak his office. *The Strategic Survey* wrote: "Almost anything that could go wrong for the Middle East Peace Process did go wrong in 2000." Like Netanyahu before him, Barak was decisively defeated in the February 2001 election. The 2001–2002 *Survey* was not out when this book went to press.

The tragic state of violence and the seeming intractability of the conflict are reflected in one particular news account. On January 16th, 2002, Palestinian gunmen killed Avi Boaz, a seventy-one-year-old American Jew who had lived in Israel for forty years. Boaz, an architect, had never applied for citizenship. He also had close Palestinian friends and one family that he had adopted as his own.

The Al-Aqsa Martyrs Brigade associated with Arafat's Fatah movement claimed responsibility for killing a "filthy Israeli agent." The charge was ludicrous. The tragedy was not. The current situation has made friendships between Jews and Palestinians increasingly dangerous and therefore less likely. The Boaz murder, multiplied many score, reflects the depth of the turmoil and terror that must be redressed if any progress is to be made in winning a peace.

The consequences are obvious. Through the last elected four prime ministers (Peres was an interim office holder), two—Rabin and Barak—had sufficient credibility to risk all for peace. For different reasons, both failed. The other two, highly conservative politicians—Netanyahu and Sharon—were not going to risk much for peace. In that regard, for the short term they were successful. For the long term, disaster looms.

Israel will continue to administer Palestinians harshly. The quest for security will no doubt produce greater restrictions on the rights of Palestinians and even Israelis. For this, Israel will be condemned by some for violating human rights. A few of the allegations will be valid. But certainly, extremists will inflate these charges and elevate them to full-fledged acts of terrorism. The Army will continue to kill and arrest suspected Palestinian terrorists. Israeli bulldozers will continue to raze Palestinian villages in attempts to punish and deter terrorism.

Meanwhile, Palestinians will be further alienated and disenfranchised. Hatred and revenge will build. Violence will beget terrorism; terrorism will beget more violence. No matter how well-intended Arafat may or may not be, controlling these passions will be impossible.

In the Arab world, resentment against Israel will grow. The notion of Israel as a democracy will be increasingly derided as Israel relies on force and violence to counter violence. Meanwhile, Israelis who by and large are anxious for a peaceful and fair resolution become more cynical. If Rabin and Barak could not come to an agreement with the Palestinians and Arafat, what other politician will? Sharon realizes this dilemma. But despite Israeli public opinion that still favors peace, there is no obvious means of achieving that goal. Hence, the situation is deadlocked and perhaps at its lowest point since Israel won its war for independence fifty-four years ago. For extremists who rely on perverting Islam for their own ends, this tragedy will be seen as heaven-sent from Allah in the war against the West and those whom these fundamentalists wish to destroy.

As this cycle of violence escalates, so does the risk of uncontrollability and further escalation. The use of some form of mass-destruction agent is far from inconceivable. As the turmoil and terror intensify, one surprise thus far has been the relative restraint shown in limiting attacks and reprisals to relatively confined areas and relatively small numbers of people. Suicide bombings are horrific. However, no event of the magnitude of September 11th has been perpetrated—yet. Hence, precautions and preventive polices must be taken now to ensure that neither side will use these diabolical agents of destruction.

## Unfinished Business: Egypt, Syria, Iran, and Saudi Arabia

Within the Arab and Muslim states of the crescent of crisis, there are two parallel conflicts underway. One is over the leadership and unity of the Arab and Muslim worlds. This is a largely external issue and not readily visible since Nasser failed decades ago.

A unified Arab and Islamic front under a strong spokesman or leader could become an unavoidable option if, as the United States continues its "war against terrorism," its methods become heavy-handed and offensive to the Islamic world. Making impositions for assistance to hunt down terrorists could overload certain states. Racial profiling by the United States of practitioners of Islam, whether inevitable or through inadvertence, will be offensive. In these circumstances, Islam and the Arab world may need a counter-weight to what appears to be unacceptable U.S. conduct in how it wages the fight against terrorists and terrorism. If this situation were to occur, the United States would be stigmatized by the same argu-

ments and allegations that are being used against the Israelis and
their treatment of Arabs and Palestinians.

The second conflict is internal to each state and pertains to the
clash between the traditional values and spiritual bases for Islam and
modernization. As the Israeli-Palestinian conflict is partly defined by
the clash between sovereignty and security, in Islam the greatest tension is between maintaining adherence to the faith and accommodating the powerful forces seeking modernization. And there are also
the differences between Sunni, Shi'a, and Wahabi sects.

No Arab or Muslim state dominates the others. Nor does any
single leader possess the charisma, legitimacy, and influence to take
on this role. However, the upsurge in violence in the Israeli-
Palestinian conflict, the threat of extremism posed by bin Laden, and
the clash of traditional values and modernization are fundamental
challenges to stability and peace in the region and elsewhere. The
need to address them is critical. But there may be few good answers.

Egypt is the largest and probably the most powerful military state
in the Arab-Muslim part of the Middle East. The challenges noted
above particularly affect Egypt. The test for its leadership is to navigate the treacherous currents in the Arab-Israeli-Palestinian conflict
while responding to the pressures for modernization at a time when
extremism remains a direct threat to the regime.

Egypt's population approaches 71 million; some 94 percent are
Sunni. It has a military of about 443,000. It is the second largest
recipient of U.S. foreign military assistance behind Israel. But Egypt
is desperately poor, with a per capita GDP of about $3,600 and an
average life expectancy of just over sixty-three. Egypt therefore suffers from economic deprivation. Deprivation gives rise to dissent.
And many Egyptians still do not support the peace with Israel and
are vocal about Israel's harsh treatment of the Palestinians.

Hosni Mubarak has been president since 1981. Egypt is a republic with duly elected political leaders. However, political instability is
real. Extremists, radicals, and terrorists abound in significant numbers. Sadat was assassinated by militants inflamed by the peace with
Israel. Islamic Jihad is Egyptian and five of the nineteen terrorists
responsible for September 11th were reported to be Egyptian nation-

als. Hence, while Egyptian intellectuals have been in the vanguard of Arab political thinking, Egypt's peace with Israel, its desperate economic condition at home, and its constant battle against extremism limit its ability to lead an pan-Arab or Islamic movement.

Egypt must therefore struggle with its fierce domestic economic and political problems. While it has an important role to play as an intermediary with other Muslim states, and is seen in that capacity by the United States, its political fragility is real. The prospect of a radical group's seizing power is no longer far-fetched even though bin Laden's sights no doubt are set on Saudi Arabia and the Gulf side of the Middle East. For the United States, the stability and longevity of Mubarak's rule cannot be taken for granted. Minimizing these risks, however, is something that most likely will be accomplished by dealing with matters external to Egypt.

Syria is unlikely to compete for any leadership role until such time as its relatively new president, Bashar al Assad (son of Hafiz al Assad, who died in July of 2000), has firmly grasped the reins of power. Syria does, however, have a critical role to play if it so wishes in forging an Arab-Israeli peace. Syria is a republic with a popularly elected political leadership although the process is tightly controlled and coups had been relatively common in earlier decades. Its population is about 17 million, two-thirds of whom are Sunni. Syria's average per capita GDP is about $7,800, twice Egypt's; life expectancy is nearly seventy. It has a military of 321,000 active-duty forces and still stations about 20,000 troops in Lebanon.

In the mid 1990s, Syria was helpful in advancing the peace process. Well before Assad died, there were reports that the Syrian president had assured Bill Clinton of Syria's interest in making peace with Israel. The Israeli withdrawal from Lebanon was a positive step in that direction. However, the unraveling of the Israeli-Palestinian situation and the failure to reach agreement over returning the Golan Heights have cooled Syrian interest. Syria too is categorized by the United States as a state that sponsors terrorism. The infamous Bekaa Valley in Lebanon has been a Syrian-run terrorist training area for decades.

Anyone who has visited the Golan Heights realizes that it is indeed an invaluable strategic asset. The heights rise high above Israel's northern border, and on a clear day both Damascus and the Mediterranean are visible. Syrian forces in command of the heights directly threaten the northern part of Israel. Remembering the near disaster in 1973 when Syria almost cut Israel in half by attacking from Kunitera, a small town south of the heights, the Golan will not easily be returned. However, that piece of territory may hold the key to future peace.

Iran is, of course, a non-Arab Islamic state. It has a population of 66 million, slightly smaller than Egypt. About 90 percent are Shi'a Muslim and the average life expectancy is nearly seventy. Also a republic with popular elections, Iran is controlled by the leader of the Islamic Revolution, Ayatollah Ali Hoseini-Khamenei, appointed for life by the Assembly of Experts. Iran's president is elected every four years. In June 2001, Ali Mohammed Khatami-Ardakani was reelected. Iran's per capita GDP is about $6,500 and its active army is about 513,000.

Before the 1979 revolution, Iran was a close U.S. ally and friend. Under the Shah, Iran was a principal buyer of U.S. arms. American strategy was to bolster two pillars of the Persian Gulf—Iran and Saudi Arabia—against Soviet encroachment. Strategy was based on blocking Soviet appetites for warm-water ports and the rich Gulf oil fields. After the Ayatollah Khomeini took over, Iran became an adversary and was eventually declared a rogue nation harboring terrorists. Hezbollah is an Iranian creation. The tension is common to much of Islam: a conservative and often repressive ruling clerical elite and a progressive, popular leader supported by a society anxious to modernize and even Westernize to raise Iran's standard of living.

Saudi Arabia is perhaps the most perplexing of the Gulf States for America. On the one hand, the Saudis regard themselves as good friends of the United States. This friendship goes back to World War II. American intervention in the Gulf War in 1990 was appreciated. However, the appreciation was defined on Saudi terms. This difference in cultural outlook did not always play well in the United States. Many Americans felt the United States was due a larger and more public display of appreciation by the Saudis and, after September 11th, far more support in waging the war against terrorism.

Saudi Arabia has large oil reserves and a source of long-term income, provided oil prices are at least economically competitive. A large state about one-fifth the size of the United States, the Kingdom has a population of about 23 million, of which 5.5 million are non-Saudis. It is a monarchy that maintains absolute control and has a legal system derived from the Sharia or Islamic law with strict behavioral rules and punishments that seem barbaric by Western standards. Women, for example, have few rights and must conform to an unyielding dress and conduct code. Punishments include beheading, lashing, amputation, and other corporal means that have been long prohibited in the West. Saudi Arabia practices the Wahabi form of Sunni Islam. Its population has an average life expectancy of about sixty-eight years and the average per capita GDP is $10,500. The Saudi military is comprised of 126,000 serving forces and a National Guard of 75,000.

For the Saudi monarchy, the threat of instability is never far away. The stationing of American forces in large numbers has put immense pressure on Saudi society. Infidels were never tolerated in large numbers. And after the 1996 terrorist bombing of Khobar Towers, where U.S. troops were quartered, the bulk of American forces were moved and sequestered in remote parts of the kingdom. This relocation may have relieved some of the societal tensions. It also kept Americans separated from their Saudi military counterparts. Hence, the value of direct military-to-military contact was marginalized.

Moreover, the Saudi leadership must deal with the forces of modernization and the traditions of Wahabism that remain very conservative. The vastly different views of women between the Saudis and the West have come into direct conflict. A female Air Force officer sued the secretary of defense over Saudi dress codes that were mandatory for U.S. servicewomen in the kingdom off base. And the seemingly hypocritical Saudi stance on alcohol, where it is forbidden in the kingdom but partaken almost anywhere else, does not go down well with Americans, who find this conduct puzzling at best.

The real strains, however, are on the many Saudis who are disenfranchised and estranged. Osama bin Laden is the world champion poster child in that category. His hatred of the regime probably started with his isolation from it. Then it was not a giant leap to accuse the royal family of religious apostasy by its countenance of large numbers of Americans encroaching on holy lands.

In part to keep extremism and extremist elements outside Saudi borders, upward of tens of billions of dollars have been donated each year to Islamic charities. How much of this money goes to legitimate purposes and how much to radical madrasses that indoctrinate young students with highly provocative and anti-Western propaganda has never been revealed. However, this practice has been recognized and occasionally condemned by the United States as another example of Saudi hypocrisy. Furthermore, unconfirmed reports of increasing social problems with drugs and alcohol among the upper classes inside the kingdom have circulated, increasing the rhetoric over Saudi double standards.

In early 2002, increasing disenchantment with the Kingdom over its lack of support for the U.S. effort to root out terrorism led a number of members of Congress to call for a withdrawal of U.S. forces from Saudi bases. Reports of unofficial Saudi requests for American forces to leave the kingdom once the current phase of Enduring Freedom has ended circulated in the U.S. media. Despite the assurances of both the Bush and Saudi administrations that no requests for withdrawal have even been discussed, the large U.S. presence is an irritant and a sword that cuts in two directions. American military presence in Saudi Arabia and at Prince Sultan Air Base has been essential for operational reasons to pursue the campaign in Afghanistan. It also is a reassurance and guarantee that Iraq will not reattack south. On the other hand, the strains on Saudi culture are great. The Saudi leadership is highly sophisticated and recognizes how domestic politics affect foreign policy, theirs and ours. America's embargo of South Africa over racial discrimination was not lost on them. The treatment of women, Saudis realize, could provoke a strong negative response.

Less visibly, the U.S. hunt for money laundering and the closing of financial conduits to extremist groups have led to new disclosure rules. Saudi investors, very sensitive to these actions since September 11th, reportedly have transferred between $600 and $800 billion to offshore accounts that are less subject to intensive inspection. Given the more independent attitude of Crown Prince Abdullah, King Fahd's chosen successor, toward the United States, the Saudis are already preparing for the possibility of distancing themselves from America. A further piece of evidence is in the Saudi education system; instead of educating the elite in the United States, the Saudis are constructing their own system of universities in the Kingdom.

No doubt the Saudis will exercise prudence in any actions they take. At the least, the royal family cannot be seen to be succumbing to bin Laden's demands that the American infidels leave holy land. On the other, American presence is essential to countering the ambitions of Saddam and Iran.

The Saudi government maintains that it is in firm control of the state. That may continue for some time. Yet the forces of globalization and modernization are powerful. To the degree that the openness of American society has become a potential vulnerability, the closed and inflexible nature of Saudi society is at least as great a potential source for political leverage. The inability or failure to empower a larger proportion of Saudi society in key sectors of that society may prove to be the undoing of the House of Saud. On the other hand, it is also possible that such actions will induce sufficient pressure on the tension between Wahabism and modernization to induce an unfraying of society. This is the predicament that challenges the future integrity of Saudi Arabia.

## Saddamicyde and Other Problems

Iraq is a separate category. Whether the United States remembers or not, Iraq was a quasi-partner during the eight-year war against Iran. Iraqis complain that just prior to the Gulf War, they were set up by the United States by inferring permission for the 1990 attack against Kuwait. It makes no difference what the truth is. But neither are the

issues as black and white as many Americans believe with the common conclusion that the time is now right to end Saddam's rule.

Iraq has about 23 million citizens. Per capita GDP is estimated
at $2,500. About three-fifths of the people are Shi'a, yet the Sunnis
have dominated the leadership. Life expectancy is about sixty-six.
However, given the sanctions and embargoes since Desert Storm and
the cynical ways Saddam has manipulated humanitarian goods and
services, it is difficult to judge the standard of living throughout Iraq.
While Iraq's military is relatively large, about 424,000, it has not fully
recovered from the Gulf War pounding it took.

By the time this book goes to press, the Bush administration may
have made up its mind how to deal with Iraq. There are three basic
options, each with many permutations and risks. First, the United
States can continue its current policy of containing Iraq through
sanctions, UN resolutions, and other international agreements.
When or if Iraq displays weapons it should not have or threatens its
neighbors, the United States reserves the right, as it has since the
Gulf War ended, to use military force.

Second, the United States can use sanctions and embargoes more
selectively to limit Iraq's acquisition of mass-destruction weapons.
The return of UN weapons inspectors could be negotiated as the
quid pro quo for permitting freer flow of noncontraband goods.
This is a "softer" form of containment backed up by military force
and a seemingly more rational policy likely to be supported by the
UN and particularly by such states as France, Russia, and China,
which view Iraq from a different perspective.

Third, the United States can finish the job. A military attack,
almost certainly with only U.S. and possibly a few U.K. forces, would
be mounted to remove Saddam. Other states, such as Turkey could
join in, particularly in enforcing the postwar peace. In the aftermath
of the Afghanistan campaign, which demonstrated the overwhelming military superiority of the United States, estimates vary as to how
long and what this expedition would require in manpower to
accomplish its task as well as probable casualties on both sides. One
hundred thousand to three hundred thousand troops set the probable range of needed forces. But the plan of attack as well as the logis-

tical support would be entirely dependent on whether access would be permitted or denied by the Saudis and other Gulf States. And there are certain to be unintended consequences.

How the so-called Iraqi opposition of Kurdish and Shi'a populations would react to a second Desert Storm is critical. Would the Iraqi Army desert or protect Saddam? And, perhaps most importantly, would Saddam widen the war through a direct attack against Israel with Scud missiles and mass-destruction weapons or other means? Indeed, to use Anthony Lake's term of national "nightmares," if Saddam did possess nuclear weapons, would he employ them and if so how? One nightmare scenario is to detonate a nuclear weapon at high altitude. The electromagnetic pulse or EMP generated by the blast could be sufficient "to turn off the lights" in much of the region by destroying electrical and electronic circuitry. American (as well as virtually all) military systems from tanks to jet aircraft to ships are vulnerable to EMP attack. The reader's imagination suffices to conjure up a situation in which much of that military equipment was rendered useless by an EMP explosion.

Similarly, Syria and Iran are problematic principally for support of the terrorist organization Hezbollah and terrorist operations against Israel. It is highly unlikely that the United States would intervene with force in either case. However, these two states are very much part of the reasons for and consequences of instability. Turmoil and terror can never be eliminated without involving Syria and Iraq as part of the solution.

## Unfinished Business: The India-Pakistan Conflict

Today, India and Pakistan are receding from the brink of war. As in three prior wars, it may not seem a fair fight. India is the largest democracy in the world with a population of nearly 1.1 billion, over 81 percent of whom are Hindi and 12 percent Muslim. Average life expectancy is sixty-three. Per capita GDP is about $2,200 a year. The Army has an active duty strength of over 1.2 million with 535,000 reserves. India is estimated to possess between fifty and one hundred nuclear warheads along with medium-range ballistic missiles.

Pakistan is roughly twice California's size. Its population is nearly 145 million with an average life expectancy of just over sixty-one and an average per capita annual GDP of $2,000. Ninety-seven percent of the people are Muslim, divided about four to one Sunni to Shi'a. Pakistan's armed forces number about 620,000 active and 513,000 reserves. Pakistan is estimated to have perhaps twenty to thirty nuclear weapons and short-range ballistic missiles.

In 1947, Britain granted independence to what had been its Indian colony. Secular and religious alternatives collided. Nehru had argued for a single state and that political solutions should be defined on a secular basis, not on the profound religious differences between Hindis and Muslims. Jinnah, a Muslim, argued that religious differences could not so easily be resolved, especially since the colonial power would not be present to adjudicate and to prevent violent disputes.

Jinnah won. India became a single, predominately Hindi, entity. Pakistan, a Muslim state, was created and divided into two parts— East and West—separated by the newly independent India. Tiny Kashmir, nestled high in the Himalayas, was caught in between. Predominately Muslim, Kashmir was ruled by an Indian maharajah. A plebiscite was never held. Such was the depth of animosity and feeling on both sides that after independence, India and Pakistan fought the first of three wars, this one over Kashmir. Pakistan believed that the majority Muslim population had the right to join with it. India, fearing that partition or independence of Kashmir would reverberate in other parts of the country, opposed anything except retaining control. As a result, Kashmir was permanently partitioned with the so-called line of control dividing the country. India controls the northern tier, Pakistan the south.

The second war, in 1965, was a standoff. In the 1971 war Pakistan was soundly defeated. The cost of defeat was the loss of East Pakistan. That became the newly independent state of Bangladesh. Since then, India and the surviving former West Pakistan have remained at gunpoint over control of tiny Kashmir. Minor skirmishes and fighting have become endemic and continue in the shadow of nuclear weapons now possessed by both adversaries.

Meanwhile, Kashmiri extremists, often trained and supported by Pakistan, use terror in the battle to end Indian occupation. The most recent attack, on the Indian Parliament on December 13th, 2001, brought both states to the brink of war. Gradually, the danger receded, at least for the moment.

During the Cold War, the United States generally supported Pakistan. India had led the nonaligned movement for decades. It was largely critical of American policy. Indeed, it may have been one of the few states to laud what it perceived as its cultural superiority over the United States with an arrogance that offended and angered many Americans. During the Soviet-Afghan war, Pakistan was an ally and a key logistical base for supporting the mujahadeen.

When the war ended, the United States went home. During the Clinton years, counterproliferation became a high priority. India had the bomb. Pakistan did not. The administration did everything it could to discourage Pakistan from going nuclear. In the spring of 1998, India and its new government tested nuclear weapons. These weapons were not simple fission devices. The Indians had learned how to use "boosted fission," a very sophisticated means of intensifying the power of the device. The world wondered what Pakistan would do. The United States applied pressure on Pakistan not to test.

The major U.S. news outlets were all over the story. On one program, CNN had invited the Pakistani minister of information and me for a half-hour coverage of what would happen next. It turned out that several students had gone on a killing spree at a high school in Colorado. The program on Pakistan was abbreviated to a few sound bites so Littleton High School could get as much airtime as possible.

With a line open to Islamabad, I asked CNN if the minister and I could continue the conversation. CNN was obliging. For an hour, we discussed the situation. When the conversation ended, there was little that I did not know or could not intuit about Pakistani intent. Whether this information was valuable or not, no one in the administration seemed interested and the White House and State Department expressed appreciation for the alert but declined the offer for any further information.

Pakistan might never have been persuaded to defer nuclear testing. But the Clinton administration simply had no reason to wish to know what Pakistan might do. Minds had been made up. Proceed at your own risk, was the clear message being sent to Pakistan.

Several weeks later, Pakistan exploded its first nuclear device and became a nuclear power. The Clinton administration was furious. In retaliation, it imposed various sanctions on Pakistan. Indeed, the United States embargoed some $800 million worth of F-16 aircraft that Pakistan had bought and paid for. Pakistan felt the wrath of American anger.

All of this changed well before September 11th. The Bush administration made overtures to India. A visit by Richard Armitage, Bush's deputy secretary of state, in the spring was a clear signal of American interest in rekindling a better relationship. The general intent was to use India as a possible lever with China, its major rival.

Now, the United States needs closer ties with both India and Pakistan. In the long struggle against terrorism, a more stable Afghanistan is critical. For that to happen, Pakistan must play an active role. Pakistan was the only state to recognize and support the Taliban. Pakistan is linked ethnically through the Pashtuns and through a long history of cooperation going back to the Soviet war. The country is also rife with Muslim clerics, many of whom are considered extremist.

Pakistan has between seven thousand and fifteen thousand Madrassas or religious schools. A substantial number of them are profoundly anti-American and teach that gospel. Education as it is known in the West is not what is offered in these Madrassas. The single subject is the Koran and the students, beginning at six or seven, memorize it. This process, not reading, writing, and other basic skills, defines education. The tragedy for thousands of Pakistani youth is that there is no other way to obtain food and shelter than through attending Madrassas. A diabolical situation results because many of the Madrassas are well-funded hotbeds of sedition and extremism and students learn accordingly, creating a supply of future extremists and bin Laden acolytes in what seems a permanent pipeline to jihad.

Musharraf understands the precarious hold on power any Pakistani government has. And without Pakistani support and cooperation, American intervention in Afghanistan would have been far more difficult. Thus, Pakistan is a frontline state and a key ally in the campaign against bin Laden, extremism, and terror. Musharraf also recalls Sadat and the vision and courage the Egyptian leader had. Whether Musharraf will become a South Asian Sadat is an interesting question.

Similarly, India is vital to the United States. India will surpass China in population in the coming decades. It is a strategic counter to China. It also has the world's largest middle class. Hence, the economic potential of India as a market, trading partner, and producer of goods and services is extraordinary.

Yet Kashmir is a veritable life-and-death issue. As Palestinians and Israelis die in the conflict between sovereignty and security, Indians, Pakistanis, and Kashmiris die over Kashmir. The India-Pakistan dispute contains a supreme irony. The United States intervened powerfully with military force in Afghanistan against al Qaeda and the Taliban in retaliation for September 11th, using Article V of the UN Charter as justification.

Kashmiri extremists attacked the Indian Parliament in New Delhi. Had it been in session, India's government could have been decimated or worse. The Indian government believes Pakistan was behind the attacks. Perhaps its evidence is as strong as that of the United States against bin Laden. India then has similar reasons and justification for attacking Pakistan. What stand can the United States take without appearing hypocritical or arrogant or both?

But the only way that conditions between India and Pakistan can be improved for the long term is through some relaxation in the tension over Kashmir. There may be no alternative except to attempt to resolve this extraordinarily difficult and intractable of problems if there is to be genuine stability in the region and beyond.

## Unfinished Business: The bin Laden Menace

No parallels are exact. Bin Laden combines elements of Bakunin, Lenin, and even Lawrence of Arabia. He is a revolutionary. His aim is to change the order of things, first on the Saudi peninsula but elsewhere as needed. Instead of Marxist ideology, bin Laden employs religious sophistry as a cloak for his intent. But like the social democrats and revolutionaries, bin Laden is clever enough to learn from past mistakes and change his tactics and strategy.

It was Marx's view that communism would take root in an advanced, industrialized European state, namely, Germany. Lenin, highly inventive, turned Marxism on its head. Russia was feudal and not industrialized and lacked the criteria classical Marxism believed crucial for revolution. Bin Laden has emulated Lenin's turnabout in recognizing Israel as a target and by his latest focus on disrupting America's economy.

Bin Laden seems to lack the tactical genius and political and organizational skills of Lenin and even Lawrence. But he has, among his acolytes, the charisma and legitimacy of Lenin and Lawrence. Lawrence tried desperately to mold an Arab force into an Arab state and failed during World War I; bin Laden has similar aspirations modeled along religious lines.

Bin Laden may prove to be more akin to Pancho Villa as a passing danger than to the Bolshevik revolution. But his message is almost certainly going to resonate with other, more capable people who could evolve into future Lenins and Hitlers not, however, bent on territorial domination. Instead, bin Laden's perverted religious ideology and jihad form the basis for amalgamating Islam under a revolutionary and radical non-territorial cause aimed at eradicating the current order.

Much is known about Osama bin Laden. The youngest son of a well-to-do Saudi family, bin Laden had an insulated childhood dominated by his mother. Well educated as an engineer, he developed resentment against the House of Saud, in part because of his very conservative view of Islam. He went to Afghanistan to fight the Soviet Union in the 1980s. His role was more that of a facilitator than a warrior.

After the Gulf War, the presence of U.S. forces in Saudi Arabia became unacceptable to him, given his radically fundamentalist view of Islam. Because of his extremism, he lost his Saudi citizenship in 1994. His involvement in the 1993 bombing of the World Trade Center and subsequent terrorist acts in Africa, Yemen, and the September 11th attack is well documented. Peter Bergen's *Holy War Inc.* is a readable inventory of bin Laden's activities.

The danger that bin Laden and his nihilist philosophy pose is a threat to both democratic and autocratic states. Saudi Arabia and the United States are the current targets. What bin Laden may not have realized before September 11th is that his perversion of Islam is a dagger with many target regimes. America's openness is at risk. Saudi political inflexibility is a huge vulnerability. Israeli preoccupation with survival is another. Pakistan cannot be excluded. Thus far, this danger has not been widely understood.

Conventional wisdom holds that Osama bin Laden's principal aim is to overthrow the Saudi government and drive the American infidels from the holy lands. But bin Laden has learned a few things. As noted earlier, he now understands that "it's the economy, stupid!" Economic warfare is an avenue al Qaeda and others will follow. Bin Laden and others like him will also take the battle wherever the opportunity is offered.

Thus, the Arab-Israeli conflict and the future of a Palestinian state can no longer be separated from the grievances of even moderate Arabs nor can they be isolated from passions that use these differences to intensify fundamentalist extremism. And if there is to be stability in Afghanistan, then India and Pakistan must resolve their fundamental differences caused and exacerbated by the standoff over Kashmir. These are the two bookends to prevent the states in between from collapsing on each other no matter what ploys bin Laden and his associates mount.

Such an undertaking will be a double Sisyphean labor. However, what may break this deadlock is that bin Laden has shown that no state is safe from terror. Without collective action by many nations, conditions will grow worse, not better. To paraphrase the Washington Treaty of 1949 that formed NATO, attacks such as those inflicted on September 11th, 2001, against the United States are attacks against all the members of the world community. This shared vulnerability creates the impetus and incentive for moving to resolve the Indian-Pakistani and Arab-Israeli conflicts with far greater force and momentum than at any other point in the past fifty years.

The threat bin Laden and his philosophy of jihad pose is directly aimed at the physical structures of the states he intends to destroy. Unlike Nazism and Communism, bin Laden does not need to capture a country or occupy a territory to impose his will on society. The United States and Saudi Arabia (plus Israel and others) are vulnerable. This is the challenge and the danger. Is America up to both?

# ★ 7 ★

## Bears, Dragons, and Eagles

### Trifecta Politics

"Triangular politics" reshaped the Cold War. The strategy worked for two reasons. The inherent hostility and rivalry between Communist China and Soviet Russia provided a strategic opening. And President Richard Nixon had the vision to understand and to exploit these profound political, ideological, and cultural hostilities that separated and conflicted Russia and China. The depth of that mutual historical animosity is underscored by the Russian word for Chinese, which translates as "bogeyman." In 1969, these differences provoked several bloody military clashes on the Ussuri River between China and Russia over long-standing border disputes.

Nixon dispatched envoy Henry Kissinger on a series of secret negotiations to keep China away from its erstwhile ideological ally and strategically closer to the United States as a de facto partner. Once triangular politics created movement toward strategic realignment, Nixon embarked on a policy of "détente" to stabilize relations with the Soviet Union. Détente would focus on limiting the nuclear arms race as a first step.

In dealing with the unfinished business that has been accumulating since the Gulf War, a newer version of triangular politics can play a powerful role. "Trifecta" is a better term for describing this strategy because it implies a three-way winner. For such a policy to prove effective, America, China, and Russia all must gain in the process. Two ganging up against one will not work as it did for Richard Nixon.

Triangular politics proved highly successful. For sophisticated (and courageous) observers, the tensions between the Soviet Union and China had been unmistakable only a few years after the end of the Korean War. But, in the United States, political "correctness" circa the Joe McCarthy era mandated that communism was "monolithic." Russia and China were simplistically viewed as part of a common threat, rationalized by the American perception that the United States "lost" Mainland China to the communists in 1949. Communist China's unexpected entry into the Korean War in November 1950 and the rabid McCarthyism that ran amok in the 1950s also made taking a rational view of China and communism politically dangerous.

After the brilliant surprise landing in September 1950 at Inchon, the seaport of South Korea's capital, Seoul, Supreme Allied Commander General Douglas McArthur disregarded all warning indicators and ordered his forces north toward the Yalu River and the Chinese border in hot pursuit of the retreating remnants of the North Korean army. In late November, around Thanksgiving 1950, Chinese People's Liberation Army (PLA) elements crossed the border into North Korea and made limited probes against the UN forces.

The limited attacks, followed by Chinese withdrawal, were intended as an unmistakable signal of China's intent to intervene if the allied advance continued to the Yalu River. Mao and his communist colleagues had been in power for a year and were still consolidating authority throughout China. A united Korea, possibly with U.S. military forces stationed all the way to the Yalu, was a clear and present danger to China and a direct threat to the regime. How Mao and China would have reacted to a partitioned North Korea with a border drawn somewhere across its narrow "neck" south of the capital Pyongyang is, of course, unknowable.

McArthur ignored the probes. UN forces continued a rapid advance north. McArthur was so certain that China was bluffing that he promoted the slogan "home for Christmas." If China were foolish enough to attack, McArthur reasoned that his superior firepower would halt the Chinese Army in its tracks. McArthur's famous infallibility failed on all counts. China was not bluffing.

The intervention came with massive numbers of ground forces deployed in "human waves." American firepower could not halt the sea of Chinese soldiers. The allies were overwhelmed and hastily retreated to the 38th parallel, the post–World War II line of division between the two Koreas. A bloody standoff raged for two years. Then, in November 1952, General Dwight David Eisenhower was elected president, promising to end the war in Korea.

Through an Indian cutout, Eisenhower warned China that if an armistice were not concluded, the United States would consider nuclear options to end the conflict. Weary of war and preoccupied with establishing political control throughout all of China, Mao agreed to a negotiated armistice with the UN that eventually ended the hostilities. Korea was and still remains divided. A peace treaty has never been signed. China would remain an enemy of the United States, however, formally unrecognized as a communist state, until Nixon began the process two decades later. Jimmy Carter would finally recognize China in 1979.

The Soviet leaders understood, of course, that the idea of a Sino-Soviet alliance was a bad joke. They also understood that the United States did not regard Moscow's relationship with Beijing in the same light that Russia did. For nearly seven centuries, China and Russia shared and contested a huge border. Mongol hordes had invaded west and Russia pushed east of the Urals, colonizing the huge territory all the way to the Pacific. Conflict between the two powers had been chronic and each regarded the other adversarily. Even their views of communism were at variance. However, until Nixon's first term, the United States chose not to recognize these conditions. As noted, the Vietnam War was fought with the belief that China was the enemy to be contained through holding Southeast Asia.

After Khrushchev rose to prominence in the late 1950s, he

attempted to cultivate China in forming a real Sino-Soviet pact. However, relations came apart specifically over Soviet reluctance to transfer nuclear technology and other military systems to China. Ironically, one of the first academic observers to recognize this split was Kennedy's deputy national security adviser, Walt Rostow. In 1954, Rostow published *The Prospects for Communist China* in which he accurately predicted the Sino-Soviet dispute. For reasons cited earlier, that view was not to the liking of the Kennedy and Johnson administrations.

Triangular politics forced the Soviet Union to revise its strategic relationship with the United States. In a political sense, China, in concert with the United States and NATO, loosely surrounded Russia. A strategic dialogue with the United States was essential for Moscow and Nixon was offering a Cold War ceasefire through the policy of détente. Arms control agreements became the currency of the new strategic relationship. The Strategic Arms Limitations Talks or SALT began in earnest. In 1972, SALT 1 was signed as an executive agreement (to sidestep a Senate fight over a treaty) to limit offensive systems and the famous Anti-Ballistic Missile or ABM Treaty was signed and approved by the Senate.

ABM remained the cornerstone of the strategic framework that helped keep the Cold War cold. The United States and the Soviet Union would clash over many issues. However, with SALT and the ABM Treaty, it was absolutely plain that both sides tacitly agreed to keep the political and ideological points of conflict peaceful. This attitude persisted in Russia after the Soviet Union collapsed. Hence, to the current Russian leadership, the central strategic and even psychological importance of ABM cannot be dismissed or ignored.

Under Mao Zedong and his extremely able foreign minister, Chou En-lai, China began the long path to modernization. Under Deng Xiaoping, who assumed power in 1978 at Mao's death, China began and continues the modernizing of its economy, infrastructure, and political system. All of the attendant risks of modernization and political control are present. As with Russia, China suffers from the twin handicaps of an entrenched socialist system abetted by a huge centralized bureaucracy and the perils of immature capitalism. Reconciling these systemic challenges and obstacles is the central problem for both states. And establishing strategic reference points and bases for long-term cooperation with the United States remains crucial to Russia and China.

## The Bear Defanged

The Soviet Union ended up not as the classic "ten-foot-tall" superpower but rather as a military giant whose vital organs had not all fully developed. The U.S. government never appreciated this condition of inherent Soviet weakness. Ironically, this lack of understanding was not confined to Western intelligence agencies. The Soviet leadership did not detect this fatal flaw until it was too late.

Despite its critics, détente eventually worked. And America's use of "human rights" and, later, Ronald Reagan's fabled phrase "evil empire" were psychological levers to affect and occasionally moderate the actions of Soviet leaders. However, whether the United States was simply lucky or was clever in applying human rights to particular political advantage remains debatable. What is clear is that ideas and values, properly translated into policy, can be very effective.

In the end, no forecasts or predictions of the Soviet Union's demise came from either inside or outside the Kremlin. The Bush administration was both delighted and surprised when the collapse occurred. However, we can learn a lesson. No government, including that of the United States, is immune to failing to anticipate or predict such extraordinary events. The collapse of any enterprise, especially one that is seemingly in control, from the Soviet Union to the Taliban in Afghanistan to Enron, the Houston trading giant that imploded in early 2002 into the largest American corporation bankruptcy in history, almost always comes as a complete surprise.

Yet this chronic inability to deal with the unexpected is directly relevant to the unfinished business that lies ahead. The nature of the new threat means that anticipation and foresight are essential. Incorporating these requirements into current government processes is a piece of unfinished business that has a very high priority for action. The least that can be done is to ensure that alternative futures are considered and evaluated, even those that not only are "out of the box" but perhaps "break the box" as well.

To deal with the uncertainties that are part of both international politics and daily life, and the need to improve the analytical process for better anticipating events that have profound consequences, the story of the disintegration of the Soviet Union offers an interesting insight into what could happen in other states and regions, particularly in the crescent of crisis. The limitations of an authoritarian, centrally controlled system and the frictions between political and economic modernization, while varying of course from state to state, still have common features and certain similar long-term results.

The dissolution of the Soviet Union is one of history's more extraordinary stories. The authoritarian Soviet government was rigid and inflexible. The economy was socialist, centralized, and bureaucratized. The combination of a highly irrational and dysfunctional economic system and Stalin's paranoia over control managed to make fraud, corruption, and the proclivity to falsify bad news endemic across society. The size and resource priority of the party-military-industrial-secret police complex provided important means for political control.

The criminal and bloody excesses under Stalin, including the purges and the ruthless activities of the secret police (MVD or, later, KGB) to hunt down all enemies of the state, forced both government and the dominant party structure to become highly compartmentalized and secretive simply for self-preservation. Compartmentalization proved highly corruptive. The veil of secrecy shrouded the agencies of government. The veil of fear induced government personnel, from high-ranking party and cabinet officials to factory managers and laborers, to falsify achievements invariably in the upward directions.

The "Hero of the Soviet Union" medal awarded for superhuman and otherwise impossible achievement exemplified the extent of self-deception. Stories such as the famous mineworker who was so honored for shoveling ten tons of coal in a single day were the butt of humor and ridicule inside and outside the Soviet Union. The political consequence of this cognitive illusion was that no one beyond a very small circle of leaders knew what was actually happening inside Russia. And those who knew were either afraid to reveal the truth or, like Stalin, apathetic about it.

In his memoirs, Mikhail Gorbachev reported how stunned he and his contemporaries were at Khrushchev's secret speech delivered to the twentieth Party Congress in November 1956 that detailed the murderous excesses of Stalinism and the deaths of millions of innocent Russians. Although that such outrages could have taken place was not surprising, the idea was planted in Gorbachev and many in his circle of young party members that the system was corrupt. But the system, to those party members who still believed in it, had to be salvageable, or so they thought. In fact, the Soviet command economy run from the center was both irrational and inflexible. There would never be enough resources to overcome the inefficiency of the economic and political systems. In retrospect, it is amazing that the Soviet system sustained itself for as long as it did.

Another reason the system imploded was the party's antiquated leadership. Brezhnev was seriously ill for years. From the late 1970s after his retirement in 1976, as CIA director, William Colby would deliver an annual lecture to the students at the National War College. Each year, he forecast that Brezhnev had only months to live. Brezhnev soldiered on. After Brezhnev finally died in November 1982, two old and sickly men replaced him in succession, each moving on to their reward rather quickly. Yuri Andropov, head of the KGB, lasted until February 1984; Constantin Chernenko, for only eleven months after that. Gorbachev ultimately became the new and penultimate leader of the Soviet Union. But for nearly a decade, there was a series of dying hands on the reins of power in the Kremlin. The Soviet Union was in grave trouble.

Because of this turnover in leadership (wags reported that Russia was approaching Italy in that category), members of the Politburo frequently gained new portfolios. Gorbachev recorded that he and his colleagues were aghast when they discovered the real state of the Soviet economy and the enormous problems that had been papered over. Hence, *glasnost* (openness) and *perestroika* (restructuring) were imposed on the Soviet system. Both required decentralization and flexibility. Neither the economic nor the political system could tolerate them. The disastrous ten-year war in Afghanistan exacerbated these contradictions. In the end, the Soviet Union simply went poof.

This is an important lesson for other tightly controlled, autocratic regimes. Gorbachev was a devoted Marxist and deeply believed in socialism. His idealism had been stripped away by the revelations in Khrushchev's secret speech. However, Gorbachev believed that the socialist system in the USSR could be made right. His solutions proved to be incompatible with the inflexibility and authoritarian character of the political system. China, of course, was a keen observer of what was happening in the Soviet Union. Its leadership was determined not to repeat Gorbachev's mistakes by unleashing irresistible forces that could ultimately prove destructive. Hence, while suffering from similar systemic handicaps, Beijing intends to control more carefully the pace and scope of modernization. That is its test.

With the dissolution of the Soviet Union in December 1999 into fifteen independent republics, the new Russia is about half the population and two-thirds the size but still spans thirteen time zones from the Baltic to the Pacific. About 1.8 times larger than the United States, Russia has nearly 146 million citizens, 80 percent Russian and the rest of diverse ethnic and religious backgrounds. Its per capita GDP is $8,000 and average life expectancy is sixty-seven. Its military forces number about one million in active service. Those forces are in low states of readiness and morale as pay and benefits have been drastically cut or simply withheld. The Russians have a powerful nuclear inventory, with 1,020 land and sea-based ICBMs and an ABM system, permitted under the treaty, with 100 interceptors.

Since August 1999, Russian forces have been engaged in a second campaign in Chechnya against rebel forces and separatists. About forty thousand troops have been committed to this campaign, including 42 Motor Rifle Division consisting of about 15,000 solders, 8,000 Border Guards, and 10,800 troops from the Interior Ministry who perform the policing and clearing functions to find or hunt down the rebels. Chechnya has become a bloody tragedy with no clear end in sight.

Russia has legitimate reason to defend against rebellion and terror. But the use of force by both sides has often been brutal. Human rights and antiwar groups have actively campaigned against Russian intervention and the harshness with which Russia has dealt with the Chechens. However, the aftermath of September 11th and America's declaration of war against terror and terrorism have reinforced the Russian hand in Chechnya. After all, the battle the Russian government claims it is fighting is against terror and terrorists directed against the homeland.

Russia is a democracy and a federation whose political and economic conditions are fragile at best. It is a nation rich with resources, but exploiting those resources has been problematic for both Tsarist and Soviet regimes. Its president holds a four-year term. Currently, President Vladimir Putin, will be up for reelection in 2004, who is very popular. However, that can change quickly.

Russia's predominant problems are politico-economic. Russia is still in many ways a backward and underdeveloped state. The legacies of seventy-five years of Soviet rule are obstacles to progress. The bureaucracy is ponderous and unresponsive. A free market and capitalism have been accompanied by several evils: inflation, corruption, and massive criminal theft of monies. Hence, organized crime is not simply a fiction but a menace to Russian society and its economic progress.

While Russian GDP has grown, Putin must ensure that workers are paid and that money is found to meet the state's expenses. Sergei Rogov, head of Moscow's Institute on the USA and Canada, one of Russia's preeminent think tanks, puts the case more directly. He says that while Putin is highly popular, that popularity is dependent on "checks being in the mail." A failure or bump in the economy could easily end his credibility and his authority.

The reasons Russia's political and economic viability is vitally important to the United States, Europe, and many other countries are neither complicated nor difficult to understand. Russia is still in transition to becoming a full democracy and a functioning market economy. Slipping back to some form of post-Soviet autocracy would be a strategic disaster and could restart the Cold War. Russia has a vast inventory of nuclear weapons, fissile materials, and experts. The subject of Russian "loose nukes" or nuclear weapons for sale as well as experts in their manufacture for hire to the highest bidder was one of the Clinton administration's most horrific nightmares. That danger has not passed.

The most profound security challenges this new Russia faces are threefold. First is continuing the economic and political transformation to a society and market that are free, open, and relatively clean of crime and corruption. Second is to reach agreement with the United States over a strategic framework that takes into account many of Russia's weaknesses and insecurities and provides a formal and consistent structure that can serve as the basis for Russia's future national security. Third is the politically egoistic need to be regarded as a regional "superpower," principally in Eurasia where it can bring its influence to bear in constructive ways.

NATO expansion east is a major part of this unfinished business. While Russia has a de facto seat as the "twentieth" member but without a formal vote, NATO's dilemma of expanding and dealing with Russia is far from resolved. If and when the Baltic States are serious candidates for membership, the decision about accession, if not adroitly handled, could precipitate a crisis with Russia. Furthermore, if September 11th and what appear to be dramatic increases in American defense spending are thrust into the European debate as reasons for NATO members to boost their defense budgets, Russia will have to respond. Since conventional forces are expensive, the response is very likely to be greater emphasis on nuclear weapons and deterrence. In other words, a new arms race could emerge.

The personal relationships between Presidents Bush and Putin and Secretaries Powell and Ivanov are currently very strong. The Bush administration's formal withdrawal from the ABM Treaty, which takes effect in the summer of 2002, in order to permit broader testing of missile defense was not the cataclysmic event many advocates of preserving the ABM treaty predicted. Perhaps the tentative agreement to reduce strategic nuclear forces to below 2,500 warheads over time was a palliative. Yet the issue of missile defense has not been resolved and if mishandled could precipitate a real problem with Russia.

Similarly, no general agreement over dealing with international terrorism has been worked out yet between Russia and America. Perhaps none will be. However, with U.S. forces using bases in former Soviet republics and even the occasional Russian base to wage the campaign in Afghanistan and elsewhere, the pressure for a meeting of the minds will grow. This pressure will increase if and when the United States takes the campaign against terrorism deeper into the crescent of crisis. Russian political, diplomatic, intelligence, and possibly military support could prove exceedingly useful. But such interactions will require a new strategic framework or modus vivendi for assuring the future security of both states. Abrogation of ABM, missile defense, and the extent of America's future war on terrorism will have a profound impact on whether broad strategic agreement on a post–Cold War equivalent of détente can be reached.

Finally, it is the economy, stupid! U.S. private and government investment and aid to Russia have been limited by corruption, absence of business and commercial law and regulation, and organized crime. On the one hand, Putin must deal with these obstacles and impediments, in many ways as serious as the abuses of the Stalin era and the irrationality of a command economy. On the other hand, the United States must be prepared to take more risks, first in helping Russia to assure the security of its nuclear and weapons arsenals and second in promoting economic growth. These are big and serious challenges. They too form unfinished pieces of business.

## The Dragon

Several vignettes and historical context demonstrate the complexity and contradiction of China. In many ways, China is both highly sophisticated and horribly backward. Imperial arrogance and cultural superiority subsumed in the phrase "middle kingdom" remain embedded in the Chinese psyche, particularly that of the elite. A sense of the challenge in overcoming this middle-kingdom complex can be drawn from an ancient example.

For centuries and through several dynasties, the Chinese solution to the problem of rodents was to build better and more sophisticated mousetraps. These devices ultimately would become literally mechanical works of genius engineered as finely as Swiss watches. But the Chinese never considered more effective and very different means of solving this problem, such as pesticides and chemicals. Culture took hold. Once a solution had been invented and implemented, cultural conditioning inflexibly led to product improvement and not derivation of a better alternative. On a larger scale, one legacy of this middle-kingdom mentality is an intellectual-cultural barrier to innovation that China must break at all levels of society if it is to modernize fully and become a truly industrialized and economically competitive state.

A senior Chinese diplomat (and good friend) was finally returning home for reassignment after nearly a decade of service in the Washington embassy that began in the late 1980s. This person had an excellent appreciation of the United States and its political system since reporting on it was his job. Over a farewell lunch, I asked how the diplomat felt about leaving the many comforts of life in America for a more Spartan existence at home. After a moment of careful reflection, the diplomat smiled. While he very much liked America, Americans, and his service, he was anxious to return to what he described as a "truly civilized country." What is more, he meant it. Despite the comforts of "conspicuous capitalism," culture won out.

Visitors to China and to Beijing up through the mid-1980s saw a largely agrarian and undeveloped society. Beijing teemed with oceans of bicycles and seas of uniformed police navigating through an old, drab city filled with ugly, Soviet-style squat concrete buildings conforming to the generally low design standards of socialist architecture. Most Chinese dressed in traditional or inexpensive Western garb. By that decade's end, Beijing architecture had not changed dramatically. However, the oceans of bicycles were being replaced by cars. The ubiquitous uniformed police had melted away. And Chinese garb was becoming more Western and fashionable.

By the 1990s, China's larger cities were modernizing even more rapidly. The architecture was decidedly Western and even stylish. In

Beijing, a series of major road arteries and ring roads had been built. Cell phones were everywhere and a very prosperous middle class was in evidence in restaurants and hotels and in the streets. But it was the pace of change and its intensity that were particularly noticeable.

In February 2000, I spent two weeks in Beijing and returned a few months later. The change in Beijing was remarkable. In preparing its bid for the Olympic Games in 2008, the Chinese had launched a crash construction and development program to refurbish Beijing. This program had been underway for some time. However, in less than a year's time, these results came together. A relatively dreary Beijing had been transformed into a modern city. The Cold War view of "communist China" no longer fit. And while the rural parts that formed most of China had not advanced in terms of infrastructure and architecture, even the most rural villages had at least one satellite dish for television and cell phones were common.

The contradictions in Chinese behavior are also obvious. The Chinese can be at once hugely sophisticated and intransigent. In early 2002, the Chinese revealed that a Boeing 767 bought by the government had been bugged by the United States. They discovered some two dozen electronic listening devices, including several in the headboard of one of the installed beds. In all likelihood, given the time needed to install the devices, the bugging had to have been approved by the Clinton administration. More likely, the announcement of the incident was due to internal Chinese politics over Jiang's successor rather than any covert action by the United States. With President Bush's February 2002 trip to China looming, the incident could have been played up. China chose not to and, after the initial story was released, clearly as a signal, went on with business as usual.

On the other hand, China's continuing crackdown on dissidents, on the Dalai Lama and Tibet, and on a sect called Falun Gong in particular seems incomprehensible to most Westerners, especially since Falun Gong advertises its practice of nonviolence. These distinct differences in attitude suggest some of the complexities of China and its politics.

For more than a quarter of a century, China's Four Modernizations, instituted by Deng Xiaoping in the late 1970s, have been the basis for changing Chinese society. China's ruling leadership had set the country on a course of economic modernization. "Capitalism with a Chinese Face" was one of Deng's favorite phrases. The first priority was "stability." Stability meant maintaining tight political control under the Communist party. The political leadership was not about to embark on any policy that risked massive social upheaval and even possible revolution. Nor was the Communist party about to put itself out of business. Modernization, sovereignty, and security are shorthand expressions for the other priorities.

Deng and his colleagues understood all too well that an economically weak China courted disaster internally and externally. But moving from an essentially feudal and backward basis to a modern economy would be a massive shock to the system. Yet that is exactly what has happened and why stability and political control are so important to the leadership. Marrying a socialist system to a free-market economy is a seeming contradiction and one that brings considerable grounds for future divorce into plain view.

China, because of its huge population and the industrious character of its people, has the world's second largest GDP, behind the United States. Cities such as Shanghai and Quanjo have become economic showpieces. China is developing a strong middle class. Although it will be overtaken this century by India as the world's most populous state, it still has the challenge of governing 1.3 billion souls, about 10 percent of whom are living in poverty. China's annual per capita GDP is about $3,600. Average life expectancy is seventy-two.

But modernization has not come without social cost. Birth control policies and male dominance have created a demographic nightmare. There are about 100,000,000 more males than females. A substantial number of Chinese males will not be able to marry or to start families, very much a departure from the Chinese tradition. Prostitution is a growing problem as is trafficking in women. Drugs are becoming more prevalent, harkening back to the mid-1850s and the Opium Wars. All of these social trends are inducing huge political pressures on government to respond.

As in much of the rest of the developing world, the clash between modernization and political control becomes stronger. Thus far, China has been able to grow its economy sufficiently to deal with many of these problems. President Jiang Zemin has privately forecast that, over time, popular elections will be coming to China as the means to select national leaders. Whether Jiang was talking years or decades is the question to ask.

China's priorities remain "sovereignty, stability, modernization, and security." Unsurprisingly, these are interrelated. China's memory is long. The colonization and humiliation in the nineteenth and the early part of the twentieth century due to the intervention of "foreign devils" will never be allowed to reoccur. However, if one examines the record, China is not territorially ambitious. There are border disputes with Russia. Tibet remains a controversial region, and a source for human rights abuses and critiques. Sovereignty applies to traditional Chinese borders.

Stability refers to political control and the authority of the party. The Chinese leadership recognizes that loss of control could lead to disruption, civil war, and worse. History has been an unkind teacher in those regards. Modernization and economic growth must be shaped in that context. No doubt Jiang Zemin and his colleagues understand that political modernization is the prerequisite for economic modernization. However, the rate and scope of change, in the leadership's view, must be carefully controlled. This is the dilemma and the weakness. Control, as the Soviets learned, could not be maintained once the powerful forces of freedom and a market economy were unleashed.

Finally, security means that China will have the military means to assure its sovereignty and to defend against encroachment. Clearly, Taiwan is the crucial issue and central fixation. Beijing almost assuredly will remain committed to a peaceful reunification worked out in the "three communiqués" with the United States. Taiwan's declaration of independence could change a peaceful process to war or to "other means," using the Clausewitzian term. However, it does not appear in Taiwan's interest to take such a rash step nor in the U.S. interest to support full-fledged independence. But there are more subtle grounds for differences and dispute.

One reason that Beijing opposes U.S. missile defense relates to the Taiwan issue. While Beijing may not have the military means to seize Taiwan, it can use its military power to intimidate the island state. If the United States were to build an effective system of missile defense and deploy it to defend Taiwan, China would be at a disadvantage in at least two ways, as it views the problem.

Both the declaratory and putative Chinese missile threat against Taiwan would be reduced by an effective defense. The deployment of U.S. missile defense to Taiwan would also be a strong and perhaps overwhelming political signal of support for Taiwan that the Chinese could not counter. Because China is unable to mount an amphibious attack and unwilling perhaps to resort to an aerial bombardment, intimidation through missile diplomacy remains the better option should Taiwan declare independence. A U.S. missile defense would shred this "hole card." Thus, if Taiwan were prepared to declare independence, American missile defense could remove China's only countervailing means for preventing that step.

Similarly, China's strategic weapons, currently about twenty to thirty relatively obsolete ICBMs, would have no value in deterring or coercing the United States since missile defense would neutralize any threat to the American homeland regardless of how well the system operated. Perception is what would count. Faced with that imbalance, China's response almost certainly would be to increase its nuclear inventory so that the "limited" American defenses could be saturated with incoming warheads. The best estimate is that, given a limited U.S. missile defense regime, China might acquire two hundred to three hundred ICBMs. If China were to embark on such a program, in all likelihood the reaction in the United States would force some form of a new arms race. Given China's relatively few resources, an arms race would be an economic disaster at worst and a huge drain at best.

On the U.S. side, there remains a huge gap in understanding the depth of Chinese passions regarding the psychological importance of "one China" and the reuniting of Taiwan with the mainland. Despite occasional crises between China and Taiwan, none have been allowed to get out of hand. Compared with the more likely danger from the crescent of crisis, China-Taiwan is a lesser probability security problem. However, should a severe crisis occur, it has the potential to become a flash point as dangerous as the Arab-Israeli and India-Pakistan conflicts.

There are three past incidents in Sino-American relations that are germane. The first was the Tiananmen Square student protests and repression on June 4th, 1989; the second, the bombing of the Chinese embassy in Belgrade on the evening of May 7/8, 1999, during Operation Allied Force; and the third, the downing of the U.S. EP-3 over Hainan Island in April 2001.

Tiananmen Square in Beijing is literally the center of the city, with the Forbidden Palace to the north and the People's Congress to the south. Pro-democracy students protested for several days. A papier-mâché replica of the Statue of Liberty was prominent and the televised image of a student staring down a Chinese T-62 tank was dramatic journalism at its best. Finally, the leadership decided that it could no longer tolerate the protests. The PLA was sent in. The result was a bloody clash in which hundreds of students were killed or injured.

The reaction in the United States was one of outrage. Despite the Bush administration's strong pro-Chinese stance (the president had served as ambassador to Beijing and National Security Adviser Brent Scowcroft had been Kissinger's deputy during the secret negotiations in the early 1970s with China), the strength of popular opinion meant that relations would be set back drastically. In 1992, candidate Clinton would run condemning the "butchers of Beijing."

The view in China was dramatically different. If a poll had been taken, it is likely that the vast majority of Chinese would have sided with the leadership in repressing the student protests. To most Chinese, the students and not the government were in the wrong. This attitude was based on the traditional Chinese view of society and respect for authority. The students had no right, as far as the public was concerned, to challenge authority.

On the evening of May 7/8, 1999, two precision-guided munitions dropped from America's most advanced bomber, the Stealth B-2 Spirit bomber, landed with pinpoint accuracy on Target 493.

Unfortunately, Target 493 turned out to be the Chinese embassy in Belgrade. By good or bad luck, the cipher room was one of the parts of the embassy that was hit. Several Chinese were killed, including at least one intelligence officer.

The Clinton administration responded awkwardly, ultimately, issuing an apology. The United States provided confidential material to the Chinese to establish that this was a tragic accident. But the Chinese government and, more importantly, the Chinese public were disbelieving. The argument from the Chinese side was rather convincing.

How could it be that having spent nearly $400 billion on intelligence over the past ten years, the United States did not know the location of the Chinese embassy in Belgrade? And why would a B-2 bomber armed with the most sophisticated weapons drop them on the wrong target? The United States could not answer these questions to China's satisfaction. In the meantime, Chinese gathered in the street at Xiu Shui Bei Jie 3, the address of the U.S. embassy in Beijing, where the crowd pelted the grounds with rocks, bottles, and other hurled projectiles.

The outrage on the part of the Chinese public was seen in the United States as manufactured. Americans could not appreciate the intensity of the reaction for what most people believed was a horrible but honest error. The Chinese government denied any responsibility for the riots. Indeed, the reaction was so intense that it took several days for the Beijing leadership to determine how to deal with the riotous crowds. Obviously, a repetition of June 4, 1989, would be avoided. However, Chinese attitudes toward sovereignty and its violation were at work.

As noted earlier, in April 2001, a Chinese PLA F-8 fighter purposely buzzed a U.S. EP-3 electronic reconnaissance aircraft. The Chinese pilot miscalculated and hit the EP-3, ripping off part of the port wing. Both aircraft were mortally damaged by the mid-air collision. However, the EP-3 pilot made a brilliant crash landing at the nearby airfield on Hainan Island, part of China. The Chinese pilot crashed in the sea and was killed. China initially claimed that the

EP-3 violated Chinese airspace and had deliberately flown into the fighter. Both claims were wrong.

This was the first real crisis for the new Bush administration. Fortunately, it had a very able diplomatic team in place. That team also had powerful military credentials not lost on Beijing. Colin Powell had been chairman of the ICS. Ambassador Joseph Prucher formerly commanded the Pacific as a four star admiral. And Admiral Dennis Blair, also a very canny and experienced officer, was in command of the Pacific.

From Beijing's perspective, the leadership did not want another public overreaction on their hands as happened after the embassy in Belgrade was hit. Hence, for the first few days after the incident, while the American crew was interned on Hainan by the PLA, the civilian politicians wrested control of the crisis from the hands of the PLA. Once that was done and public reaction could be kept in check, a sensible path toward negotiations could be followed. Jiang and his colleagues skillfully played the crisis to obtain an "apology" from the United States. The United States never apologized fully. Both sides were satisfied and the crew was returned safely.

The concern in many American circles, especially Congress, was that the Bush team would overreact in order to display toughness. A small sampling of that attitude had surfaced over Korea in February when Powell's attempt to engage North Korea was rebuffed by the White House. Cooler heads prevailed in this crisis. Sensibly, Powell's view was to emphasize getting the safe return of the crew and not worry about the aircraft. After debate with the more aggressive Pentagon leadership, who held out for a tougher line with China, the administration opted for Powell's course, and the crew and ultimately the aircraft were returned.

In this progression of events, Sino-American relations were improved as both sides developed a better understanding of the other. In the case of the United States, Chinese attitudes toward sovereignty and the degree to which historical humiliation was still a sore point became clearer. China's leadership learned that even such an extraordinary situation as the Belgrade bombing, which seemed inexplicable, was possibly not premeditated. And the Beijing leadership learned how to cope with public reaction—something that had not previously been a source of concern in an autocratic and centrally controlled state.

Yet the huge divides over culture, history, and possible misunderstanding still exist. Because China's leadership has a much longer tenure than that in the United States, where presidents have a maximum of eight years and cabinet officers usually serve for far less, these are matters that the U.S. leadership must continually relearn. And discussion has not included the Congress, where, while there is longer tenure, there are also harder divisions of both left and right that limit flexibility in dealing with or understanding the Chinese perspective more fully.

## The Eagle

The criticism that the United States lacks a coherent strategy, or has adopted the wrong one, has been leveled at every administration. But, since World War II, there have been certain continuities that contradict this critique in the main even if an explicit strategy has been lacking. During the first part of the Cold War, the Soviet Union and China were the joint enemies. The United States applied containment to both. A string of alliances, from NATO in Europe to CENTO and SEATO in the Pacific, was constructed to surround China and the Soviet Union and to prevent the further spread of communism. Vietnam was the ultimate and unsuccessful extension of active containment with the failed U.S. involvement in Southeast Asia. South Korea and Japan became firm American allies and troops stationed there since the end of World War II still remain.

Nixon, of course, brought a strategic design into office and successfully changed the entire calculus. China became a de facto ally. Détente relieved many of the worst Cold War tensions. And in the Persian Gulf, the United States crafted its two-pillar strategy using both Saudi Arabia and Iran as bulwarks against Soviet advances into the oil-rich region.

The Carter administration continued the Nixon strategy, ultimately recognizing China and consigning Taiwan to lesser status although with the assurance of American assistance if attacked by

China. Arms control was pursued as the key currency for keeping U.S.–Soviet relations on track and pursuing détente. But events in Eurasia made that track with the Soviet Union difficult to navigate smoothly. In 1979, the shah fell, Iran became an American adversary, and the Soviets invaded Afghanistan. Carter failed to win reelection as Ronald Reagan soundly defeated him in 1980.

Reagan's strategic view was strongly anti-Soviet eventually becoming pro-Chinese. In essence, it was an ideological sharpening of the Nixonian era. Reagan, of course, brought with him the idea of the Strategic Defense Initiative, announced on March 23, 1983. And, in retrospect, Reagan was able to advance U.S.–Soviet and U.S.–Chinese relations through this relatively tougher policy toward Moscow. The phrase was not used then, but Reagan had fashioned a policy of détente with "tough love." The interregnum provided time for the irrationalities of the Soviet political and economic system to spin out of control.

Bush I and Clinton faced a world in which the monolithic communist threat dissolved. Neither administration was able to fashion a new strategic framework that would persist. For Bush, the collapse of the Soviet empire came too late in his administration. For Clinton, the absence of clear-cut and consistent policy aims with sufficient specificity to drive programs made deriving a workable strategic framework elusive. For Bush II, this remains the largest challenge.

It is by no means clear that Bush II has the instinct and comfort level to develop and implement a strategic framework beyond following certain principles as his predecessors did. September 11th created a momentum of its own. Had that tragedy not occurred, it is uncertain whether the Bush administration would have sorted itself out. The first eight months of his presidency were not filled with great achievement and the shakedown period was not complete.

## The Eagle's Axis of Evil

President Bush's State of the Union Address, delivered to Congress on January 29, 2002, introduced the term "axis of evil." The presi-

dent made it clear that it was time to face up to reality in international politics. And, in his view, the reality was plain: the three states
that made up this axis—Iraq, Iran, and North Korea—had regimes
that could only be described as "evil." The phrase created both consternation and praise.

Abroad, the reaction to this axis and its implicit reference to
World War II and the German-Japanese-Italian alliance was largely
negative. A key criticism was the lumping of three very different
states in the same category. Iraq could easily be singled out for special treatment. Saddam Hussein was no one's friend. But Iran and
North Korea, many of America's overseas friends would argue, were
not Iraq. At home, those wishing to end the menace of Saddam
applauded the president's initiative.

No doubt part of the president's intent was to build the case for
possible military action against Iraq. As the axis of evil became better
defined, the administration's concerns were impossible to miss. Iraq
and Saddam had ambitions for weapons of mass destruction. If left
to his own devices, Saddam would eventually acquire nuclear weapons to add to his inventory of chemical and biological agents. An
Iraqi nuclear bully was a clear and present danger to the region and
to the world.

Furthermore, the administration believed that a future September 11th-type of attack was inevitable. Unless checked, terrorists will
seek weapons of mass destruction to use in these assaults against the
United States. Bush sees Iraq as a supplier of these weapons to terror
organizations. Hence, forcing a regime change in Iraq to eliminate
Saddam is the most effective way of preventing that state from
becoming a nuclear danger and passing weapons of mass destruction
to terrorist groups out to attack the United States.

The administration subsequently declared that it has made no
decision on whether it would use force to change the regime in Iraq.
Vice-President Dick Cheney was sent to the Middle East via London
to consult. However, operational planning continued apace in the
Pentagon and analysts were predicting an attack, in the event the
decision was made, in the fall of 2002. Clearly, this view of the axis
of evil will play a significant role in the conduct of the Bush national

security policy. It will cut across most U.S. relations since the three members of this axis are located in proximity to the regions of most vital importance to America.

Regarding Russia and China, many critical issues are at stake. Administrations rarely project where and how U.S. relations with these states should be headed and what outcomes are preferable or acceptable. For example, while Congress finally granted China most favored nation (MFN) status, no vision or statement has been offered to suggest what U.S. economic policy is toward China or Russia except in general terms. That may be the only possible course but it also may not be.

Regarding strategic matters, while the United States and Russia appear to have reached agreement on further nuclear arms reductions, the consequences of the abrogation of the ABM Treaty remain unclear. America's missile defense program is still very much in the formative stage and will depend on further testing. The United States has no agreement whatsoever, or even any negotiations, with China over nuclear armaments.

Regarding alliances, expansion of NATO and Russian participation are unclear outside very general possibilities. NATO is likely to expand. Russia has a twentieth chair if not at the table perhaps within the room as more than just an observer. How much more has yet to be decided.

The United States remains committed to Japan and Korea. But the role of those states and of China in the northeast Pacific particularly in dealing with the North Korean member of this new axis has yet to be defined and thought through on a public basis.

The war on terrorism continues. Intelligence and other information-sharing arrangements between the United States and Russia and China have been reported as excellent. After Bush's Asian trip in late February 2002, China clearly decided that the fight against terror, given similar conflicts inside that country, overrode concerns with the abrogation of ABM Treaty. China's leadership demonstrably moved to embrace better relations with the United States. However, the extent of these new relationships and what they will mean for Russia and China in how they deal with indigenous terrorism remain unresolved. And should the United States determine that it will use force to remove Saddam, gaining even tacit support from Russia and China will be crucial.

When the United States began its bombing campaign in Afghanistan on October 7, 2001, it clearly had broad objectives for its strategy. The Bush administration was determined to "root out" terrorism and those who support it. In an interview with the *Washington Post*, Bush described the process as a series of concentric circles. The innermost circle is Afghanistan, al Qaeda, and the Taliban. A second circle, still being defined, includes at least one member of the new axis of evil—Iraq. Other candidates are the Philippines, where U.S. forces are already deployed with the Filipino Army in pursuit of terrorists on Basilan Island, Somalia, Yemen, and Indonesia. But no clear-cut strategy has yet emerged.

The inherent dilemma is that the first stage of this campaign—or war, as Bush calls it—against terrorism is only that. There is no scorecard or other means to determine who is winning or losing. Hence, both good and bad news emanated from Afghanistan and Operation Enduring Freedom. The good news was that the first phases of the military campaign against al Qaeda and the Taliban went far better than most observers expected.

Afghanistan has an interim government, the promise of international support to rebuild at least part of the infrastructure that was destroyed in over two decades of strife, and the chance of becoming whole again. The presidency of George W. Bush has been rejuvenated by his actions as a war president, and American credibility in many quarters has been strengthened.

American casualties have so far been modest: ten killed in action and, tragically, another two dozen dead by friendly fire and aircraft mishaps. By all accounts, collateral damage was minimized and the reputation of U.S. military power burnished. For a time, the fight was over—so much so that Defense Secretary Donald Rumsfeld's famous daily press conferences turned to lesser questions ranging from treatment of detainees in Guantanamo Bay, Cuba, to how many special forces were sent to the Philippines and other hot spots to track down al Qaeda cells.

Operation Anaconda was launched in early March to destroy what were assumed to be the surviving pockets of al Qaeda resistance. However, more phases lie ahead. The most immediate is keeping Afghanistan from again falling into the abyss of civil war. This means providing tools to assist the government of interim Prime Minister Hamid Karzai in establishing a modicum of peace, stability, and the rule of law and in rebuilding the nation.

The subsequent and longer-term phases will be continuing the fight against "terrorism with a global reach" and apprehending or dismantling whatever remains of the al Qaeda network and its base of support. In these next phases, given the complexity of stabilizing Afghanistan, the probable outcomes cannot be guaranteed as good and may be very bad. And, if the concentric circles extend to the "axis of evil," the news would become worse.

America's memory, even after an event as horrific as September 11th, is often short. Despite the highly visible six month commemoration of the event, headlines quickly returned to peacetime issues. Dramatic images of Special Forces troopers riding to battle on horseback and contrails in the sky from circling warplanes waiting to pound Taliban positions have ended. The Enron debacle, economic recovery plans, the Super Bowl playoffs, and even Congressman Gary Condit, the representative whose affair with an intern became front-page news when she disappeared, fill the headlines and nightly news shows.

The scent of really bad news comes from several directions. While Afghanistan has an interim government, warlords still reign. Its neighbors, whether Iran to the west or the three "stans" to the north, will no doubt be providing aid and comfort to the cliques they support rather than doing what is best for Afghanistan. Most of the Taliban have melted away to homes and hideouts. Many may become recrudescent. And the possibility of a major attack or ambush that kills Americans should be taken as a near certainty.

India and Pakistan have stepped back from the brink of war, but the fifty-five-year-old conflict between them is not over. As Pakistan struggles to contain its extremist elements and radical clerics, the government of Pervez Musharraf will be taxed. If further attacks in

India occur, such as an attack in January 2002 against a U.S. information office in Calcutta, there can be no guarantee that a new and more serious crisis will not erupt, one the United States may have less leverage to contain. In many ways, the ability of the regime in Kabul to restrain the centrifugal internal forces that threaten to divide Afghanistan again will have direct relevance to Pakistan and its political stability.

Whatever the strength of the U.S.–Saudi relationship, Riyadh cannot be complacent about U.S. presence in the kingdom and the long-term American campaign against terrorism. U.S. military presence may well continue. However, the Saudi rulers must confront the clash between the need for modernizing society to relieve internal political pressures while maintaining control and the traditional values of Islam.

Saudi Crown Prince Abdullah moved to confront these matters. First, in January 2002, he gave an unprecedented interview to the *New York Times* and the *Washington Post.* Abdullah emphasized the persistence and strength of the U.S.–Saudi friendship. He also issued a clear warning: unconditional support of Israel at the expense of Palestine by the United States would have consequences. Then, in February, in an interview with *New York Times* columnist Tom Friedman, Abdullah referred to a "peace plan" in his desk—in reality, more a vision statement than a plan. Abdullah told Friedman that a settlement among Israel, Palestine, and the Arab world was possible. Relations with Israel might be normalized if the Palestine state were constituted around the old 1967 borders specified by the UN resolutions. This plan was presented to the Arab League meeting in late March and could have a profound impact on the region and the conflict with Israel.

Finally, there will be critiques on this first phase of the war. Initially, estimates of opposition forces numbering upward of eighty thousand Taliban and fifteen thousand al Qaeda fighters were reported in the media. While there has been no confirmation of how many enemy forces indeed remained in Afghanistan during Enduring Freedom, it may well turn out that these numbers were exaggerated by a factor of ten.

Milt Bearden, former CIA station chief in Pakistan during the Afghan-Soviet War and regional expert turned author (his novel *Black Tulip* is a riveting story about covert operations during that period), believes that there may have been no more than three thousand Taliban arrayed against the coalition. As the actual number of enemy forces is determined, the magnitude of the military achievement may be diminished.

## A Long Look

It may be wishful thinking to believe that any administration is prepared to embark on serious and public review of what it will take to keep America safe. A leak of any size could be politically destructive. In March 2002, a copy of the administration's Nuclear Posture review was leaked. The mere mention of new nuclear targeting considerations caused a firestorm. Answers to basic security questions may be impossible because no consensus can be developed on some or any of them. While the long-term dangers posed by bin Laden and others like him are taken very seriously, the U.S. government has a visceral aversion to sweeping changes whether in strategy or organization.

Writing in the *Washington Post* on January 31st, 2002, the co-chairs of the National Security Strategy Commission, Hart and Rudman, pleaded with the Bush White House not to allow "business as usual" to prevent the sweeping institutional reform needed to transform America's security organization to meet twenty-first-century needs. And the internal problems of political and economic modernization in China and Russia may be so intense that any effort by the United States to structure new relationships could be an unacceptable shock to the system.

All of these reasons that argue for change at the margin or policies of steady as you go can be powerfully persuasive. On the other hand, it would appear that the need for some modus vivendi among the United States, Russia, and China on matters of national interest and importance may be growing more crucial. The danger during the Cold War was nuclear destruction, but the likelihood was low that it would be in anyone's interest to let the nuclear genie loose.

Nineteen men with box cutters killed over three thousand people and obliterated perhaps half a trillion dollars from the U.S. economy. What could a similarly diabolical and cunning plan do to disrupt not only the United States but Russia and China as well? How possible is it that someone would undertake such a task? And how much damage and disruption would be caused? If the answers to these questions are not negligible, then there is no excuse for not considering strategic frameworks and plans for containing this danger much as nuclear war, in a different sense, was contained for over fifty years of Cold War.

# ★ 8 ★

## Finishing Business—
## What Must Be Done

### First Principles

In an age of visible turmoil and terror, no sane person would disagree with the sentiment that the United States and its friends must be kept safe. But the precise question is safe from exactly what? The Bush (43) administration has provided one answer to that question. Terror and terrorism are the clear and present dangers. Hence, the war is on to eliminate both terrorists and those who support or sponsor them.

H. L. Mencken, the renown journalist, was credited with the observation that anyone who had a short, simple answer to a tough, complex problem was invariably wrong. The problem with the Bush declaration is more than simply definitional. Terror and terrorism are tools, weapons, and tactics. As Lenin said, "The purpose of terrorism is to terrorize." But containing both, while necessary, is not sufficient. The *causes* of terrorism must be addressed as well if there is to be any chance of keeping the nation safe for the long term.

Why was the United States attacked on September 11th? The reason is not only hatred of the United States, although that sentiment is widespread. The reason for the attacks is related to a psychotic interpretation of Islam that sees the presence of American forces in

Saudi Arabia as desecrating the most sacred values of Islam. No doubt the image of unwavering U.S. support for Israel to the detriment of the Palestinians, rightly or wrongly, further fires rabid anti-Americanism.

Terrorism, which arises from the larger danger of extremism, has several parallels with America's drug war. Coping with the drug infestation has two sides: supply and demand. U.S. government counterdrug policies have visibly emphasized reducing supply. Thus, billions of dollars have been dispensed to antidrug patrols and as aid to Colombia and other Andean states in the effort to choke off supply. Demand is addressed with ad campaigns, education, and law enforcement. However, the fact is that unless demand is reduced, the drug war can never be won. Both sides of the problem must be cured.

Terror also has two sides: cause and effect. To "win the war," causes (i.e., supply) must be reduced and effects—applying terror against targets—must be neutralized (i.e., demand). Protection can be achieved by physical defenses and proactive or preemptive means to eliminate the terrorists before any acts of terror are perpetrated. In essence, sometimes the bad guys must be struck first. This is what Israel is currently practicing in its program of "targeted assassination." Clearly, a set of moral and legal issues must be readdressed if preemption is to become a weapon of choice, something that has been obscured by the palpable American revulsion to September 11th and the deaths of more than three thousand innocents.

The Bush response has not yet fully addressed the causes of extremism (a more appropriate term for understanding terrorism). Nor has it fully explored the limits and consequences of any preemptive policies no matter how seemingly justified. And, in dealing with the means to eliminate terrorist actions, its definition of an axis of evil has added the prevention of the proliferation of weapons of mass destruction as a key objective. The question, however, is whether North Korea, Iran, or Iraq would make these mass-destruction agents available to extremists. Prudence would argue that any likelihood of such dissemination is too great. On the other hand, the added objective can easily dilute the main effort against terrorism, especially if regime change becomes the next aim.

How dangerous, then, is the world today for the United States and its allies and friends? During the Cold War, while the potential danger was catastrophic nuclear war, the reality was otherwise. Despite the tens of thousands of nuclear weapons (and vast quantities of biological and chemical mass-destruction agents), after the atomic bombing of Nagasaki in August 1945, none was ever used in anger. For many in the United States, September 11th "changed everything." America would never again be safe from devastating attack.

The Bush administration has argued that post–September 11th, the United States should expect "vastly more damaging" forms of attack. This forecast was based on the Bush view of the high likelihood that terrorists ultimately would gain access to weapons of mass destruction. In turn, these weapons would be used here. Hence, the axis of evil that specifically listed Iran, Iraq, and North Korea was constructed because each of those states had ambitions for acquiring weapons of mass destruction and direct links to terrorist organizations. The supposition was that the first would lead to the second: these states would find it in their interests to provide certain groups with weapons of mass destruction or technology to enable their acquisition. And, each regime is considered evil.

So what then is the Bush intent and how is it likely to play out given what is known about the nature of the world today? The first element in the Bush plan is to continue the fight to "rout out" al Qaeda wherever its cells are operating. Some eighty states are suspected of harboring al Qaeda members within their borders. Second, certainly in 2002, Bush seems determined to take the fight to regimes that support or sponsor terrorism whether al Qaeda or other groups such as Hezbollah and Hamas. Third, the administration suggests that it is prepared to strike first if necessary to prevent weapons of mass destruction from falling into the hands of terrorists and terrorist organizations. While allies and coalitions of the willing are critical to succeeding in these phases of strategy, the administration has left no question that it will take the lead. If friends and allies follow, that is preferable. If the United States has to act unilaterally, it seems willing to do so.

## The Biggest Danger

The Bush approach has merit and, for the time being, has attracted powerful public support. The policy, however, has potential flaws. The biggest danger to the United States is not from weapons of mass destruction. Fifty years of Cold War provided ample opportunity to learn how the use of weapons of mass destruction could be contained or deterred.

Iran, Iraq, and North Korea, no matter how intense their anti-American hostility, are not the Soviet Union. Unless the United States loses its nerve or its competence, containing these states should not prove impossible or even questionable. Changing the nature of their regimes, however, is an entirely different matter and has a far greater index of difficulty. If that is the intent, then another strategy and an unyielding coalition backed by unbreakable international support almost surely will be needed.

*The real danger is far more diabolical. As one of the world's most open societies, the United States is fundamentally vulnerable to attack. As bin Laden has discovered, "It is the economy, stupid." Disruption rather than destruction of huge amounts of American infrastructure is the aim. And mass destruction weapons, however frightening, are not the only means of causing great damage. If terrorism is to be kept in check, much of the effort must go in the critical area of reducing societal vulnerabilities to the future equivalent of box cutters used with devilish and enormously destructive skill. Furthermore, an explosion in the crescent of crisis is certain to spread. In its path, the international economic system will be put at risk. Hence, prevention means dealing with the conditions from which extremism arises. There is no alternative.*

## Some Realities

The first reality is that, while the United States is the strongest economic and military power in the world, without a countervailing threat to leverage that influence such as the "evil empire" and the Cold War, its authority and legitimacy no longer can be derived solely from that strength. Good reason or overwhelming evidence for action is vitally needed if other states are to be brought along. It is interesting that while few Americans doubt that Osama bin Laden and al Qaeda are responsible for September 11th, no convincing case or formal document has been released to show the proof of guilt. Such a case is vital if the international community is to be a willing partner for the long term.

Second, in an age of instant communications and no broad international agreement on common enemies beyond generic wars against crime, disease, poverty, and terrorism, targets for American counteraction such as Iran, Iraq, and North Korea have many political and diplomatic alternatives. Iran can draw on Russia, France, and the other Islamic states as counterweights to the United States. Saddam can embark on a peace initiative with his neighbors as Libya's Qadaffi has or Iraq can permit UN inspectors back in, thereby neutralizing U.S. preferences for a regime change. North Korea can court the South and turn to China for support. Any of these steps would play against the United States as propaganda and in the media.

Third, while the U.S. military and the CIA seemed to perform well in Afghanistan, the number of Taliban and al Qaeda forces they overcame may have been substantially overestimated. Their dispersal and escape to other hiding places do not mean the danger has been eliminated. Should the war be expanded to Iraq or North Korea, the same rapid and decisive results cannot be taken for granted. That the United States is the most formidable military power in the world should not automatically be translated into invincibility in all cases.

Fourth, the attention of the American public cannot be indefinitely kept on the war against terrorism. Calls for ever greater vigilance and warnings of imminent attack ultimately will go unheeded. Maintaining full public support will be a full-time job. And, if domestic terrorists strike first, the evil axis may have to be jettisoned to deal with this imminent danger.

Fifth, it is by no means clear that the American economy will

achieve high levels of growth quickly. The administration can argue
that further increases in spending for defense and homeland security
are critical. The issue is not whether the nation can afford $379 bil-
lion for defense in fiscal year 2003. At a cost of just over 3 percent
of GDP, the nation can. The critical questions are whether this additional spending actually makes the United States safer and what
actions will be needed regarding future budgets to account for Social
Security and health care in order to keep expenditures in line with
receipts so that deficit spending can be controlled.

Sixth, there are three levels in the terror hierarchy that must be
neutralized. The first is the actual terrorists and organizations,
whether individuals such as a McVeigh or a Unibomber, groups such
as al Qaeda or Islamic Jihad, or states that directly or inadvertently
support terror as suggested by the designation "axis of evil." Second
are the actual causes of extremism and terrorism. And third are the
actual "things" of value to be protected against terror, from populations to infrastructure.

Finally, administrations will have to learn to deal with multi-
crises, that is, several crises that occur more or less simultaneously.
During the Cold War, multi-crises were relatively rare. In 1956, there
was Suez followed by the Hungarian Revolution; in 1958 the United
States intervened in Lebanon and China threatened the offshore
Nationalist islands of Quemoy and Matsu. In 1961 the Bay of Pigs
was followed by a crisis over Berlin. In January 1968, the Tet Offensive in Vietnam was being reversed when North Korea pirated the
USS *Pueblo* in international waters. And in 1973, the Yom Kippur
War was raging when the United States went to DefCon Three to
head off the possibility of Soviet intervention in the Middle East.

That has all changed. The United States faced three simultaneous
crises during Enduring Freedom: the campaign in Afghanistan, the
escalation of the Israeli-Palestinian conflict, and the latest India-
Pakistan standoff following the bombing of India's Parliament. Con-
figuring any government to deal with several simultaneous crises
approaches the limits of the possible. Yet this is what is suggested if
the axis of evil becomes the basis for action.

## Three Paths

The Bush (43) administration has three basic courses for action. First, it can continue its present plan to rout out terrorists and deal with the axis of evil as it must. Clearly, other chronic problems such as the Israeli-Palestinian and India-Pakistan conflicts will be critical but will be dealt with on an ad hoc basis, not necessarily as part of a broad, integrated strategy. Rebuilding Afghanistan will be important. However, a massive type of new Marshall Plan to deal with the causes and consequences of extremism and terrorism globally is unlikely to emerge.

Second, the Bush administration can choose to pursue a broader strategy that incorporates means to rectify causes of extremism that are common to the territory on which bin Laden has preyed, namely the Islamic world, on a largely unilateral basis. By leading in this manner the United States could rightfully expect others to follow. A coalition of the willing suggests how such a strategy would evolve.

Third, the Bush administration could develop a broader strategy, that is, a comprehensive plan to attack the causes as well as the culprits of terrorism where they arise and to defend our homeland and those of our friends through physical protection and preemption if necessary but on a multilateral basis. As NATO was fashioned during the Cold War, a new form of alliances and international partnerships would be constructed to these ends. Clearly, this most ambitious of the three options will be the most difficult to execute and will bring the largest risks. However, it almost certainly will bring the biggest rewards.

## Re-Learning from the Past

Every administration enters office with a particular personality, mind set, and agenda. Every administration has to deal with crises whether internal or external and regardless of cause. Every administration has to deal with the harsh realities and occasional tyrannies of the political system that tend to skew judgment. And every administration since Truman's, less Bush 41 (who lost reelection), has had to cope with some form of political calamity that threatened the political survival of the president from Watergate to Monica and from Vietnam to the Iran-Contra scandal.

Making course directions or admitting to error and failure when policies or judgments proved detrimental or erroneous occurred infrequently. Arrogance invariably infected government and judgment. Similarly, preconceptions often overcame fact and analysis. Vietnam is the most tragic example.

On the other hand, administrations do well when they get first principles correct by fully understanding the facts and circumstances of each issue. Truth and candor are crucial antidotes to ideology and preconception. So too, comprehension of cultural and societal differences between the United States and other states must be given more than lip service.

The Truman administration, despite Harry Truman's low ratings at the time, managed to get the Cold War right. It understood that the Soviet Union could be contained short of war and short of major rearmament, although the Korean War changed that consideration. NATO and the Marshall Plan were among its finest moments. Where Truman had greatest difficulty was with the extreme right in Congress and what would become rabid McCarthyism that distorted and skewed rational policy.

The Eisenhower administration also had a sound understanding of the security needs of the nation. Eisenhower's strategic "new look" emphasized nuclear deterrence and gave rise to the phrase "massive retaliation" as the means to contain Soviet ambitions. However, Eisenhower, with his extraordinary wartime experience, recognized the nature of the Soviet Union and Joseph Stalin (to whom some have mistakenly compared Saddam Hussein and Kim Jung Il). Hence, under Eisenhower's leadership and guidance, America was kept quite safe.

The Kennedy administration entered office with the "best and brightest" and the promise to "pay any price and bear any burden" to protect freedom. Unfortunately, the Kennedy preconceptions did not conform to reality. The United States became trapped in Vietnam and in a larger arms race with the Soviet Union. It is arguable that the nation was made safer by the stunning rhetoric and charm and style of the Kennedy administration.

Poor Lyndon Johnson inherited the mantle and Vietnam. It probably killed him. By 1968, when he withdrew from consideration for another term, the war had ripped America apart. While the physical danger from the Soviet Union had not grown, America was not safer. Vietnam, the counter-culture, drugs, and other unhappy legacies eroded the greatness and the promise of the United States. It would take several decades to recover.

Richard Nixon was the most accomplished foreign policy president the nation would have, perhaps including Ike. Inexplicably, the Nixon administration tolerated and then covered up Watergate, the sleazy break-in at Democratic National Headquarters in the building of that name, for reasons that still are not known or fathomed three decades later. Nixon paid a dear price. But Nixon also showed that it was indeed possible to create and implement a comprehensive security strategy. And, with the opening to China, the gradual withdrawal from Vietnam (which many criticized as too slow), and the arms negotiations with the Soviet Union, Nixon indeed helped make the nation safer.

The Carter administration, driven by the president's emphasis on human rights and decency, was voted out of office after one term. The best lesson perhaps is that there is no easy way to negotiate the huge cultural gap between what a president tries to impose as values and standards and what the rest of the world accepts. Carter's failure was not intellectual; it was cultural. And even American citizens finally turned against the perception of Carter's self-righteousness and sense of integrity.

Reagan remains a mystery. His administration had three main aims—cut taxes, increase defense and reduce the government—that rarely lost focus. Clearly, there was an ideological imprint stronger than in many other White Houses. And clearly there were disasters, from the Beirut bombing in October 1983 that killed 241 Marines to the Iran-Contra debacle that nearly ended his presidency. On the other hand, the Soviet Union began its death spiral. The "malaise" of the Carter administration was reversed. And while Reagan's reelection slogan "it is morning in America again" was entirely form without real substance, it conveyed a certain message of America's rekindled sense of self-confidence.

The Bush's forty-first administration, for reasons already noted, had at its apogee the Gulf War. Whether Bush was physically drained by Grave's disease or simply too aloof from the political fray to win reelection will be debated. However, it is clear that foreign policy triumphs cannot be assumed as fungible to domestic politics.

The Clinton administration is a treasure trove of lessons. Clinton learned from past mistakes and aggressively changed policy directions, invariably to the center, "triangulating" on where supporting public opinion was strongest. Clinton also had the vision to appreciate longer-term security dangers. His administration correctly assessed the dangers from terrorism, proliferation of mass-destruction weapons, instability in the Middle East, and the requirement for bringing China and Russia into the circle of civilized nations. The problem was the inability to execute, not a failure to understand.

## Unfinished Business I and II—Unleashing the Eagle

The first piece of America's unfinished business deals with the inherent vulnerability of an open society and particularly one as open as the United States. There are two levels of vulnerability. The first is the inherent difficulty in taking, justifying, and sustaining major action exacerbated by the weaknesses of a political system that often overly constrains choices and options for action. For example, if any administration finally concluded (for argument's sake, correctly) that the only alternative to another war in the Middle East was to impose a settlement on all sides, a firestorm would be created at home. That reaction could too easily derail any action no matter how vital. Or, more likely, the prospect of such a reaction could preclude even the consideration of a step as bold as this one.

Included is the inherent vulnerability of America's physical infrastructure to disruption and damage. The reality is that this vulnerability can be reduced but it never can be fully eliminated. And the further dilemma is that additional actions to safeguard the nation can too easily impinge on individual rights and do real damage to the nature of freedom.

September 11th certainly provided the Bush administration with an irresistible motivation to fashion a powerful, sweeping, and effective response. Time will tell how long the war on terrorism will coalesce bipartisan and public support. Even in crisis, the openness of the American political system, with its checks and balances, often dilutes or stops action well short of what is needed. The most relevant example was Congress's inability to pass an economic stimulus package after September 11th.

Many will argue that this economic package was not needed. That misses the point. To most Americans and to the White House and Congress, there was urgency and reason for action. Yet none was forthcoming. What happens when action is needed and there is no way to galvanize the political system? The current birthing pains of the Homeland Security Office suggest that even in a matter as political vital as homeland security, effective action is rarely certain. The administration has no doubt made the wise decision to allow this new office some room to settle in before perhaps making it a cabinet-level department. Meanwhile, despite National Guardsmen posted at airports, fighters flying combat air patrols overhead, and a blizzard of warnings and alerts to maintain greater vigilance, is the nation's infrastructure any safer than it was on September 10th?

The second and related piece of unfinished business is the dysfunctional organization of government to deal with the nation's security. The combination of these first two pieces of unfinished business has produced three huge deficits—in strategy, in institutional organization, and in recruiting and retaining the best and the brightest to serve.

## Recommendations

General George Marshall, a great American hero who was largely responsible for America's victory in World War II and was one of the chief architects for the structure that eventually won the Cold War demanded getting the objectives right. In dealing with the new dangers of the twenty-first century, it is essential to define the correct objectives.

To keep the United States and its friends safe, there must be full and sophisticated, as well as accurate, understanding of what the real threats are and how they can be contained, deterred, and eliminated. The largest danger is not simply terrorists armed with weapons of mass destruction. The danger is extremism. Bin Laden may prove to be a passing danger. But he has fashioned a formula for revolution and change as Lenin did. The fertile fields for future disciples will be found in the crescent of crisis that stretches from the Mediterranean to the Straits of Malacca.

The key objectives for keeping America safe must deal with both causes and effects of this radicalism. First and foremost, the United States must refute the legitimacy and basis for this perverted interpretation of Islam. Bin Laden and his formula for exploiting the openness of America and other societies based on religion and holy virtues must be exorcised. This will require the full support of Islamic clerics and politicians, literally around the world. A long-term program for education and discourse to these ends is essential. It will also require a strong and well-funded commitment to reducing many of the economic, social, and political disparities that are the breeding grounds for terror and extremism. This commitment will be shaped by the next problem.

A root cause of extremism is the inequality of societies, particularly those that are autocratic, inflexible, and ruled from the center as the Soviet Union was. States in the crescent of crisis including Egypt and Saudi Arabia fall into this category. Both are also friends and allies of the United States. Hence, great care and diplomacy as well as firmness in moving these states toward modernization are prerequisites. The Bush adminstration is disposed toward regime change in the axis of evil, but it must also persist in helping friends in these regions to make positive change as well.

In this light, a new version of the old Marshall Plan is essential. Given America's unprecedented wealth, there is no economic reason why a percent of GDP or about $100 billion a year could not be applied to dealing with many of the economic and societal inequities worldwide. Clearly, this will not happen overnight. Any program will have to be carefully crafted, with fine political judgment. The American public must be persuaded that such a program is needed, that it will be efficiently and effectively administered, and most significantly that the aim to eliminate these social disparities is achieved in credible and measurable ways.

With this program in place, or at least in the first stages of inception, the United States will have the political legitimacy and clout to deal with specific regimes from the Saudis to the Pakistanis. In Saudi Arabia, there is every prospect for a clash between the security interests of the United States, particularly access to oil, and human rights abuses with specific reference to women. If not handled with care, U.S.–Saudi relations could easily disintegrate.

Saudi leaders argue that their nation is young, only seventy-odd years old, and, as it took time in the United States for African-Americans and women to achieve full standing as citizens, so too it will take time in the kingdom. These leaders promise that change will occur. Critics draw on the South African example of apartheid and the success of the economic boycott that ultimately ended that horrid practice. Others note that while the secular leadership in the royal family is pro-American, many in the clergy, dominated by Wahabism, view Americans as infidels. Hence, within the kingdom, to the degree that this observation is valid, tension between the ruling family and many of the clergy is real and problematic.

The United States will have to determine the better course. From a security perspective, the distinction between friends or allies and adversaries is critically important. With friends such as Saudi Arabia and China (or other autocratic regimes), a set of policies that accepts the longer view to remedying societal and political inequities is appropriate. For belligerent or adversary regimes as in the axis of evil, aggressive policies that include the threat or prospect of regime change and the necessity of behavioral change are justifiable. The vital issue is that these distinctions are publicly and frequently explained to reduce the possibility of any misunderstanding or unfair criticism on grounds of hypocritical or double-standard behavior.

To deal with the effects and consequences of extremism, namely to thwart attacks against many homelands, not only the United States, there must be an office or agency that is chartered specifically to conduct vulnerability analyses and to propose reasonable responses. The combination of the skills employed at Bletchley Park during World War II, in this case to break the codes of extremism, and the equivalent of a Manhattan or Apollo Project to derive extraordinary technical solutions should be replicated, possibly under the Office of Homeland Security. However, without the analytical skills and tools combined under a single agency for this purpose, the diffused nature of the organization of government will make the task of effective vulnerability analyses and protection impossible.

Regarding specific steps for keeping the nation safe, the checks and balances and the divisions of power specified in a constitution that is over two hundred years old must be brought in line with the twenty-first century. The inherently centrifugal nature of government must have a few restraints placed on it. And some of the excesses of the system, such as the campaign-centric focus and trend toward criminalization of politics, must be reversed. The process and mechanisms for coordination and advice and consent between Congress and the presidency must reflect today's realities. A clear and agreed upon statement of strategy and policy pertaining to national and homeland security with sufficient clarity to drive programs and set proper demarcations of assignment and responsibility of duties and roles is key.

To that end, Congress should establish a joint committee on national security and homeland defense equivalent to the NSC. The membership of this Congressional National and Homeland Security Council (CNAHSC) would be determined by Congress and would include as charter members (but not be limited to) the majority and minority leaders of both houses; the Speaker of the House; the president (the nation's vice-president) and president pro tempore of the Senate; and relevant committee chairmen and ranking members. The CNAHSC would be provided a separate staff to support its functions.

The principal responsibility of the CNAHSC would be to develop both the sense of Congress and policy pertaining to national and homeland security. This committee would draft a Congressional Resolution on national and homeland security for every Congress (i.e., at least every two years). The purposes would be to align Congress and the executive more closely. The president would still maintain his role as commander in chief without infringement. Congress would maintain Article I, Section 8 responsibilities. However, such a mechanism is essential to reduce the partisanship that is increasingly threatening to disrupt a cogent plan for the common defense.

A second responsibility for the CNAHSC would be to oversee streamlining and simplification and then codification of the rules and regulations that govern all national and homeland security functions and related agencies. A third responsibility would be to propose a plan for restructuring the committee and budgeting systems in Congress to fit current and future demands and realities.

The next action is to update the National Security Act of 1947. That act must be revised to recognize the current world, not the Cold War for which it was designed. The National Security Act could define security in terms of defense, diplomatic, intelligence, and economic components. Over time, these distinctions evolved into strict barriers that were breached only at bureaucratic peril. "Vertical" solutions along these lines worked against the paramount Soviet threat. As bin Laden so vividly shows, the dangers are no longer vertical. They are "horizontal" and cut across many agencies of government.

The purposes of a revised National Security Act are to reconcile the differences between the vertical organization of the Cold War and the horizontal nature of dangers in the twenty-first century. The many competing, overlapping, and redundant assignments across law-enforcement, terrorist, intelligence, counterintelligence and counter-terrorist, military, and related humanitarian missions and tasks of this vertical structure must be realigned. And perhaps as important, state and local homeland security capabilities must be integrated into a national tool kit. Organizational barriers must be eliminated. The convergence of security capabilities among military, law-enforcement, and intelligence agencies illustrates this point.

Fifty (or even twenty) years ago, there were huge differences in how soldiers and police officers were trained and equipped. Soldiers carried rifles, wore helmets, and were trained to kill enemy soldiers and destroy enemy weapons systems. Police officers generally carried revolvers and were trained for standard law-enforcement tasks. Today, police SWAT (special weapons and tactics teams) units in full battle gear are hard to distinguish from their military opposite numbers. Both carry the most lethal automatic weapons, wear body armor, use advanced and encrypted communications, and are trained to deal with deadly force. Minimizing collateral damage and civilian casualties is common to both. Furthermore, SWAT units also are trained in techniques for dealing with terrorists and mass-destruction weapons. And, in Afghanistan, CIA officers were operating Predator and Global Hawk unmanned aerial vehicles for both reconnaissance and strike, emulating traditional military missions. In other words, there has been a convergence in actual operations, capability, and training as law-enforcement and battlefield threats grow more similar.

Part of this revision must change the basic organization for assuring the nation's security. One option is to expand the current NSC system into a national and homeland security structure. This broader structure could then be overlaid onto the Department of Defense's Unified Command Plan (UCP). The UCP has regional commanders in chief responsible for military operations in specific geographic areas. These staffs would be expanded to include all national security functions including defense, diplomacy, intelligence, and law enforcement, leading to a National and Homeland Security Command Plan (NSAHSCP).

The NSAHSCP would be organized on a regional basis and could be co-located at or with the regional CinC headquarters. Each headquarters would be staffed with senior officials across government— DoD, State, Treasury, Justice, CIA, Energy, Commerce, and other relevant agencies. Headquarters would probably remain focused on Asia and the Pacific; the crescent of crisis, namely the Middle East, Persian Gulf, and South Asia; Europe; Latin America; and North America. The NSAHSCP would exercise routine command authority within specific regions and, as appropriate, in crisis. The NSC staff structure in the White House would mirror this structure and would coordinate and adjudicate policy responses among the key national and homeland security offices and agencies.

In this regard, over time, further consideration should be given to making the Office of Homeland Security a Senate-approved cabinet post and to integrating law enforcement and intelligence. A general model for consideration in this latter instance is that used by the British—MI-5 has domestic intelligence responsibilities and MI-6 is assigned the overseas functions. In part, such a realignment would use the nation's principal intelligence agencies—CIA, DIA, NSA, national imagery and technical surveillance, as well as FBI assets—assigning them, in accordance with the law and the Constitution, to separate domestic and international organizations. The FBI would retain principal law-enforcement functions. Other departments would have smaller offices for coordination and as checks. However, the bureaucratic counterweight would be the Bletchley Park-Manhattan Project creation working under the Secretary for Homeland Security, who would also draw on local law-enforcement intelligence services. Finally, to deal with covert operations, the ability of British forces to operate more broadly than those of the United States suggests a division of labor that can be negotiated.

There are two other critical areas for this new National Security Act. Both are designed to involve the public more intimately in understanding the character of the new security challenges and in attracting the nation's best to service. A National and Homeland Security Information and Awareness Office (NSAHSIO) should be established. Headed by a presidentially appointed and senatorially confirmed chief executive, this office's purpose would be to inform a variety of publics about these key issues. As with the Institute for Peace or a greatly expanded Radio Free Europe, public awareness is the aim. This office would probably function under a board of cabinet officers to ensure that there was full coordination and integration and, most importantly, that this office would "stay on message."

To attract able people and to respond to the need for far more comprehensive education and training of national and homeland security professionals, the National Security Act should be amended to establish academies for that purpose. A controversial but practical solution is to use the nation's four service academies—Army, Navy, Air Force, and Coast Guard—as the institutions to provide officer-level entries. Graduates would be required to spend time in the reserves unless they chose the military as their profession. Class sizes would be expanded from the approximate four thousand at each of the three military-service academies as appropriate. Graduates would be able to choose service in either the executive or legislative branch for a set number of years in addition to reserve commitments. Such a step would also expand the number of Americans who had some form of military experience.

## Unfinished Business III and IV—The Crescent of Crisis

The Arab-Israeli-Palestinian conflict, containing Iraq and possibly Iran, and the India-Pakistan conflict have become linked by the threat of bin Ladenism. An explosion in one place cannot reasonably be expected to remain contained. And the stakes and dangers are growing, not receding. Hence, bold and even risky options must be considered. While simultaneous pursuit of several aggressive initiatives exceeds good judgment, application of a high-risk high-payoff option in just one of the crisis spots could be a firewall to prevent explosions from extending throughout the entire crescent.

Former Israeli Prime Minister and now Foreign Minister Shimon Peres publicly worries that the state of the Israeli-Palestinian conflict has never been worse. This condition could be called the *Wafa Idriss phenomenon*. Idriss was a twenty-eight-year-old Palestinian woman who was killed by a bomb that she was carrying. If this was not an accidental detonation, the event suggests that gender is no longer an inhibition for suicide bombers. The whole cycle of violence could escalate to ever more dangerous and destructive levels as both male and female Palestinians find means of political expression in suicide attacks. How the Israelis would react to female suicide bombers and whether the policy of targeted assassinated would be gender-blind are impossible questions to answer except to say that any forceful reaction is likely to exaggerate the dangers.

The Bush administration has not yet engaged heavily as peacemaker and facilitator of peace. Both Israel and the PA have been largely and unsuccessfully left the task of ending the violence and finding a road to peace. The heightened violence, especially if it worsens, could force a bolder initiative on the part of the United States. Such an initiative was suggested nearly a quarter of century ago by Malcolm Toon, a former American ambassador to Israel and to the Soviet Union.

Toon thought then that the only alternative for peace was direct intervention by the United States and the Soviet Union and the stationing of ground forces to guarantee the security of both warring parties. If the United States decides that solution of the Israeli-Arab-Palestinian conflict is vital in the larger context of calming the entire region, then the Toon option must be weighed. Some form of U.S. and possibly NATO-supported intervention along the Yugoslav model might be fashioned. The prospect of German troops serving in Israel as part of a NATO peace-assurance force may have seemed ridiculous a few months ago. Yet, if the alternative is another war, possibly with mass-destruction weapons, is that acceptable?

The external forces would guarantee the survival of Israel and the security of both states. Establishment of some form of a Palestinian state would occur along the lines of prior UN resolutions. The risks would be enormous. Israel would find it impossible to accept a position in which other parties determined its security. Palestine would want assurances of sovereignty and dignity. Violence and terrorism would not be instantly ended and no doubt there would be casualties among the peace-imposing forces. Americans would be wounded and some would die. The political furor would be fierce in many states, not only Israel and America. But what is the alternative?

The Iraqi options were noted earlier. The highest risk rests in using armed force to change the regime. Upward of one hundred thousand to three hundred thousand troops, presumably all or mostly American, would mount an attack and advance to Baghdad and other key cities. The Iraqi army would have to be engaged and neutralized. Saddam would be killed, captured, or forced to flee. An interim government would be imposed, possibly under UN supervision.

Huge dangers are associated with such an endeavor. The military intervention could bog down and the successes of Desert Storm and Enduring Freedom might not be replicated if Iraqi soldiers chose to fight to defend the homeland. Certainly, support in the Arab world would evaporate. Without access to the Gulf and bases in Saudi Arabia, sustaining any intervention would be excessively complicated. Almost certainly, Saddam would fire something nasty at Israel. Provocation could bring Israel in regardless of the American attitude. This would further deteriorate relations in the Arab world, probably precipitate an oil embargo, and no doubt give momentum to anti-Americanism and the extremism advocated by bin Laden. And, Iran would be a wild card.

Still if intervention succeeded, the most immediate problem of Saddam and mass-destruction weapons would be alleviated. Possibly the United States could withdraw or greatly reduce its presence in the Gulf, thereby ending the grounds for bin Laden–like charges of defiling Islam. And the message to other would-be enemies would be powerful. The benefits would be great. But the risks and dangers appear far larger.

Given the axis of evil, Iran is no longer off America's "most wanted" list. While not considered as significant a piece of unfinished business as the other hot spots in the region, Iran is clearly a high priority for the Bush administration. Two thoughts are offered. Grounds for grievances and animosities are present on both sides. It was the United States that overthrew the Mossedegh government in 1953 and replaced it with the shah, a ruler the United States supported to the very end in 1979. The United States also shot down an Iranian Air Bus in 1987 (later abruptly apologizing and providing compensation for its negligence).

Iran's government of course viewed America as the Great Satan. It supported the takeover of the American embassy and the imprisonment of fifty-two Americans. It conspired to bring down Pan American Flight 103 over Lockerbie. And its support of anti-Israeli terrorist organizations has been strong.

Still, it is unlikely that the United States would intervene with military force absent an extreme provocation. More likely, the United States will continue to rely on a double containment policy against Iran and Iraq to halt the spread of mass-destruction weapons through embargoes and if need be selected military strikes, and to prevent support of terrorist organizations.

A fertile region for a bold initiative is the India-Pakistan dispute and the confrontation over Kashmir. If India and Pakistan can redress their major animosities and grievances, the far bookend of the crescent of crisis will be made secure. However difficult this task may prove, it is arguably less difficult than the bold initiatives suggested for the other bookend states.

Kashmir must be resolved. Permanent separation on each side of the Line of Control legitimizes the status quo without adding additional value to either side. Reverting control of Kashmir to one of the parties is impossible. The only feasible (although not necessarily achievable) option is to grant Kashmir independence. Home rule, given the majority of Muslims over Hindus, would provide many points of conflict. Perhaps a board of control to supervise an independent Kashmir with Indian and Pakistani membership could help.

Assurances and the stationing of peacekeepers would follow. Assistance and financial aid would be prerequisites for success. The net effect would be to stabilize India-Pakistani relations and ultimately produce a rapprochement. The alternative is instability and the risk of another nuclear confrontation. And, given the reach of Islamic extremism with or without bin Laden, the opportunity for mischief and the destabilization of Pakistan remains a real danger.

Each of these options is high-risk. Benefit is neither assured nor necessarily likely. Yet, if each of the hot spots in the crescent of crisis is linked in a potentially explosive chain, then uncommon measures are needed to destroy those links. Business as usual will not work no matter how attractive a lesser-risk policy appears.

## Unfinished Business V—Harnessing Bears and Dragons

The United States, Russia, and China are ripe for a new version of triangular politics, in this case, "trifecta politics." Each of the three must benefit from this arrangement. The basis for discussion could be strategic stability talks. Initially, these talks should focus on items of immediate security interest: bin Laden's version of extremism and the future of nuclear deterrence and defense. From those starting points, broader agendas can be developed.

The thesis underlying these talks is that it is in each of the three powers' interest to agree to a strategic framework that incorporates the aims and objectives to keep each nation safe from the dangers of the twenty-first century. The abrogation of the ABM Treaty creates the responsibility and opportunity for the United States to come to some arrangement with the other two powers about how deterrence and defense should be viewed. Ultimately, sharing missile defenses (if indeed they work), as Ronald Reagan promised, should be an American commitment. And lowering the number of offensive nuclear warheads and ensuring the integrity of nuclear weapons are two areas where three-way agreement should be sought.

From these talks, the discussion should be expanded to include all nuclear states. Britain, France, India, Pakistan, and even Israel as an observer should be invited. The purpose of these stability talks is reach a modus vivendi over the future of nuclear weapons and perhaps agreement on no-first-use pledges, something the United States has previously refused to consider. Once that agreement—formal or tacit—is reached, the next step is the UN General Assembly and Security Council.

The UN should pass a new resolution that declares any unprovoked or terrorist first use of weapons of mass destruction a crime against humanity. Such crimes may not have specific sanctions other than the authority of self-defense provided for in the charter for joint or independent action to make the user accountable. Without strong international pressure to preclude use of these weapons, prevention will be difficult. But, to obtain international support and cooperation, the United States must demonstrate willingness that even though it is the largest possessor of these weapons and the only state to use a nuclear bomb in anger, it has the responsibility to move toward their eventual elimination. That process may take decades. Indeed, it may never happen. However, unless the United

States takes the lead in moving in that direction, its plea for preventing proliferation will be countered by many states who resent American hypocrisy and arrogance in having their nuclear cake and eating it too.

These are all bold suggestions. The saw that there are fighter pilots who are old and fighter pilots who are bold but no fighter pilots who are both old and bold applies. Yet, if the dangers are as pronounced as Secretary of Defense Donald Rumsfeld so eloquently argues and as different from the Cold War, then new venues must be examined. There is no alternative.

## Action This Day Keeping the Nation Safe

Each of these tasks, from revisiting the National Security Act of 1947 to proposing new initiatives for peace and stability, is enormous and possibly insurmountable. How can any of this be done? First, the groundwork starts now. The president must begin by expanding his war on terror to dealing with the causes and consequences of extremism. This means laying out a bold and comprehensive strategy for dealing with national and homeland security both at home and abroad. The best means for assuring homeland security is not guarding every piece of infrastructure here but (to the extent possible) eliminating and reducing the dangers where they arise abroad.

To do that, words and deeds count. The societal inequities that foster and create the bases for extremism must be attacked. Money and other kinds of assistance are part of the solution. Clarity of action is another. And clear-cut statements, repeated and broadcast for as long as is necessary, to make the case for ending extremism are as important as military and law-enforcement agencies to successful outcomes.

The United Nations clearly has a critical role. However, the UN often lacks the resources and skills to handle one crisis, let alone two crises at once. Hence, while the UN must pass appropriate resolutions calling for fair and equitable solutions, more than likely, it would be involved in dealing with only one of the bookends. Kashmir is the conflict the UN should focus on. While actual terms must be negotiated, stability between Pakistan and India can be won only through defanging the Kashmir problem.

Meanwhile, the United States, perhaps in concert with NATO, must tend to the Middle East. In the Middle East, solutions also must include Iran, Iraq, Syria, and Saudi Arabia if the Arab-Israeli conflict is to be diminished or resolved. This is a very tall order. But, what is the alternative? As al Qaeda so vividly showed, an attack against one is an attack against all. The international order cannot permit itself to collapse like unanchored books on a shelf. And, the bookends are available.

## The Clarion Call

The Bush administration's war on terrorism and on those who support or sponsor terror and the identification of an axis of evil for the purpose of sealing off any links between terror groups and weapons of mass destruction are necessary declarations of intent. However, as comprehensive strategy, they are incomplete. Unless or until the causes of this terror—namely, the roots of extremism—are eliminated or neutralized, the consequences in the form of future catastrophic attacks against the United States and its friends will almost certainly be planned. The danger is that some will be executed. As Secretary of Defense Rumsfeld has warned, future attacks may be "vastly more destructive."

Similarly, the Bush administration focus on weapons of mass destruction highlights a major danger. However, that danger perhaps can be more easily contained than the administration suggests. Fifty years of Cold War experience against the Soviets should not be so easily consigned to "the rubbish dump of history," to use a favorite Leninist expression. A larger danger has been concealed in the process.

The larger danger is the formula concocted by bin Laden. It draws on the openness of American society as the key weakness to be exploited. It is prepared to use diabolically clever measures, whether airliners turned into mass-destruction missiles or even nastier tricks to disrupt the American way of life. Clearly, the U.S. economy, its citizens, and supporting infrastructure are the top-priority targets.

If this assessment of danger proves accurate, far bolder steps and actions are required. The unfinished business of the past must be finished. This is the test and challenge for the United States, its public, and its government. George W. Bush has been given a historic opportunity and a mission of supreme importance but extraordinary difficulty. He has selected a team with impeccable credentials, enormous talent, and vast experience to advise and support him. This is the best America has. The challenge, however, may be the greatest that America has ever faced. The answers to the question of how well a political system designed by the best minds of the eighteenth century will deal with the rigors of the twenty-first century are no longer academic. The future of the nation will ride on them. Unfinished business, no matter how intractable and laden with danger, must be finished if the nation is to be kept safe.

# Acknowledgements

This book has one author but many contributors. The idea originated in the mid-1990s. With the end of the Cold War, neither the Bush nor Clinton administration had, in my view, fashioned a sufficiently relevant strategic framework for the vastly different circumstances that challenged the nation's security. Both policy and organization remained largely creatures of the Cold War. And attracting and retaining enough quality people for government service was perilously close to a crisis point.

Armed with these concerns, I sought funding. . . . In 1998, the Smith-Richardson Foundation awarded me a generous grant and the National Defense University provided a home for the project. A manuscript called *"Who Will Listen, Who Will Lead"* resulted. The draft assessed these dangers and their causes, prescribed remedies, and offered five scary scenarios that forecast the probable risks that lay ahead. The draft was well received by the policy community. However, publishers saw little commercial value. All of that changed after September 11th, 2001.

My agent, Peter Rubie, had the foresight to pass the manuscript to Kensington Books. Fortuitously, Walter Zacharius, CEO and Founder, wanted to do a book that looked closely at those events. And Michaela Hamilton, Kensington's editor-in-chief, liked my writing enough to become my editor. In this, my first commercial book, the experience has been a pleasure and I am very grateful for the support, professionally and personally.

In military service, a risk in extending appreciation and thanks is omission of even a single person. If that happens, I apologize. Many individuals provided insight, critique, and guidance. I am particularly grateful to the following who read *Unfinished Business* (and some who read both it and *Who Will Listen*) and shared their reactions: Zbigniew Brzezinski; Frank Carlucci; Arnaud DeBourchgrave, Bruce George, Chuck Horner, Robert Hunter, Bill Owens, James Schlesinger, R. James Woolsey as well as David Abshire, John Barry, Michael Bayer, Hans Binnendijk, Richard Chilcote, Wesley Clark, Bud Edney, John Foster, Fred Franks, Alexander Haig, Bruce Hoffman, Jonathan Howe, Jerry Hultin, Dan Kaufman, Geoffrey Kemp, Charles C. Krulak, Anthony Lake, Ian Lesser, Gary Luck, Barry McCaffrey, Philip Merrill, Thomas Morgan, Robert Morse, Robert Oakley, Dave Oliver, Norman Ray, Robin Raphel, Tom Ricks, Donald Rumsfeld, Brent Scowcroft, William Sessions, Leighton Smith, and (AVM) John Thompson. I also appreciate the support of my close colleagues at CNAC: Robert Murray, Mike McDevitt, Steve Tela, Brenda Caldwell, and Bill Bell (to whom I wish a speedy and successful recovery).

David S. Bill IV was an invaluable research assistant (as well as the son of Rear Admiral David Bill, mentioned in the book for his service in Desert Storm). .

Although in my sixth decade of life, I can still have heroes. Senator John S. McCain is one whose extraordinary profile in courage has spanned two careers. A second is a former student, or so he claims, who went on to be Chairman of the JCS and Secretary of State. Whatever Colin Powell may have learned from me, I assure the reader that it is inconsequential compared to what I have learned from watching him in the service of his country.

Finally, my greatest debt is to my wife, Julian. She is the dominant intellect and personality of our life together. I sensed that the first time I saw her from afar on a golf course in Portugal thirty years ago. It turned out to be the most expensive round of golf I ever played—she claims that she hardly saw me because I hit so many errant shots. That we were both right suggests the strength of our bond.

For any flaws and errors in the preceding pages, the responsibility is mine alone.

# Source Notes

To aid the reader in navigating the prior pages, I deliberately omitted footnotes and endnotes. That does not suggest any laxity in research, however. Of the source materials, particular use was made of U.S. Government archives and published material. The many commission reports cited in this book as well as committee hearings before Congress, expert testimony, and the abundance of congressionally mandated reports are treasure troves of information. And, for sheer data and comprehensive information on regions, events, and other related items, the publicly available archives and web site of the Central Intelligence Agency are first-rate sources for research.

Since September 11th, 2001, the print media have, in my view, done an excellent job of reporting on these and related events. The *Washington Post* and the *New York Times* deserve mention. Also, *The Military Balance* and *Strategic Survey* published annually by the International Institute for Strategic Studies offer essential reference information and insight.

The following books were particularly helpful and are listed without comment:

Allen, Frederick Lewis. *Only Yesterday: An Informed History of the 1920s.* New York: John Wiley and Sons, 1959.

Barer, Shlomo. *The Doctors of Revolution.* London: Thames and Hudson, 2000.

Beals, Carlton. *The Great Revolt and Its Leaders.* New York: Abelard-Schulman, 1968.

Bergen, Peter L. *Holy War, Inc.* New York: Free Press, 2001.

Borkenau, Franz. *European Commission.* London: Faber and Faber, Ltd., 1951.

Bowden, Mark. *Black Hawk Down.* New York: Atlantic Monthly, 1999.

Bush, George. *All the Best.* New York: Scribner, 1999.

——, and Brent Scowcroft. *A World Transformed.* New York: Vintage Books, 1999.

Clark, Wesley K. *Waging Modern War.* New York: Public Affairs, 2001.

Crenshaw, Martha. *Terrorism in Context.* University Park: Pennsylvania State University Press, 1995.

Franks, Frederick M. *Into the Storm: A Study in Command.* New York: Putnam, 1998.

Friedman, Thomas. *The Lexus and the Olive Tree.* London: Little, Brown, and Co., 1996.

Gorbachev, Mikhail. *Perestroika.* New York: HarperCollins, 1987.

——. *A Time for Peace.* New York: Richardson, Steinman, and Black, 1985.

Halberstam, David. *The Best and the Brightest.* New York: Random House, 1969.

——. *War in a Time of Peace.* New York: Scribner, 2001.

Hoffman, Bruce. *Inside Terrorism.* New York: Columbia University Press, 1998.

Horner, Chuck. *Every Man a Tiger.* New York: Putnam, 1999.

Ikle, Fred C., *Every War Must End.* New York: Columbia University Press, 1991.

Jacker, Corinne. *The Black Flag of Anarchy: Anti-Statism in the United States.* New York: Charles Scribner's Sons, 1968.

Kennedy, Margaret. *A Century of Revolution.* London: Methuen and Co., Ltd., 1922.

Lake, Anthony. *Six Nightmares.* New York: Little, Brown, 2000.

Laquer, Walter. *The Age of Terrorism.* Boston: Little, Brown and Company, 1987.

Lesser, Ian, ed. *The New Terrorism.* Santa Monica: Rand, 1999.

McLean, George N. *The Rise and Fall of Anarchy in America.* New York: Haskell House, 1972.

Owens, Bill, with Ed Offley. *Lifting the Fog of War.* New York: Farrar, Straus, and Giroux, 2000.

Powell, Colin L. *My American Journey.* New York: Random House, 1995.

Schwartzkopf, H. Norman. *It Doesn't Take a Hero.* New York: Bantam Books, 1993.

Trainor, Bernard E., and Michael Gordon. *The General's War.* London: Little, Brown, and Co., 1996.

# Index

# About the Author

Graduating with honors from the Naval Academy, Harlan Ullman went on to serve twenty years in the Navy including five tours in destroyers, one in command.

In the Vietnam war, he skippered a Swift Boat and, later, led a subdivision of Swifts in over one hundred fifty patrols and operations from combat assault to gunfire support and special operations. He later spent nearly two years in the Royal Navy, much of it at sea as ship's company in a frigate and later on the staff of the Royal Britannia Naval College at Dartmouth, England.

Ashore, the Navy sent him to the Fletcher School of Law and Diplomacy, where he was awarded a master's degree, a master's in law and diplomacy, and a Ph.D. with emphasis on international affairs, finance, and economics. He became a professor at the National War College, where he directed the course of instruction in Military Strategy. Before returning to sea, he served as a special assistant in the Office of the Secretary of Defense with responsibilities for overseeing a substantial portion of the entire defense budget. Prior to his retirement, he was Head of Navy Extended Planning.

After leaving the service, Ullman joined the Center for Strategic and International Studies as Senior Fellow and director of the political-military and strategy programs, the largest at that institution. He oversaw a number of important national security and defense projects on strategy, force structure, acquisition reform, nuclear posture and terrorism.

During this period he began consulting with a number of Fortune 100 companies and was elected to the board of directors of the

Wall Street Fund, one of the country's oldest mutual funds. He formed his own company, the Killoween Group, an advisory and consulting firm with broad financial interests. He is currently chairman of the advisory board of a high technology company, as well as a distinguished visiting scholar at the Stevens Institute of Technology in New Jersey.

Ullman still enjoys senior (part-time) appointments at several of the nation's most prestigious research institutions in Washington, D.C. At CNAC (the former Center for Naval Analyses), he is a senior fellow and chairs the Senior Seminar Program, which brings distinguished speakers in contact with senior naval leadership and CSIS. He remains with CSIS. For 1998–2000, he was made a Distinguished Senior Fellow at the National Defense University, where he worked on a grant from the Smith-Richardson Foundation and co-chaired a major project, "Globalization and National Security." He also served on a number of presidential "transition" studies, principally at the RAND Corporation and the Center for the Study of the Presidency.

He writes a weekly column for UPI, has written a number of books, and is a well-known media commentator on American and foreign television and in print media. He and his wife reside in Washington, D.C. where his hobbies include golf and care and feeding of two Welsh Corgis. His next book is tentatively titled "Bullet Proofing the Organization."